Advance Praise 1

" PKI is fast becoming the cornerston⌍ ⌍⌍ ⌍⌍⌍⌍⌍ ⌍⌍
provides an excellent perspective on PKI for both technology and
business people."

—*Fran Rooney, CEO, Baltimore Technologies*

" The organization of the book, and the choice and weighting of
topics, are excellent. I am not aware of any other books on PKI that
emphasize deployment and acquisition concerns like this one. The
case studies and example RFP were particularly useful. This book
will appeal to those in charge of procuring and operating a PKI."

—*Rich Ankney, Vice President, CertCo*

" A must read for anyone who will be involved assessing,
recommending, approving, buying or implementing digital asset
security at any level in a enterprise. Austin brings together an
impressive array of authoritative experts, and attains seamless
topic integration presenting the right flow of ideas to the reader.
Hard to imagine, but he succeeds delivering a PKI treatise with
sufficient depth and breadth to please the initiated, yet easy to
read from the boardroom to the heart of the IT function."

—*Juan Rodriguez-Torrent, PKI Forum founder,*
President & CEO Aposematic Corporation

"...grounded in the real world of the business benefits PKI provides.
Case studies show how PKI has been implemented by a variety of
companies today, allowing readers to learn from the experiences
of others without vendor hype or bias. Austin's conversational style
that explains the nuts and bolts of PKI along with substantive,
practical case studies make this book a must-have resource for
anyone considering PKI deployment."

—*Debra Cameron, President, Cameron Consulting*

"This thorough look at PKI will help to enrich understanding in
the industry and help to move efforts in e-business forward."

—*Laura Rime, Global Marketing Manager, Identrus*

PKI

A Wiley Tech Brief

Tom Austin

Wiley Computer Publishing

John Wiley & Sons, Inc.

NEW YORK · CHICHESTER · WEINHEIM · BRISBANE · SINGAPORE · TORONTO

Publisher: Robert Ipsen
Editor: Margaret Hendrey
Managing Editor: Angela Smith
Text Design & Composition: Benchmark Productions, Inc.

Library of Congress Cataloging-in-Publication Data:

ISBN 0-471-35380-9

Printed in the United States of America.

10 9 8 7 6 5 4 3 2 1

Wiley Tech Brief Series

Other titles in the series:

Steve Mann and Scott Sbihli, *The Wireless Application Protocol (WAP)*. 0471-39992-2

Ray Rischpater, *Palm Enterprise Applications*. 0471-39379-7

Chetan Sharma, *Wireless Internet Enterprise Applications*. 0471-38382-7

William A. Ruh, Francis X. Maginnis, and William J. Brown, *Enterprise Application Integration*. 0471-37641-8

Jon Graff, *Cryptography and E-Commerce*. 0471-40574-4

Contents

Acknowledgments

In the nearly two years it took to complete this book, I've had the opportunity to meet with some great people that contributed to this book, offered their assistance in one way or another, or simply shared their thoughts and ideas.

The idea for this book became reality as a result of the fine people at Wiley. I'm especially grateful to Marjorie Spencer and Margaret Hendrey. Marjorie, who believed in me, the concept for this book, and made it happen. Margaret, from start to finish, was always available to see this project through. Her expert direction, patience, and prompt response to my many questions and requests is the mark of a true professional. Equally, thanks go to Carol Long for her ongoing support, encouragement, and objectivity as well as Angela Smith and Kerstin Nasdeo for their painstaking efforts in taking this draft to production.

The case studies presented in this book would not have been possible without the efforts of many people, especially Wayne Austad, Gavin Grounds, Richard Karon, Art Purcell, John Taylor, and Ron Szoc who made a tremendous effort in responding to my numerous list of questions. The essence of what you'll learn from these case studies are a direct result of these people willing to share their experience and wisdom with you.

Special thanks go to Tracy Shouldice, Susan Hannah, and Roger Sabourin of Entrust Technologies. This book would not have been what it is without them. Their untiring and ceaseless efforts on my behalf helped make this book what it is. They are truly the best!

With topics ranging from biometrics to cryptography, from legacy systems to time stamping, few people, if any, can be an expert in all areas of PKI. The knowledge and depth of experience of the people that contributed to this book are more than one writer alone could ever match. I'd especially like to thank Jeff Stapleton, Roseanne Day, and Steve McIntosh. In addition to contributing chapters to this book, they've all helped to make it that much better. Jeff, for agreeing to contribute to this effort and for putting me in touch with other experts that also contributed to this book. Roseann, for always sharing her thoughts, insights, and valued friendship. Steve, for his many offers of help, and for also improving my writing.

Of course, no book would be complete without illustrations. The outstanding visuals you see in this book are the masterful work of Richard Eberly. Richard has the unique skill of taking a simple sketch and creating artwork that contributes immensely to helping us understand beyond just the written word.

I'd like to recognize Laura Rime of Identrus, and Richard Guida of the Federal PKI Steering Committee, for their guidance and responsiveness as well as Brian Iverson of Novell, Gary Miller of EXOCOM, Carl Norell of CeloCom, and Michael Thieme of International Biometric Group.

For reviewing and critiquing this book, I sincerely appreciate the time and efforts of Rich Ankney of Certco, Dr. Burt Kaliski of RSA Laboratories, Juan Rodriguez-Torrent of Aposematic Corporation, Roger Sabourin of Entrust Technologies, and Dr. Richard Y. Yen of The Chase Manhattan Bank.

Most of all, I'd like to thank my wife Bonnie, for all the support she provides me. Not only has she freely and unconditionally supported all of my endeavors, but she also read and provided me with her feedback, even after many a long day at work, on all that I wrote for this book. I couldn't ask for more.

About the Contributors

Santosh Chokhani is the founder, President and CEO of CygnaCom Solutions Inc., an Entrust Technologies company specializing in PKI.

Roseann Day is a security consultant who works with a wide range of systems and software vendors on their marketing and product development strategies. Her professional career spans over 25 years which includes positions at Digital and IBM.

Todd Glassey is the creator of Certifiable Time Data and its use models in modern eBusiness systems. His 20+ years of experience include strategic and industry specific technology assessment, network, project operations, and security consulting, as well as hardware and software development.

Sven Hammar is CEO, Celo Communications Ltd. and President, Celo Communications Inc. He has 15 years experience as a consultant in the security field and has been president and vice president of various Swedish consulting companies.

Diana Kelley is the General Manager for Jawbreaker, a security software development effort, at Symantec Research Labs. Ms. Kelley has ten years of experience creating secure network architectures and eBusiness solutions.

Sathvik Krishnamurthy is vice president, marketing and business development at ValiCert. Prior to ValiCert, he held various positions at Worldtalk Corporation, Deming Internet Security and Retix.

Steve McIntosh. Focusing primarily on PKI, network security, and UNIX in his 20 years with technology vendors, Steve McIntosh has held product management positions at nCipher, CertCo, and Digital.

Samir Nanavati is a partner at International Biometric Group, LLC, a biometric consulting and integration firm he co-founded in 1996 to help companies investigate, design, and implement biometric solutions.

Ruven Schwartz is an attorney with over 15 years experience in the technical and legal communities and is currently Vice President of Trust Practices at CertifiedTime. He also serves as vice chair of the American Bar Association Information Security Committee.

Jeff Stapleton is a manager with KPMG, LLP in the Information Risk Management practice focusing on Secure Electronic Commerce and PKI services. He is the chair of the ANSI/ASC X9F4 working group and has participated in developing Financial Industries security standards with ISO TC68 and ANSI/ASC X9.

Introduction

W hether it's to build market share, develop new business, increase productivity or profitability, there's no doubt your organization needs to take advantage of the Internet to stay competitive. However, with stories today about Internet security problems about as frequent as weather reports, doing business online clearly represents risks as well as benefits. When conducting crucial business over the public Internet, we need to have certain assurances. The question is, just what are those assurances?

Those assurances are a set of security services that are provided through a technology we refer to as Public Key Infrastructure, or simply PKI. The essential services that PKI can provide are confidentiality, authentication, integrity, and non-repudiation. These services are important because:

➤ Confidentiality *assures you* that your information is protected.

➤ Authentication *assures you* that you know with whom you're doing business.

➤ Integrity *assures you* that information is not being modified or substituted.

➤ Non-repudiation *assures you* that the originator cannot deny originating a message or business transaction.

Of course, these services do come at a cost—but just how much? What impact will PKI have on your organization and your customers? How complex is it to implement, and just how long will it take? While it's easy to learn the benefits from vendors, it can be much harder to get answers about the costs. You'll find many of the answers in this book.

Moreover, you'll learn the fundamentals of just what makes up the various components of PKI, such as cryptography, certificates, directories, key management, and time stamps. It also includes background information on government and industry initiatives, ongoing efforts for industry standards, and legislation that affects how you conduct business online.

Who Should Read This Book

This book is intended to help technology, business, and sales professionals understand PKI technology and how it can be applied to meet business requirements. Its goal is to help readers quickly get a grasp on what's involved, whether your role is selling, buying, planning, or implementing a PKI. The book also illustrates key business and competitive reasons for PKI through a set of case studies that underscore what others have found to be critical success factors, their lessons learned, and what they would do differently.

You may or may not already be familiar with PKI. For those just starting out, this book will provide a great starting point to learn what PKI is all about. You'll gain a sound understanding of basic concepts and principles, realize what others are doing, and learn about the security services and solutions that PKI can address. In short, you'll have the background information you'll need to be able to ask serious questions about PKI, and be able to begin planning one.

For those who are more advanced in their knowledge of PKI, the case studies will help you with your business justification for PKI, and should also provide added insight in what others have accomplished and the process they followed to really implement their PKI. Additionally, if there's a need to understand more about auditing, biometrics, hardware mechanisms, time stamps, and creating a Certificate Policy and Certification Practice Statement, you'll find the right information in this book to help you get the job done.

What You Will Find in This Book

This book covers the fundamental technology and business topics that are critical when considering and deploying a PKI. Furthermore, it delves into the experiences of others who have implemented PKI, the outside influences that affected them, and more importantly, the impact it has had on their business.

Part One: Security Basics

Part One introduces you to the underlying mechanisms present in a PKI, and the essential security concepts and standards required to maintain an appropriate working environment. In addition to the various technology disciplines within a PKI, basic business requirements and issues are discussed.

Chapter 1, "PKI Explained," looks at the need for PKI, factors to consider in authentication, how cryptography works and enables digital signatures and certificates, and the environmental security that's necessary before a PKI can be implemented.

Part Two, "PKI Technologies," delves into the heart of a PKI. The life cycle and necessary supporting disciplines that ensures the security and continued operation of a PKI are presented, along with the roles that certificate and validation authorities perform. Considerations are also offered about directories, time stamps, and hardware mechanisms and the business value they bring to a PKI.

Part Three, "PKI and Business Issues," takes an in-depth look at Certificate Policies and Certification Practice Statements and issues around auditing a PKI. Besides factors to consider about qualifying vendors, and at the looking the costs involved, you'll learn how to obtain your own digital certificate to help familiarize yourself with its basic features and functions.

Part Four, "Case Studies" offers you insight into how PKI is being used in the real world. Comprehensive case studies include government, financial, and service sectors that feature how these organizations proceeded to build their PKI and what they've accomplished. Moreover, it captures internal migration issues and the external forces that are at work that could have a direct effect on how you might proceed with your PKI.

It also reveals the details behind the usual technology planning and implementation by looking at concrete business requirements that necessitated PKI, the investment they made, the impact it's had on their business, and how they're measuring results. Discover what they would do differently and what they found to be the most helpful in getting their PKI up and running.

Part Five, "PKI Efforts," gives you an overview as to what government and industry consortia efforts are underway, as well as a synopsis of related standards, laws, and regulations. Which biometric technologies are best for PKI, and what potential approaches can be taken are also discussed, in addition to listing and describing the technical issues you'll face when integrating existing enterprise applications.

In Appendix A, "Request for Proposal for Public Key Infrastructure," you'll receive some help in getting started with a sample, generic Request for Proposal (RFP) that you can use that includes general guidelines and descriptions, and specific questions you can tailor to your needs.

Looking Forward

Getting your arms around PKI isn't easy. Yet, more organizations than ever are planning or actually deploying PKI, because it's the technology that effectively provides the necessary foundation for electronic commerce.

Lastly, the interest and activity surrounding PKI has never been greater. When I attended the first Entrust PKI conference in 1998, the level of interest of 700-plus attendees in a vendor's first conference amazed me. The next year, attendance at the Entrust event more than doubled. And it's not just the Entrust Conference. Both the conferences for Baltimore Technologies and RSA are also experiencing record attendance. It's a strong signal of where business is headed.

While you can learn a lot from going to these conferences, this book will provide you with perspective to the point you'll be prepared to implement a PKI in your own environment.

PART ONE

Security Basics

PKI Explained

Today, there's little doubt that electronic information assets represent a significant share of an organization's value. Customer and employee databases, transaction records, trade secrets, and scientific research are just a few of the items that represent the lifeblood of many companies. What used to be paper-based information, stored in file cabinets with traditional physical locks, is now found on a myriad of computer disks and networks.

With electronic capabilities, we're able to communicate easily with others, provide essential information and services, and even conduct business transactions. Before the Internet opened up our private networks to others, access to these information assets was restricted to the select few authorized within the company, and there was minimal risk and a high level of control.

However, in their efforts to increase market share, profitability, and stay competitive, business managers demanded that information assets be readily accessible to customers, suppliers, and partners. Where Information Technology (IT) managers once had strict internal controls and minimal risk, they were now exposing their systems and networks to outsiders with little or no control and at a much higher risk. Moreover, despite any internal system problems or external environmental factors (such as power outages, fire, or floods), customers, suppliers, and other users now expect accessibility 7 days a week, 24 hours a day (see Figure 1.1).

Unfortunately, with this increased access to electronic information, the same level of protection afforded to its physical counterpart has not yet been satisfied. Similarly, in its *Year 2000 Survey of Fortune 1000 Companies*, Pinkerton Service Corporation also discovered that *"Corporate reliance on technology has given rise to unprecedented exposure to software bugs, viruses, and other security issues."* The survey further commented that the number-two concern voiced in the survey was Internet / intranet security, which had

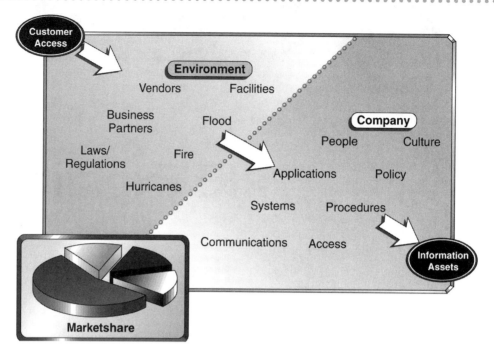

Figure 1.1   Access to information.

the greatest one-year movement in the rankings, up from number seven just the year before. To put this in perspective, fraud and white-collar crime, a $400 *billion* annual problem, ranked fourth.

There's no question that critical business information must be protected. Management not only has a fiduciary responsibility to demonstrate due diligence in its actions, but it's also now required to do so by law. To be sure, the U.S. Economic Espionage Act (EEA) of 1996, redefined the term "trade secret" to mean *"all forms and types of financial, business, scientific, technical, economic, or engineering information…"* which has made it incumbent upon management to have *"taken reasonable measures to keep such information secret…"* For more information on this, see Chapter 19, "Initiatives, Laws, and Standards."

Indeed, even the National Association of Corporate Directors recently issued a challenge to boards of directors to take action regarding information technology security. Among the responsibilities cited, directors *"should insist that systems and their uses provide adequate management control and accountability balanced against the needs of the organization. Similarly, they should require that information be protected from unauthorized or unintended modification, destruction, disclosure, or other endangerment."*

Are organizations structured to manage these issues? In most cases, no. According to the Pinkerton Survey, just 7 percent of security departments report directly to the

CEO or company president, with the largest group, 21 percent, reporting to human resources. There's a lack of holistically looking at security. While many of us feel somewhat physically secure in seeing the security guard at the door, the locks, dogs, fences, and closed-circuit television cameras in our facilities, those only address the more traditional, physical model of security. It's certainly an essential function, but it also leaves out two other points in an important triangle of security: the boardroom and the IT systems people (see Figure 1.2).

While most of us realize the need for physical security, and now with demands from the boardroom to executive management, whose responsibility is it to develop and implement the infrastructure for secure e-commerce? Management understands the value information, the intangible assets of the corporation; traditional security understands the value of physical protection; and IT security understands the value of systems and network security in fulfilling the business requirements. All three functions need to better communicate and work together to protect the interests of the organization. Fundamentally, however, it comes down to appointing one senior, management person who's responsible for ensuring it all happens. At least that's what the U.S. Federal Sentencing Guidelines considers as part of performing due diligence under the EEA.

So then, why PKI? Because PKI is a technology that can provide the infrastructure, the controls, and the underlying security services necessary to support the requirements business executives now face. Let's look at PKI more closely.

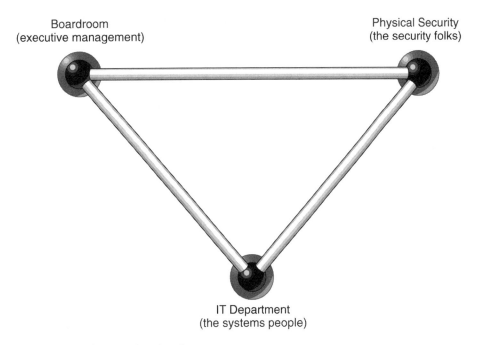

Figure 1.2 The security triangle.

What's a PKI?

Before asking what components make up a PKI, let's first ask, "what exactly is a PKI?" The acronym literally means "Public Key Infrastructure." The term "public key" is the more common name for *asymmetric cryptography*. So, what's asymmetric cryptography? Well, it's a different way of doing cryptography that is distinct from the more traditional way called *symmetric cryptography*. So, what's the difference between symmetric and asymmetric cryptography? Let's hold that discussion for *Basic Crypto* in Chapter 2, "What's in a PKI?". Suffice it to say that PKI is named for a particular type of cryptography.

So, how does the term *infrastructure* fit into this? Think of a bunch of computers communicating across a LAN, WAN, or the Internet. Numerous applications can be run on each computer, talk to each other, exchange data, and perform transactions. For all of that to occur, there has to be a communications architecture in place; otherwise, the computer and their application wouldn't be able to talk to each other. Similarly, in order to run all of those applications securely, that has to be a security architecture in place. Security today between computers is achieved mainly through cryptography. That cryptography architecture is also called an *infrastructure*.

However, the acronym PKI is a bit of a misnomer, in that the cryptography is not limited to just asymmetric cryptography. Both symmetric and asymmetric cryptography work together in a PKI to provide the overall security. This is much like a toolbox to build a house. You don't attach ceiling joints, walls, roofing tiles, and the like with the same nail. Different types of fasteners are used for the correct job—thus, it takes the right tools for the right job. It's the same with cryptography: It takes the right cryptographic algorithm and security mechanism for the right job. So, what are the security mechanisms in a PKI?

A PKI contains security mechanisms that provide security services. What are those services? We introduce yet another acronym, CAIN, for confidentiality, authentication, integrity, and something called non-repudiation.

Confidentiality

Confidentiality is the protection of data against unauthorized access or disclosure. This service is typically provided via access controls (possibly in conjunction with encryption) for data storage, and via encryption during data transmission. It's the encryption part that the PKI can provide. Access controls are really a combination of authentication and authorization.

Think of confidentiality as an opaque envelope. The message inside is not visible from the outside. Of course, almost anyone can open an envelope and read the contents. However, encryption is like an incredibly strong envelope that cannot be opened except by the authorized person(s) to whom the envelope is addressed.

Authentication

Authentication is the verification of an individual's identity and/or the verification of data origin. In other words, a person (or even a computer) needs to verify that the entity (computer or person) he or she is communicating with, or receiving data from, is indeed who he or she thinks it is, and who the other entity claims to be.

We humans verify other people all of the time. The telephone rings, and immediately we recognize the voice. A knock on the door reveals a face that we know. The airline ticket agent asks you for a photo identification. Computers and networks ask for a password, and the ATM machine requires that you enter your PIN after inserting your ATM card.

Authentication can be achieved by one or more of three ways:

➢ Something you know, such as a PIN or password

➢ Something you have, such as a door key or an ATM card

➢ Something you are, called *biometrics*, such as a fingerprint, voice pattern, or your iris

The section *Authentication Basics, Alternatives* later in this chapter provides a more detailed discussion of various authentication techniques, their strengths, and their weaknesses.

Integrity

Integrity is the protection of data against unauthorized modification or substitution to information. This service is provided by cryptography mechanisms called a *message authentication code* (MAC) or a *digital signature.*

Think of integrity as a transparent envelope. The message inside can be read from the outside, so there's no confidentiality. However, the envelope is what's called tamper evident. The addressee can look at the envelope and verify that it has not been opened, ripped, or even substituted.

Non-Repudiation

Non-repudiation is the combined services of authentication and integrity that is *provable to a third party*. This implies a legally unproven presumption that the originator cannot deny having originated the message. Asymmetric cryptography provides a mechanism called a *digital signature* such that only the originator could have produced the digital signature. Therefore, anyone else, including the receiver of the signed message, can verify the digital signature. This has strong implications, such as in a court of law, that the signer of the message cannot deny having originated the message.

Furthermore, the digital signature also has the same property as the transparent envelope mentioned earlier. The message can be read, but in addition to authenticating the signer, the reader can also verify that the message has not been modified or substituted.

Now that we've laid out the security services, the next section presents a more detailed description of authentication techniques. The section *Basic Crypto* in Chapter 2 provides an overview of general cryptography, and ties the security services presented here with the specific cryptographic mechanisms that provide these services.

Authentication Basics, Alternatives

As mentioned, authentication can only be achieved by one or more of three factors:

➤ **Knowledge Factor.** Something you know.

➤ **Possession Factor.** Something you have.

➤ **Biometric Factor.** Something you are.

Knowledge Factor

Knowledge Factors in the guise of passwords for system and network logon, and personal identification numbers (PIN) for ATM and credit cards, have both strengths and weaknesses. The user provides a claimed identity such as a name and the Knowledge Factor. The Knowledge Factor provided by the user is matched against the reference Knowledge Factor obtained via the user identification. This is referred to as a *one-to-one verification*.

Strengths

Ubiquitous. This implies they have high awareness and wide acceptance.

Reliable. Either it matches or it does not; there is no ambiguity in their verification.

Virtually free. Typically, every application and system relies on passwords for access controls. Of course, this doesn't take into consideration the cost of administration and management.

Easy to use. The user only needs to enter two items.

Weaknesses

Subject to memory loss. People easily and often forget passwords and PINs.

Subject to guessing. Dictionary words and personal associations, such as family and pet names, are too often used.

Subject to social engineering. Someone implying or posing as someone that they're not to improperly gain information or system access.

Subject to poor administration. Passwords are often not properly chosen, assigned, or managed.

The relative strength of a Knowledge Factor is dependent on its size and randomness. Its size is defined as the length of the character string and the possible number of potential values. For example, a six-character password allowing alphanumeric characters (A to Z, and 0 to 9) and special characters (e.g. ~ ! @ # $ % ^ & * _ + = < >) provides $50^6 = 15,625,000,000 \approx 15$ billion possible permutations. In contrast, a four-digit PIN provides $10^4 = 10,000$ possible permutations. Its randomness is defined as the uniqueness of each Knowledge Factor. For example, a poorly chosen password is a valid word, and a poorly chosen PIN is a person's birthday date or address.

Possession Factor

Possession Factors are used to provide assurance that the user has authorization, and cover a wide range of devices, such as door keys, driver's licenses, employee badges, and cryptographic keys. In general, Possession Factors also have both strengths and weaknesses.

Strengths

They are common. While not as ubiquitous as passwords, they are in widespread use in various instances, such as credit cards.

They are reliable. For example, credit cards using magnetic stripes are proven technology.

They are costly. Physical tokens must be manufactured and purchased.

Weaknesses

They are often difficult to use. For example, the magnetic stripe must be swiped against the reader.

They can be left behind. Employees routinely forget their ID badge at home, and users forget to take their credit cards when they go shopping.

They are subject to duplication. For example, the magnetic stripe data can be copied, and a counterfeit card can be manufactured.

They are subject to social engineering. Again, someone implying or posing as someone that they're not to improperly gain access or information.

They require asset management. Physical devices must be procured, they must be issued to the users, and they must be replaced when lost or stolen.

The relative strength of a Possession Factor is difficult to define, due to the wide variety of possible tokens. However, in general, strength is dependent upon the possible number of devices and the difficulty of counterfeiting a device. When the Possession Factor is a cryptographic key, the strength is a combination of its size defined as the number of bits and the underlying cryptographic algorithm. The section *Cryptographic Strengths* in Chapter 4, "Key Management" discusses cryptographic strength.

Biometric Factor

Biometric Factors embody a wide variety of technologies, including fingerprints, iris, voice, hand geometry, and face images. The user must first enroll his or her biometric information, called a *biometric template*, using a biometric reader. Authentication occurs when subsequent biometric data is validated against the template. Unlike the other authentication factors, biometrics can be used for either verification or for identification. *Verification* is where the user provides a claimed identity via a name, the template is obtained via the user identity, and the biometric data is validated against the selected template. Verification is a one-to-one process. *Identification* is where the user submits his or her biometric data for comparison against multiple templates, typically stored in a database. Identification is one-to-many process.

Strengths

> Somewhat costly, but pricing hasvastly improved and is becoming more competitive.

> Easy to use. The user only needs to touch, look, or speak into the biometric reader for authentication.

> Cannot be forgotten, lost, or stolen.

> Difficult to counterfeit, and if the biometric system adheres to industry security requirements, cannot be forged.

> Cannot be loaned or given away.

Weaknesses

> Limited to niche markets. This is rapidly changing, as biometrics have become more reliable, cheaper, and accepted.

> Inherent ambiguity that can lead to false matches or non-matches, depending upon the threshold settings. However, reliability has improved.

> May be difficult to manage. Users must be enrolled, and the biometric templates must be securely distributed.

Figure 1.3 shows how the threshold setting impacts the reliability of biometrics. The curves represent histograms, where the *x*-coordinate is the score (0% to 100% match), and the *y*-coordinate is the number of attempts. Unlike other Factors, there is an overlap between high scores (match) and low scores (non-match). When the biometric data is compared to the template, the resulting score determines whether the individual is successfully authenticated. Scores above the threshold are matches, and scores below the threshold are non-matches, by definition.

In the figure on the left, the shaded area represents low scores that are valid matches, but are interpreted as non-matches because they fall below the threshold setting. This

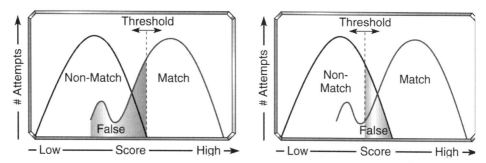

Figure 1.3   False match and false non-match.

results in false non-matches where a valid user is denied access. In the diagram on the right, the shaded area represents high scores that are non-matches, but are interpreted as matches because they fall above the threshold setting. This results in false matches where an unauthorized user is permitted access.

Biometrics also suffer from non-universality in that for any given biometric, there is a small percentage of the population that cannot use that biometric. Some construction workers, such as dry wallers and bricklayers, have built up calluses such that they essentially do not have fingerprints. Certain eye diseases can damage the iris. Some people are speechless. Also, accidents or illness can render a biometric useless. Despite the benefits and enhanced security from using biometrics, alternative Factors should always be incorporated.

Multiple Factors and Strong Authentication

So, which authentication factors are best? It depends on the user population, the application environment, and the business needs. Quite often, strong authentication is required. Strong authentication is where two or more Factors are used. This is a common practice, and many access control products offer two-factor authentication. For example, access to financial transactions at an ATM is two-factor authentication, a Knowledge Factor (PIN) and a Possession Factor (ATM card). Even credit card transactions at a brick and mortar merchant require a credit card and a written signature.

Figure 1.4 depicts the increasing security gained by using multiple factors. Clearly, three-factor authentication is stronger than two factors, and two-factor authentication is stronger than a single factor. Note that the graph for both single factor and two factors is a sloped line. For single-factor authentication, this implies that the factors are not equivalent in strength. Until a quantitative analysis has been performed, this is purely speculative at best. Consequently, the same argument applies to two-factor authentication.

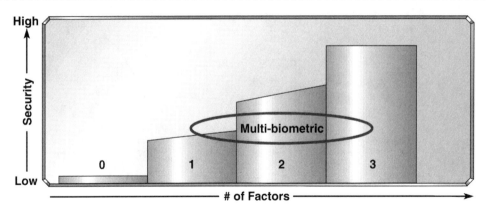

Figure 1.4 Multiple authentication factors.

Finally, there is the issue of how to treat multiple biometrics. Clearly, multi-biometrics is less robust than three factors, possibly less than two factor, and arguably stronger than single factor. Until a quantitative analysis is available, this is debatable.

CHAPTER 2

What's in a PKI?

Basic Crypto

As mentioned earlier, cryptography is organized into symmetric algorithms and asymmetric algorithms. Each field of study has commonalties and differences. Let's address symmetric cryptography first, and then contrast its characteristics with asymmetric cryptography.

Symmetric Crypto

To explore the characteristics of symmetric cryptography, it is easiest to begin looking at encryption. Figure 2.1 depicts a classic flow. The lock icons represent the symmetric algorithm, the blocked words indicate the inputs and outputs, the key icons represent the symmetric keys, and the arrows show the data flows.

Beginning on the left, the cleartext data and the symmetric key are input into the symmetric algorithm. The output is the ciphertext. In this diagram, the ciphertext is transmitted from left to right; however, the data can flow in either direction. On the right, the ciphertext and the same symmetric key are input into the same symmetric algorithm. The output is the cleartext.

The same cryptographic key is used for encryption and decryption. This is the definition of symmetric cryptography. Both parties must share the same symmetric key. The transmission of the ciphertext provides data confidentiality. It does not, however, provide data integrity or by itself enable authentication, and certainly does not provide non-repudiation. So, the question should be, can symmetric cryptography provide integrity, authentication, or non-repudiation?

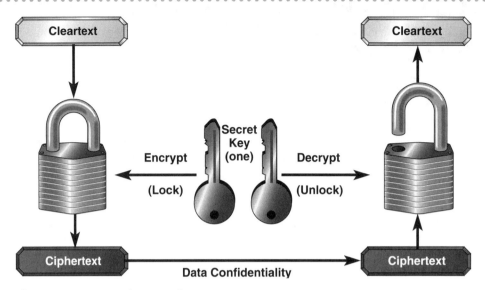

Figure 2.1 Symmetric encryption.

To address the question, let's take a look at another cryptography mechanism called Message Authentication Code (MAC). Figure 2.2 depicts a classic flow. The lock icons represent the symmetric algorithm, the blocked words indicate the inputs and outputs, the key icons represent the symmetric keys, the arrows show the data flows, and the diamond icon represents a comparison process.

Beginning on the left, the cleartext data and the symmetric key are input into the symmetric algorithm. The MAC output is actually truncated ciphertext. In this diagram, the cleartext and the MAC are transmitted from left to right; however, the data can flow in either direction. This is different from encryption, in that both the cleartext and the ciphertext (MAC) are transmitted. On the right, the received cleartext and the same symmetric key are input into the same symmetric algorithm. The output is the recalculated MAC, which is compared to the received MAC. If they match, then the cleartext has not been modified or substituted. If they don't match, then either the cleartext or the MAC has been altered.

The same cryptographic key is used by both the sender and receiver. As noted earlier, this is the definition of symmetric cryptography. Both parties must share the same symmetric key. The transmission of the cleartext and MAC provides data integrity. It does not, however, provide data confidentiality. Furthermore, since only the sender and the receiver share the symmetric key and therefore no one else can generate the MAC, and the receiver did not send the cleartext to itself, the sender is also authenticated to the receiver. However, neither the integrity nor the authentication is provable to a third party, since either of the parties could have generated the MAC. Therefore, the MAC cannot provide non-repudiation.

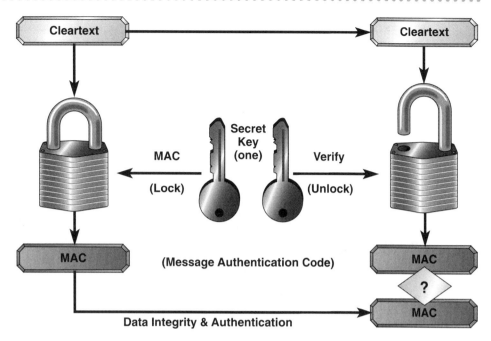

Figure 2.2   Message authentication code.

The presentation on symmetric cryptography assumes that only authorized parties share the keys and that the keys have been generated, exchanged, and stored securely. Chapter 4, "Key Management," discusses this topic in detail. Now, armed with a basic understanding of symmetric cryptography, let's review the aspects of asymmetric cryptography.

Asymmetric Crypto

Figure 2.3 depicts asymmetric cryptography. The lock icons represent the asymmetric algorithm, the blocked words indicate the inputs and outputs, the key icons represent the asymmetric keys, and the arrows show the data flows.

Beginning on the left, the cleartext data and the asymmetric public key are input into the asymmetric algorithm. The output is the ciphertext. In this diagram, the ciphertext is transmitted from left to right. On the right, the ciphertext and the corresponding asymmetric private key are input into the asymmetric algorithm. The output is the cleartext.

The public and private keys are mathematically related, but different values. Ciphertext created by encrypting the cleartext with the public key can only be decrypted with the corresponding private key. The ciphertext cannot be decrypted using the public key. Hence, anyone can encrypt cleartext using someone's public key, but only the holder of the corresponding private key can decrypt the ciphertext. Conversely, if

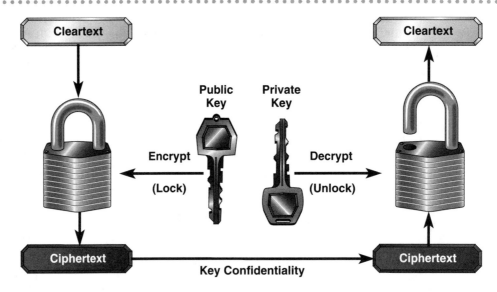

Figure 2.3 Asymmetric encryption.

the cleartext were to be encrypted using the private key, anyone having the corresponding public key can decrypt the ciphertext. Clearly, this does not provide any useful form of data confidentiality.

Asymmetric cryptography is computationally intensive and always uses modular arithmetic. Modularity is simply the remainder from division (e.g., 23 *mod* 7 = 2 is 23 divided by 7 is 3 remainder 2; that is, 3(7) + 2 = 23). Because of the size limitation imposed by modular arithmetic and the costly other mathematics, asymmetric cryptography is not used for large pieces of data, and is typically reserved for encrypting and decrypting symmetric keys. Hence, asymmetric cryptography provides key confidentiality (versus data confidentiality). This topic is further discussed in Chapter 4.

One needs to realize that who owns the public key is a critical issue. Let's assume that Alice wants to send encrypted data to Bob using Bob's public key. No secrecy is needed, as Bob's public key is public, so Bob decides to send his public key to Alice electronically. Further suppose that Eve is our technically savvy adversary. Eve intercepts Bob's public key and substitutes her public key. So, Alice, thinking she has Bob's public key, encrypts her cleartext and sends it electronically to Bob. Our adversary Eve intercepts again. Eve can decrypt the ciphertext and read the cleartext. Even worse, Eve can encrypt different cleartext using Bob's public key, and Bob will think the cleartext came from Alice.

So, the obvious next question should be, is there any useful security service achievable by using the private key to protect cleartext? Surprisingly, the answer is a resounding "yes," and in fact offers one the most powerful cryptographic mechanisms we've seen yet: a digital signature.

Digital Signatures

Figure 2.4 depicts this mysterious mechanism. The lock icons represent the asymmetric algorithm, the blocked words indicate the inputs and outputs, the key icons represent the asymmetric keys, and the arrows show the data flows.

Starting on the right, the cleartext is first input into a hash algorithm, whose output is simply called a *hash*. By definition, a hash algorithm is a mathematical function that maps a string of arbitrary length (like a document for example) to a fixed-length string, typically 128 or 160 bits long. The result is a unique value for that document or file. If anything in that document were altered, the value would change. The hash and the asymmetric private key are input into the asymmetric algorithm, whose output is called a *digital signature*. The cleartext and the signature are transmitted from right to left. On the left, the same cleartext is first input to the same hash algorithm to generate the same hash. The newly generated hash, the public asymmetric key, and the digital signature are input to the asymmetric algorithm to verify the digital signature. Similar to the MAC we saw for symmetric cryptography, if the digital signature verifies, then the cleartext has not been modified or substituted. If the digital signature doesn't verify, then either the cleartext or the digital signature has been altered.

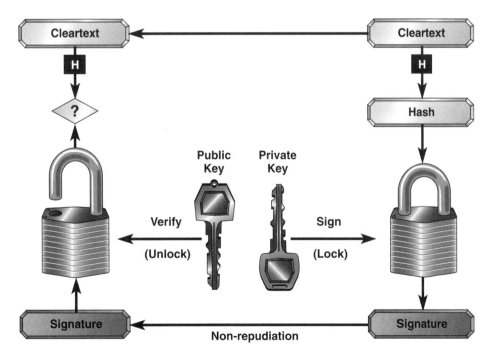

Figure 2.4   Digital signature.

For some asymmetric algorithms, the digital signature is generated by encrypting the hash with the private key (see Figure 2.5). The signature is verified by using the public key to decrypt the digital signature and recover the original hash. The original hash is then compared to the newly generated hash, and if they match, the digital signature is verified. Other asymmetric algorithms do not decrypt the digital signature to recover the original hash; rather, the public key is used to create intermediate verification values from the digital signature, and the newly generated hash is used to validate these intermediate verification values. Regardless of the actual algorithm, the digital signature provided data integrity.

As we observed with key confidentiality, the digital signature can have only been generated by the holder of the private key. Therefore, the signer can be authenticated by the verifier, if the verifier knows that the corresponding public key belongs to the signer. Furthermore, since only the signer could have generated the digital signature, the integrity and authentication is provable to a third party; therefore, the digital signature also provides non-repudiation. The signer cannot deny having generated the digital signature, since only the signer could have done it.

Let's return to our adversarial scenario, where Eve has substituted her public key for Bob's public key to Alice. Now, Bob generates a digital signature using his private key, and sends the signed cleartext to Alice. Eve again intercepts the message, alters the cleartext, and generates her own digital signature using her private key. When Alice gets the signed cleartext, she uses what she thinks is Bob's public key, and the digital signature verifies. Recall that Alice actually has Eve's public key, and that Eve generated the digital signature using her own private key. Alice now erroneously believes she has non-repudiation with the signed cleartext. Needless to say, the issue of knowing who belongs to the public key is of paramount importance and cannot be underestimated. As it turns out, digital signatures can address this issue with a mechanism called a digital certificate, discussed in the following section.

Digital Certificates

So, how do we provide assurance that an entity's public key belongs to the entity? Let's describe this as a requirement. We need to provide a secure binding between an entity's identity and his or her public key, such that we have data integrity, authentication, and non-repudiation. In another words, we need to digitally sign something that contains Bob's name and his public key.

However, Bob cannot just sign his own public key. Although this would provide data integrity, Alice would have no assurance that the public key actually belonged to Bob. In addition to the binding, we need an independent third party to certify that Bob is who he claims to be, and Bob needs to provide proof that he holds the corresponding private key. This independent third party is called a *certification authority* (CA). Figure 2.6 shows the basic elements of a digital certificate, more precisely called a *public key certificate*, and the relationship to the various entities involved.

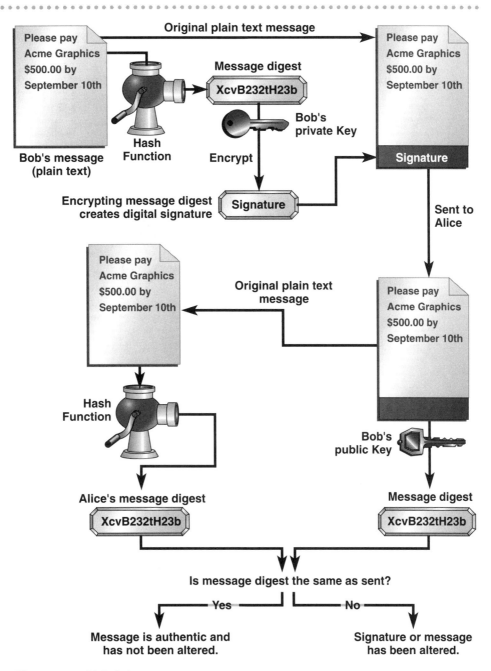

Figure 2.5   Digital signature.

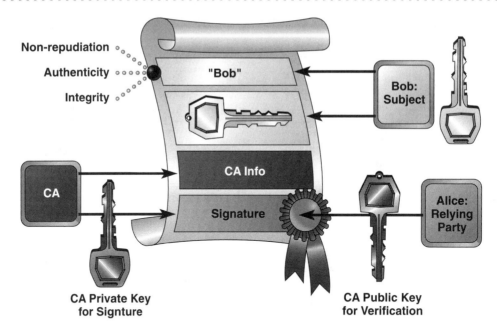

Non-repudiation

Authenticity

Integrity

"Bob"

Bob:
Subject

CA

CA Info

Signature

Alice:
Relying
Party

CA Private Key
for Signture

CA Public Key
for Verification

Figure 2.6   Digital certificate.

The first two elements are Bob's identity and his public key, where Bob is the subject of the certificate. The third element is where the CA typically adds other information, such as the issuance date, the validity period, its own identity, and the like. These three elements are hashed, and the CA's private key is used to generate the digital signature, the fourth element of the certificate. The digital signature of the certificate provides data integrity, authenticates the CA, and provides non-repudiation to users of the certificate, such as Alice, also called a *relying party*.

Any relying party can verify the certificate by verifying the digital signature using the CA's public key. Given that the digital signature verifies, the relying party trusts that the certificate is whole and sound; therefore, the binding between Bob's identity and his public key is preserved. Thus, the relying party (e.g., Alice) can now use Bob's public key with confidence.

Of course, there are many issues surrounding the validity of the certificate and the CA's public key. Further details are discussed in Chapter 5, "Certificate and Validation Authorities." The management of Bob's private key, along with any other symmetric keys, is discussed in Chapter 4.

Protection Techniques

Hardware mechanisms provide protection techniques to prevent and/or detect the unauthorized disclosure, modification, or substitution of sensitive information, such as symmetric keys, asymmetric private keys, and other sensitive data. Such hardware mechanisms include:

➢ Tamper-evident mechanisms that result in visual evidence that an attack has been attempted, such as smooth-molded casing or discoloration due to chemical attacks.

➢ Tamper-resistant mechanisms that resist physical penetration, such as hardened casing to resist drilling or compounds that resist acid washings.

➢ Tamper-responsive mechanisms that detect unauthorized access and initiate counter-measures, such as zeroizing memory or placing the system into a security state.

The type of attack the mechanism is designed to thwart is related to the sophistication of the attacker, as described in the following taxonomy of attackers in *Transaction Security System,* as published in the *IBM Systems Journal.*

Class I (clever outsiders) These attackers are often very intelligent but may have insufficient knowledge of the system. They may have access to only moderately sophisticated equipment. They often try to take advantage of an existing weakness in the system, rather than try to create one.

Class II (knowledgeable insiders) Class II attackers have substantial specialized technical education and experience. They have varying degrees of understanding of parts of the system, but potential access to most of it. They often have highly sophisticated tools and instruments for analysis.

Class III (funded organizations) Class III attackers are able to assemble teams of specialists with related and complementary skills backed by great funding resources. The are capable of in-depth analysis of the system, designing sophisticated attacks, and using the most advanced analysis tools. They may use Class II adversaries as part of the attack team.

The actual design and implementation of such protection mechanisms are problematic, and are described in the Federal Information Processing Standards 140-2. FIPS 140-2 specifies four security levels ranging from lowest (Security Level 1) to highest (Security Level 4). The National Voluntary Accreditation Laboratory Program (NVAP) accredits laboratories to test and certify vendors' products against these security levels. Chapter 8, "Hardware Mechanisms," discusses FIPS in more detail.

CHAPTER 3

Securing the Environment for PKI

B efore tackling an actual PKI implementation, it is important to step back and examine the security basics in place for the entire enterprise. A well-designed PKI implementation hinges on having a secure foundation in place. A PKI architecture built upon a poorly secured set of networks and systems is unlikely to perform as predicted. This chapter will address some basics for designing that secure foundation.

IT security, like security in every other arena of life, is not an absolute. Every action has some potential risk. However, action is the basis for success and for profit. An absolutely risk-free environment would actually be one with no potential for profit. A totally secure computer is often characterized as one shielded in concrete and buried underground, totally secure but totally useless. The challenge is to design *useful systems* with a *high degree of trustworthiness*.

Enterprises looking to integrate PKI solutions into their business model are usually embarking on business initiatives with significant potential for new business profit and both expected and unexpected risks. IT security involves planning and control to minimize those risks, so that the positives for profit outweigh the negatives of risk.

The Fifty-Thousand-Foot View

IT security is often described in military or castle fortification terms. This analogy is popular not just because IT security gained earliest attention in the government and military sectors. The fortification analogy is popular because planning and fortification are the essentials for good IT security. Most important is the fact that with IT security, just as with military security or castle fortification, security is only as good as its weakest components. A castle with the strongest walls will not survive long if it's built atop a fault line. Similarly, an e-commerce server running on the highest-performance servers may not keep running if it lacks basic protections from unauthorized outsider access.

Security design, like the planning of a military campaign or of a fortified castle, hinges on several building blocks. In both the medieval world and today's e-business environment, assets must be protected from deliberate or accidental destruction; friends must be differentiated from foes; and controlled activities must be facilitated. The basics of IT security include:

➢ Ensuring that data is not lost or altered by assuring *data integrity*

➢ Ensuring that the user is who he says he is, or *authentication*

➢ Ensuring that the user is allowed to do what she is allowed to do and is trying to do, or *authorization*

➢ Ensuring that data is protected while in transit

➢ Maintaining the environment via *monitoring and control*

These functions are comparable to the fortification offered by medieval castles as shown in Figure 3.1. Castles were built of the strongest materials, carefully situated to look down over the dominion, had strongly protected perimeters, and employed scores of guards to monitor who and what passed in and out of the castle gates. All of these protective functions reflected strict enforcement of the crown's policies for who was friend and who was foe.

The challenges in today's business climate also demand serious IT fortification. With corporate financial assets and reputations on the line, no business can afford to have its billing database altered, or have confidential client data accessed by outsiders. Modern IT security deploys a combination of hardware and software under strict policy guidelines to enforce a level of high security appropriate to today's networked environments.

Business Drivers for Increased Security Awareness and Preparedness

Today's business climate has generated new pressures and security concerns. Electronic commerce has created a global 24×7 business environment. The reputation and viability of an enterprise may hinge on providing non-stop global computing access for online business initiatives. As the major denial-of-services attacks to popular Web sites have demonstrated, a Web site that cannot be accessed is a closed shop.

Some downtime can be expected in an environment built upon hardware components. In fact, hardware components require scheduled maintenance, and software components require regular updates and patches. A total system plan involves planning for such necessary maintenance. However, unplanned downtime is more of a problem.

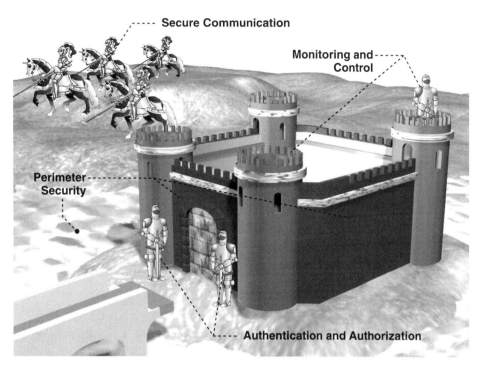

Figure 3.1 Securing the assets.

The Gartner Group has used data from its clients to model the major causes of unplanned downtime. They estimate that about 20 percent of the time, hardware failures and environmental factors are the cause. More interesting is their estimate that 40 percent of the time, failures were caused by a variety of "bugs" or performance problems with application code. Another 40 percent of unplanned downtime was attributed to operational errors where tasks were done incorrectly or not at all (see Figure 3.2).

Good security practice dictates that IT systems must operate in a controlled and predictable fashion. This chapter will address how using a variety of technologies and systems, including non-automated elements, can improve the IT manager's ability to ensure maximum uptime and graceful disaster recovery.

The Thousand-Foot View: Beginning with a Good Security Policy

A good security policy should involve input from all business units and span both physical and IT security. A security policy may be as simple as articulating that all IT

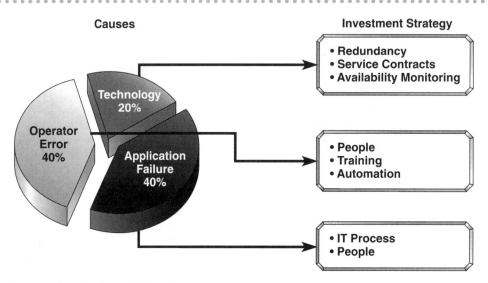

Figure 3.2   Unplanned downtime.

Source: Gartner Group

and physical resources provided by the corporation are to be used only for authorized work purposes, and permission for all actions require valid badges or passwords. Or it may be a detailed, living document. In any case, a good security policy is one that is clear, published to all, and is *consistently enforced*. It should address *what* is expected, *who* has authority to grant permissions or modify them, and *how* action is to be taken if a threat or crisis arises.

Underlying a successful policy are *resources* to support enforcement, educate users, and modify the environment as external and internal conditions change. Resources from every arm of the company united in support of a well-structured policy are essential to supporting the highest-level business goals of the enterprise.

By bringing together representatives of finance, human resources, engineering, plant security, and other business units, the enterprise can operate as a whole with a unified view of security. In addition, having resources from representative groups within the enterprise facilitates efficient follow-through on threats. A threat model can be created based on historical and business data as to who and what factors are likely to represent threats. In most enterprises, threats are as likely to occur from employees with knowledge of the physical resources and IT systems as from outsiders.

In developing a useful policy, special attention should be given to the areas discussed in the following sections.

Identification of Valuable Assets

Both physical and IT assets must be inventoried and assessed for value before they can be properly protected. Assets as varied as buildings, employees, servers, and data require attention. Tagging of office equipment and badging of employees and authorized contractors are visible steps that identify an asset as managed by the enterprise. Equally important are the databases that maintain the corporate records of where each of these assets should reside and who should supervise it.

Classification of Assets

Different assets demand different types of treatment. Once assets are inventoried, they can be classified. Most corporations use a data classification system to differentiate data as company confidential, personal and confidential, general use, and so forth. Unfortunately, many companies fall short and limit data classification to only some parts of the organization. Data that is not classified are likely to be unprotected.

Differentiation of employees is another valuable differentiation step. In addition to receiving badges and employee identifiers, employees can be classified into categories (such as full-time, contractor, regular part-time, temporary, etc.) that help differentiate where and when they can be allowed access to enterprise facilities and IT assets.

Separation of Work and Employee Assets

Recent trends in non-work-related surfing on the Internet have drawn attention to the problems that arise when employees misuse work assets for personal amusement or gain. According to the Computer Security Institute ALERT newsletter, employee misuse of enterprise e-mail can be costly to both the corporate reputation and the corporate bottom line. Moreover, an allegedly racist e-mail message was the basis of a $30M discrimination suit against Morgan Stanley Dean Witter & Company.

The first step in reducing misuse is to properly identify which assets are for corporate use only, and which assets may be used under certain specific conditions for employee personal use.

Different Security Levels for Different Times

Every enterprise is impacted by outside change. Different times of day or days of the year may merit different types of physical security if they are more likely to be times when theft or unwanted access increases. Automated locks that control physical access outside of regular working times can increase physical security. Software such as firewalls and intrusion detection can be set up so that security is stricter during hours or days when administrative support is less likely to be onsite.

Overall Coordination of Separate Security and Availability Features

Deploying a well-designed security policy, good physical security, and the system architectures addressed in the next sections in a consistent and coordinated fashion provide the best foundation for reliable and resilient computing.

Addressing Physical Security

Physical security and resource availability are fundamental to ongoing IT operations, yet often get far less attention than higher technology application or infrastructure security products. With so much visibility for new e-business initiatives and new customer relationship management programs, attention to the basics of physical security often only comes up after an audit or a natural disaster.

As with so many areas of security, effective physical security hinges upon a well-reasoned security policy. In many enterprises, physical security issues are handled separately from IT security issues, and report to separate parts of the corporation. Organizational separation may be very practical, particularly for staffing and maintenance, but it is important that both physical and IT security be coordinated closely in terms of policy and planning.

Major steps toward effective physical security build upon good planning and administration. Once a security policy has been written and articulated, the areas of physical security discussed in the following sections can be addressed.

Building on a Strong Foundation

Most enterprises recognize the need to invest in well-engineered stores or factories. Quality components are as important in IT systems as in buildings. An IT system is only as good as the parts that go into it. In IT security terminology, the concept of a "trusted computing base"—the totality of protection mechanisms within a computer system including hardware, firmware, and software responsible for enforcing a security policy—represents the foundation of reliable and well-managed parts on which an application can be layered. Just as a crack in the foundation can lead to problems in a physical structure, shoddy or poorly controlled components in an IT implementation can compromise the integrity of the entire implementation

The need to build upon best-in-breed components helps determine which operating systems and which hardware platforms are selected to host an IT application. The benefits of having 24×7 global support may far outweigh the cost benefits of freeware for many application environments. The decision of which platform to use for critical applications, especially those on which e-business initiatives are built, should address not only the initial price of the hardware and software, but also the total life cycle costs of installing and maintaining the platform and operating system.

Separation of Public and Private Areas

After classifying personnel and assets, creating physical separation can help in tighter control. Door locks, locked file cabinets, and even locked systems and databases can help protect assets from unauthorized usage.

Removal of Dependencies on One Site or One Resource

Decentralization of mission-critical computer, telecommunications, data storage, and data management systems is another proactive step that can be taken to reduce the risk that a disaster at one location will impact the entire enterprise. Single points of failure can be minimized, and rapid recovery from outages facilitated, by the installation of decentralized, distributed, and redundant systems.

Protection from Theft or Accidental Loss

Traditionally, locks, burglar alarms, and security guards provide basic protection of tangible assets. As employees have become more mobile and electronic equipment of all types has become smaller and lighter, protection from theft and loss has become more challenging.

The first step toward controlling theft and loss is to recognize that some enterprise assets may be used off corporate grounds and to differentiate them. Next comes articulating that usage policy to all classes of employees. In concert with that, it can be valuable to train employees on how to use laptop locks, and cell phone and PDA lockup features. Finally, it is essential to train employees about the risks of working with and copying sensitive data in highly mobile or replicated environments.

Protection from Natural Disasters

Automated facilities protection systems provide basic protection again fire, smoke, and water damage. As an added protection for both natural disasters and theft, offsite storage and outsourced disaster recovery services can be contracted. If corporate headquarters are in a geographical area prone to earthquakes or terrorism, a redundant site in a very different geography can be worth the expense. Uninterruptible power supplies (UPS) and surge protection systems can be used to keep electronic systems running during power losses and protected from power surges.

For many environments, it may also be important to design in access to multiple power grids and TCP/IP backbones. When servers or applications are outsourced, the Service Level Agreement (SLA) between the enterprise and the service provider should address the extra protection needed to maintain access across a wide range of environmental impacts.

While we tend to believe disasters usually occur in other's backyards, U.S. Government statistics prove otherwise. According to the Federal Emergency Management Agency (FEMA), U.S. Presidents have declared over 1200 disasters, sparing few communities (see Figure 3.3). Statistically, it is just a matter of time before a disaster strikes.

Controlling the Physical Environment

Safe, clean, and controlled physical environments support efficient operations of both people and machines. Some environments may demand special types of equipment

Figure 3.3   Presidential disaster declarations.
Source: Michael Baker Jr., Inc.

because of the extremes to which equipment is subjected. Special equipment or shielding to protect it can be purchased to help ruggedize equipment for extreme temperatures, heavy vibrations, special altitudes, and a variety of conditions.

Air conditioning is important in keeping IT equipment operating safely over a wide range of temperatures. Without adequate air-conditioning resources, hardware may fail, including UPS devices, which are necessary to provide power backup and power conditioning services. Air filtration is another proactive measure that can be taken to increase the reliability of hardware components.

Monitoring the Physical Environment

Finally, as with all other security measures, physical security should be implemented with a plan for ongoing monitoring in place from the start. On the basis of alerts and log files, increased security measures can put into place at times of higher risk. If smoke alarms are going off regularly, or wide temperature swings occur, for example, more investigation can lead to solving physical environmental problems that might have gone undetected before a major problem would have caused major downtime.

Planning Ahead for Problems

Avoiding problems 100 percent of the time is not possible. Planned and unplanned events dictate that there will be unavoidable system downtime or unanticipated changes in system behavior. The rapid, graceful, and robust restoration of mission-critical functions after an unplanned outage or after a hacking incident can prevent an interruption from turning into a disaster. Such a restoration of services can occur only if there has been advanced business continuation planning.

The economics of today's commerce and computing system architectures dictate that substantial effort be invested in *proactive* planning for downtime-avoidance, rather than in *reacting* to downtime occurrences. In fact, more insurers are recognizing the value of proactive planning for outages and security problems, and are making insurance available at lower costs for those who deploy good practice in disaster anticipation. According to the *Wall Street Journal*, one broker recently began offering up to $200 million in coverage in its NetSecure policy and has sold well over 100 policies within months.

The steps noted in the previous section address the proactive security steps that can help protect physical assets. Protection of telecommunications infrastructure, including local and wide area networks, is another area that must be addressed separately. Data protection is the third important step. This section addresses some of the numerous cost-effective and highly reliable IT mechanisms for protecting business data assets from the impact of inevitable problems. These mechanisms can be implemented in both the hardware and the software elements of IT systems architectures.

What Is System Resiliency?

Assets of any kind have real value only when they fulfill their expected purpose. Computing resources are valuable when they perform *when* required and *as* expected. In the real world, systems are subjected to a variety of factors that cannot always be controlled. These factors include natural disasters, power outages, changes in political and social environments, shifting population demographics, and scores of other non-computing pressures. Ideally, computing systems operate in a predictable fashion under as wide a range of external factors as possible. Continued improvements in IT hardware and software and their performance characteristics have led to dramatic improvements in the level of reliability and availability users can aim for with their systems.

Systems that are *resilient* operate in a predictable fashion because their design addresses operation not only under ideal conditions, but addresses in advance the need to operate under far less than ideal conditions. Resilient systems are engineered to operate predictably, even when individual components fail or natural disasters occur. Resiliency is an ideal—like security—in that even the best-designed system will suffer occasional outages. Mechanical systems, biological systems, electrical systems, chemical systems, optical systems, and any combination thereof, will eventually wear down and stop working. Even when the system itself is in working order, it may be forced to respond to some environmental or external impact by shutting down.

Well-designed systems will have an orderly and predictable shutdown process for such occasions, and tools for smooth resumption of computing. Well-designed systems are also built to continue functioning as long as possible, even when individual components fail or extra factors stress the system. All systems fail—well-designed systems fail gracefully.

Systems, processes, and objects can be made resilient by replicating them over multiple sites. Most computers are now connected to networks so that most systems are becoming, to a greater or lesser extent, distributed systems. This allows businesses to take advantage of the redundancy of processing and storage that distributed systems provide.

Business Implications for System Resiliency and Availability

Total and complete security is not possible. Similarly, 100-percent uptime at all times is not a physical possibility. Planned and unplanned events dictate that there will be unavoidable system downtime or unanticipated changes in system behavior. No system, whether standalone or networked, can provide one 100-percent uptime. However, very high levels of both security and uptime can achieved through good design and the deployment of specialized IT technologies that improve system security and resiliency. With these inevitable challenges noted, maximum uptime can remain one of the primary targets of a good system design.

To handle the demands of electronic commerce, IT systems must not only be designed with sufficient bandwidth and computing resources, they must also be engineered to perform predictably across sometimes staggering levels of peak demand. The reputation of several online commerce sites has been established or destroyed by the site's ability to serve demand during holiday seasons.

The business justifications for the introduction of new applications or new systems into an enterprise-computing environment usually focus on opportunities, benefits, expected financial return, and general risk. Applications launched on the Internet are also likely to be scrutinized for their potential to introduce unwanted system access, viruses, privacy violations, or other major risks. Assessing each of these individual factors helps determine what type of systems, staffing, and financial investments are necessary to launch an application. Equally important is the need to evaluate IT systems not only in terms of a checklist of discrete factors, but also for their ability to operate predictably over time and across a variety of changing external factors.

Options for Protection against Failures

The first steps toward reducing the impact of the inevitable problems that occur revolve around good IT operations practices. Essential protective steps include:

Keep current backups, and be sure the system will rebuild from them. Frequent, planned backups are essential to smooth operations. However, backups are only useful if the systems can actually be rebuilt or databases restored from them. It is essential to have a regular schedule for backups, and to test that the media work correctly.

Limit access to resources to only those users who are specifically authorized. Good security practice is built upon granting specific privileges to specified users, rather than enabling anyone to do everything with all resources. Obviously, tight control demands a well-reasoned plan for granting specific privileges via a tight exception policy.

Eliminate unauthorized users who have left the company. No work environment is static. People leave, get fired, or even die. Accounts left behind can provide tempting entry points for undesired access by either the departed employee or someone inside who wants to mask his own identity. Good policy dictates removing all accounts, remote access, and physical plant access privileges for anyone whose status with the enterprise has changed.

Disable unnecessary services. Just as abandoned accounts can attract misuse, unwanted or unnecessary services can lead to misuse. If there is no business need for something like Internet chat services or audio broadcasts within a corporation, such services should be disabled on the network until a business case and proper security controls are established.

Keep all systems up to date with the latest security patches. Every major hardware and software vendor invests in keeping up with security problems in the industry. Since critical security problems can arise between system updates, vendors offer interim patches to solve critical issues. Part of keeping systems healthy and secure is keeping them updated as new patches and releases come out.

Reduce system complexity so that operations do not hinge upon frequent support calls. Users are more likely to use security features if they are easy to understand and do not require frequent calls to the help desk.

Automate all actions that keep systems running smoothly. Updates to anti-virus products, backups, and other steps that keep systems and networks healthy are more likely to get done if automated.

Keep log files and use the reports they generate. It is not enough that software generates good log files. It is essential to generate useful reports from the data and have administrative staff monitor the output.

Maintaining Data Integrity

Well-managed operations are just part of a well-designed solution. Databases are an invaluable asset. There are multiple options for increasing data integrity. Many overlap with the steps for good physical security and disaster planning. However, it is essential to recognize the special value of data as an enterprise asset, particularly with databases often spread across heterogeneous networks and across multiple time zones.

The basic steps to maintaining data integrity include:

➤ Redundancy using RAID (Redundant Array of Inexpensive Disks)

➤ Regularly scheduled backup and restoration

➤ Off-site storage to reduce the possibility of losing all data when one site is impacted

➤ Electronic vaulting to protect stored data

➤ Secure transmission of data over networks via encryption

In a PKI implementation, digital certificate data is essential to the user/resource authorization process. Certificate databases may require using a variety of techniques for increasing physical security and data availability. Two steps are essential. First is focusing on physical security for all systems on which the certificate database is replicated. Second is protecting the certificates while in storage as part of normal business continuity practices. The certificate database is the linchpin of a PKI database. The effort in designing and securing that database is an investment that goes a long way toward increasing the success of the implementation.

Deploying Security Products

Finally, a well-designed IT solution can benefit from commercial security products and services. These products and services include:

➤ Security software for anti-virus, firewall, and intrusion detection

➤ Authentication software that verifies a user is the person he or she claims to be

➤ Data protection, consulting, and site audits

➤ Disaster recovery plans, restoration products, and recovery services

➤ Insurance for IT disasters

Individual commercial security products and security suites are available for multiple operating systems and hardware platforms. Similarly, support services are available from system vendors, major SI and consulting firms, applications service providers and outsourcers, and from a variety of specialized security service providers.

Insurance is the final complement to policy, products, staffs, and services. A variety of coverage options are available to help enterprises recover revenues lost because hacking, denial of service, or service outages. The insurance process can help protect the enterprise by providing protection against losses and for liabilities incurred when the unexpected occurs at an enterprise Web site. Perhaps even more important is that the process of applying for insurance protection generally involves a site audit that can help improve the overall security of the Web site and the enterprise behind it.

Using Standards to Help Select Operating Systems and Security Software

There are several criteria that can help with the operating system choice. The U.S. Department of Defense established basic definitions in the early 1980s with its *Trusted Computer System Evaluation Criteria*, which is often referred to as "The Orange Book." These classifications range from D, which has no security controls, up to A1, which is a conceptual definition of provable high security. Germany, the Netherlands, and the United Kingdom have collaborated on a similar set of definitions with the ITSEC (Information Technology Security) effort. More recently, the U.S. and European bodies pooled their resources to develop an international standard, *The Common Criteria for IT Security Evaluation.* In June 1999, an important step toward international standardization occurred when ISO accepted version 2 of the *Common Criteria* as its International Standard 15408.

The software vendor community also uses the *Common Criteria* to categorize operating system security. The levels help differentiate operating system environments with no basic security features enabled from those that are suitable for general commercial environments on up to those that have specific features for high-security environments. While few commercial sites require the complex solutions that government intelligence agencies demand, most sites require platforms where the vendor's solution conforms to the basic ITSEC E2 or Orange Book C2 level. For example, Microsoft's Windows NT Server version 4.0 is classified as C2, while Compaq's Secure VMS version 6.0 is classified as B1.

Using any of these standards-based ratings for operating systems is valuable for users, software developers, and evaluators (see Table 3.1).

Security Classifications

For security products themselves, there are also useful standards to consider. As earlier sections of this book detail, digital certificates have been defined in the X.509 standard. There is standards work going on in other security product areas. The IETF has issued the IPSec standard to increase the usability and interoperability of virtual

Table 3.1 Ratings for Operating Systems

USES OF *COMMON CRITERIA* AND *ORANGE BOOK* RATINGS	
Users	■ To find requirements for security features that match their own risk assessment. ■ To shop for products that have ratings with those features. ■ To publish their security requirements so that vendors can design products that meets those requirements.
Software Developers	■ To select security requirements that they wish to include in their products. ■ To design and build a product in a way that can prove to evaluators that the product meets requirements. ■ To determine their responsibilities in supporting and evaluating their product.
Evaluators	■ To judge whether a product meets its security requirements. ■ Provide a yardstick against which evaluations can be performed. ■ Provide input when forming specific evaluation methods.

Table 3.2 Security Classifications

ORANGE BOOK LEVEL	ITSEC LEVEL	USE IN ACTUAL PRACTICE	COMMON CRITERIA
D: MINIMAL PROTECTION	E0	Single user systems	
C: DISCRETIONARY PROTECTION			
(C1): Discretionary Security Protection	E1	Basic protection in multi-user environments	EAL2
(C2): Controlled Access Protection	E2	Most modern commercial operating systems	EAL3
B: MANDATORY PROTECTION			
(B1): Labeled Security Protection	E3	Specialized government or finance usage	EAL4
(B2): Structured Protection	E4	Only practical in customized installations	EAL5
(B3): Security Domains	E5	Only practical in customized installations	EAL6
A: VERIFIED PROTECTION			
(A1): Verified Design Beyond Class (A1)	E6	Theoretical	EAL7

private networks or tunnels that help facilitate secure communications over public networks.

Standards have not been developed for all product technologies that help secure systems and networks. The ones that do exist often take a long time to be finalized. Sometimes, too, the standard leaves a lot of room for interpretation across vendor implementations. Yet, standards can be helpful. Standards efforts can help IT decision-makers by defining some of the essential features that vendors should address in designing their products, such as those defined in ITSEC and the common criteria (see Table 3.2). Asking technology providers and integrators about how their offerings meet established standards or criteria can open a dialogue about just how these offerings can increase security in complex, heterogeneous environments.

Summary

Security is neither an absolute nor a guarantee. Underlying good IT design is the acceptance of self-responsibility for security. No government agency or business partner will fill the void if an enterprise does not accept responsibility for establishing good policy, designing systems for resilience to failure, and staffing to keep assets functioning.

Good security practice also extends to auditing systems and networks and applying post-disaster forensics tools to identify what happened. Using such feedback tools, design improvements can then be made to continuously improve and harden the environment against future attacks.

PART TWO

PKI Technologies

Key Management

K ey management is the necessary discipline to ensure the security of cryptographic keys throughout their life cycle, and consists of key:

➤ Generation
➤ Distribution
➤ Storage
➤ Usage
➤ Recovery
➤ Termination
➤ Archival

Before we delve further into each phase of the key life cycle, there are some fundamental rules, called *key management axioms*.

Key Management Axioms

The importance of these axioms cannot be overly emphasized. You need to absolutely understand and commit these axioms to memory. Without naming names, there are many instances where entire systems have been broken or hacked into due to bad key management.

Axiom #1: Keys Are Secret

Cryptographic keys and sensitive keying material (with the exception of asymmetric public keys) should be secret, meaning no one knows the value of a key.

Strange as this may sound, there are many people who either never understand this concept in the first place, or forgot it in the middle of a crisis such as a "production problem" or disaster recovery. Axiom #1 says exactly what it means, that nobody should ever see or know the value of a cryptographic key. Unlike passwords where at least one person must know the password (you must know your password, otherwise you cannot log on), cryptographic keys are the ultimate secret. Needless to say, this makes managing keys very difficult.

The reason behind this is very simple. The best cryptography does not rely on the secrecy of the specific algorithm; rather, it relies on the secrecy of the key. Therefore, if a person (one or more) knows the value of the key, the security provided by the cryptography must be suspect. People are the weakest link in the security fence because they can be bribed.

For instance, in the case where data confidentiality is provided by encryption, an adversary knowing the cryptographic key could easily capture and decrypt all of the messages, completely thwarting the security. Let's consider digital signatures: If the private key was known, then an adversary could falsely sign messages and documents that would seriously jeopardize data integrity, authentication, and even non-repudiation.

Axiom #2: Permissible Key Forms

Cryptographic keys (with the exception of asymmetric public keys) can only exist in the following forms:

➤ As *cleartext* inside the secure confines of a tamper-resistant security module (TRSM)

➤ As *ciphertext* outside a tamper-resistant security module (TRSM)

➤ As *fractions* outside a tamper-resistant security module (TRSM), using split knowledge and dual control

This axiom meets the requirement defined in Axiom #1. The first two forms are straightforward, except for the difficult part as to what exactly constitutes a tamper-resistant security module (TRSM). Refer to Chapter 8, "Hardware Mechanisms," for a discussion on cryptographic hardware. It should be obvious that keys inside cryptographic hardware or encrypted keys outside cryptographic hardware keeps them very secure.

The third form is a bit trickier. First, the term "fractions" was chosen so as not to stipulate any specific technique. There are several methods to accomplish fractionalizing a cryptographic key, for which we will look at several of the better known methods. Second, "split knowledge" means that no single person has sufficient information to determine the key; however, collusion between two or more individuals could potentially compromise the key. Third, "dual control" means that access to the key fractions is always under the supervision of two (or more) authorized individuals, which effectively reduces the risk of collusion. Key fractionalizing includes the following techniques:

➤ Key components

➤ Key shares

Key Components

Key components use the bit-wise logical operator called an "exclusive or" commonly abbreviated as XOR in text and $\oplus$ as a symbol. XOR is a function having two bits as input and a single bit as output, where $0 \oplus 0 = 0$, $0 \oplus 1 = 1$, $1 \oplus 0 = 1$, and $1 \oplus 1 = 0$. Succinctly put, if two bits are the same value, the result is a zero bit, and if different, the result is a one bit. Believe it or not, this simple function is an extremely powerful technique. Let's choose a rudimentary example where we need to exchange a single-byte (8 bits) symmetric key between two hardware boxes, without ever knowing the key. How is this possible? Figure 4.1 provides an overview of our example.

We need four individuals: Alice, Bob, Chris, and Dan. Alice chooses a random hexadecimal number between 0 and F (see the "Glossary" for an explanation of hexadecimal). Let's say Alice chooses the value 3. Alice does not show, reveal, or tell anyone her number. Alice and Chris now walk up to one of our infamous TRSMs we mentioned earlier, and under Chris' supervision, Alice enters her number into the TRSM. At this instance in time, Alice's TRSM has the number 3 inside of it. Alice now writes her number on a piece of paper and seals it inside a tamper-evident device, commonly called an

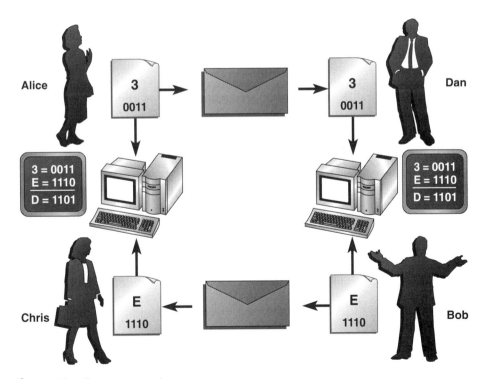

Figure 4.1 Key components.

envelope. Alice hands her envelope to Dan. Realize that only Alice knows her number is 3, and per Chris' supervision, has never revealed her number.

Dan takes the envelope from Alice and, after determining that the envelope has not been tampered with (recall that the envelope is tamper evident), opens the envelop, and under Bob's supervision, Dan enters Alice's random value into Bob's TRSM. At this instance in time, Alice's TRSM and Bob's TRSM hold the random value 3, and only Alice and Dan know the value.

Bob now performs a similar set of steps, and chooses the value E. Bob does not show, reveal, or tell anyone his number. Under Dan's supervision, Bob enters his random value into their TRSM. The TRSM having Alice's value 3 and now Bob's value E, combines the two values using XOR to produce the new value D. Bob now writes his number on a piece of paper, seals it inside an envelope, and hands his envelope to Chris.

Chris takes the envelope from Bob and, after determining that the envelope has not been tampered with, opens the envelope, and under Alice's supervision, Chris enters Bob's random value E into Alice's TRSM. The TRSM having Alice's random value 3 and now Bob's value E, combines the two values using XOR to produce the new value D.

Although this rudimentary example is rather lengthy to describe, it clearly shows how the *Key Management Axioms* can be satisfied using key components. More importantly, this example emphasizes how critical sound key management procedures are to PKI. Furthermore, this scenario also exemplifies how difficult and complicated key management procedures may need to be in order to secure establish cryptographic keys.

Key Shares

Key shares use linear algebra to divide a secret value into multiple fractions, say *M*, where not all of the key shares are needed to reconstitute the secret value. This is called an *N of M* scheme, where *N < M* is the minimum number of key shares needed to recreate the secret value.

Axiom #3: Key Deployment

Cryptographic keys are deployed in the fewest number of places that are operationally feasible.

In order to reduce the potential exposure of any cryptographic key, the key should be distributed and stored in as few locations as possible. The fewer locations, the lower the risk, as the probability of a successful attack would be easier identified. Furthermore, the fewer locations, the easier to establish and maintain proper key management procedures.

Axiom #4: Key Separation

Cryptographic keys are generated and used only for their intended purpose.

There are cryptographic attacks that undermine the security of the PKI when keys are misused. These attacks are outside the scope of this book. However, even the best intentions can be thwarted if key functionality is not separated and enforced. Therefore, keys must be separated by functionality. For example, symmetric PIN encryption keys cannot be allowed to be used for any other purpose. Likewise, asymmetric digital signature keys should not be used for other purposes, and may even need to be restricted as to the type of information they are used with, such as e-mail versus legally binding contracts.

Axiom #5: Key Synchronization

Mechanisms are in place to verify that the same key has been deployed and is in use without risking the security of the keys.

Since keys are secret by definition, it is often difficult to determine whether the correct keys have been deployed. System errors are sometimes caused by keys not being synchronized; therefore, key synchronization should be verified and eliminated as a potential problem. The simplest method is called a *key checksum*. The key to be verified is used to encrypt a string of binary zeroes, and the resulting first four bytes are used as the *key checksum*. If both checksums match, then there is a high probability that the keys are the same value.

Axiom #6: Event Journal

Key management events are captured in an event journal that is itself securely managed.

Event journal entries may be captured electronically, such as system logon, or manually, such as sign-in sheets. The purpose is to track all events that may directly or indirectly affect the security of any cryptographic key. The integrity and the authenticity of the event journal must be established and maintained throughout its retention period. Information that should be included as part of the event journal includes the following:

➤ Time stamp (data and time)

➤ Key management event (key generation, door access, etc.)

➤ System and/or personnel involved

➤ Results of the event (successful, authorized, unauthorized, etc.)

Now that we have established some basic principles that we call our *Key Management Axioms*, let's explore in more detail their implications relevant to the key life cycle.

Key Life Cycle

Perhaps the best way to convey and understand the nuances of sound key management techniques and procedures is to look at the life cycle of cryptographic keys. Keys have a definite beginning and do not last forever. All keys have various strengths due to their size and mathematical properties.

Key Generation

Key generation is when keys are initially created. All keys require randomness, such that any key is not predictable. As predictability is a problem for passwords, it is devastating for keys. If the key is guessable, or the potential search space is reduced sufficiently such that an exhaustive attack is feasible, this severely weakens the cryptographic strength of the entire PKI. Proper key generation is crucial to the overall security of a PKI. For example, in 1995, a bug was discovered in Netscape's browser where the random-number generator was not so random, and allowed a research team to crack earlier implementations of SSL (Secure Sockets Layer).

Symmetric keys are nothing more than a random number, generated using either a Random Number Generator (RNG) or a Pseudo Random Number Generator (PRNG). An RNG is a hardware-based algorithm whose bits are generated by the hardware. A PRNG is a software-based algorithm that accepts a smaller number as a *seed* to generate a random number. The implication here is that an RNG will produce a true random number, whereas a PRNG can only produce a random number that is as random as the *seed*. Realize that the same *seed* will always produce the same random number.

Asymmetric keys are more complex to generate, as they require not only random numbers, but also require prime numbers for the more popular algorithms and potentially other values depending upon the algorithm. Recall that a prime number is divisible only by the number 1 and itself, (e.g., 2, 3, 5, 7, 11, 13, 17, etc.). Notice that 2 is the only even prime number, and all other prime numbers are odd. Any other even number is divisible by 2, and therefore not a prime number. Also realize that not all odd numbers are prime, and in fact finding prime numbers is an active research effort. Further realize that given a large odd number, determining whether it is prime is a non-trivial effort. This field of study is also an active research effort.

To summarize, the technical accuracy of key generation is paramount. Furthermore, the purpose for which keys will be used should be established during generation and maintained throughout its life cycle. Depending upon the business risk and the criticality of the key being generated, in some circumstances it is appropriate that key generation be performed under dual control. Regardless, key generation is an event that should be captured in an event journal.

Key Distribution

Key distribution is when keys are moved from one location to another. There are two distinct stages of key distribution: the initial key, and subsequent keys. The initial key is established and used to distribute other cryptographic keys. Establishing the initial key in a secure fashion is critical to the overall security of the PKI. The initial key can be permanent and reused, or temporal and only used once. Subsequent keys are securely exchanged using the initial key. There are numerous schemas to achieve secure key distribution.

Master key/session key. This is a schema whereby an initial symmetric key, called a master key, is established using key fractions between two communicating parties. Let's assume that Alice and Bob have established such an initial symmetric key. Alice can now generate a subsequent key, encrypt the new key using the initial key, and sends the ciphertext to Bob. Bob can recover the subsequent key by decrypting the ciphertext using the initial key.

Key establishment. This is a schema whereby an asymmetric key pair is used as the initial key to exchange subsequent keys. Let's assume Alice has generated an asymmetric key pair, and provides the public key to Bob. Bob can now generate a subsequent key, encrypt the new key using Alice's public key, and send the ciphertext to Alice. Alice can recover the subsequent key by decrypting the cipher-text using her private key.

Key exchange. This is a schema whereby two parties generate asymmetric key pairs, and using each other's public keys can generate a shared secret value that is used as the initial key. Let's assume Alice and Bob have both generated asymmetric key pairs and have now exchanged public keys. Alice uses her public key and Bob's public key to generate a shared secret value, and Bob uses his public key and Alice's public key to generate the same secret value. Alice and Bob now derive a symmetric key from the shared secret value, and securely exchange subsequent keys using the newly derived symmetric key.

Of course, if the asymmetric public keys are to be used directly, then key distribution becomes reduced to the secure distribution of public keys. Notice that security is still necessary. The confidentiality of public keys is not needed; however, the integrity and authenticity of a public key is still very much a requirement. This is accomplished using public-key certificates, as described in Chapter 2, "What's in a PKI?" The equivalent key management requirements for certificates are discussed further in Chapter 5, "Certificate and Validation Authorities."

Key Storage

Key storage is when cryptographic keys are stored following key distribution in preparation for actually using the keys in a production environment. The protection afforded a cryptographic key must maintain its integrity, authenticity, and, where appropriate, confidentiality. Access controls can provide integrity and authenticity, but only physical hardware (i.e., TRSM) or cryptography can provide key confidentiality.

Key Usage

Key usage is when keys are in their production environment and are being used for their intended purpose. A production environment is where keys are used to protect transaction data, be it electronic mail, financial transactions, or file transfers. A production environment should provide the ability to verify whether keys are synchronized at the application level.

Key Recovery

Key recovery is when keys have been backed up for reasons of reconstituting a cryptographic key due to hardware or software failure or loss of authorized access control. For example, keys stored inside a TRSM can be lost due to damaged equipment or processing failure. Replacement equipment can be installed and the cryptographic keys can be recovered for business continuity. Another example would include the loss of an employee due to job termination or untimely death, where encrypted information can be recovered by reconstituting the appropriate key. For this reason, key recovery is often referred to as *data recovery*.

Procedures must be in place to maintain the security of the overall PKI. The recovery of one key should not compromise the security of any other key. Mechanisms for key recovery include storing encrypted keys under a special storage key, storing cleartext keys in TRSM, or storing key fractions under dual control and split knowledge.

This description of key recovery is different from what has been a hot political topic called *key escrow*. Key escrow is the recovery of a key by a law enforcement agency without the knowledge of the particular key owner or the PKI owner. Once an escrowed key has been knowingly reconstituted, the key should be considered as compromised.

Key Termination

Key termination is when a key has reached the end of its life cycle, either due to a predetermined validity period or a suspected or known compromise. For symmetric keys and asymmetric private keys, with the possible exception of key archival, key termination is where all copies of the key are destroyed. In this manner, the key is no longer available for use in a production environment. Public keys are further addressed in Chapter 5.

Key Archival

Key archival is when a key has been terminated and a copy of the key is kept in secure storage for the sole purpose of validating data that was previously protected by that key. Asymmetric private keys used for generating digital signatures should not be archived, as this would undermine the overall security of existing digital signatures. Furthermore, an archived key cannot be placed back into the production environment.

Cryptographic Strengths

Probably one of the most-asked questions is about key size. Indirectly, the questioner believes he or she is fully addressing cryptographic strength, which is a misnomer. Key size does play an important role of overall strength, but there is tremendous confusion on this topic. Let's look at symmetric keys and asymmetric keys.

Symmetric Algorithms

Symmetric algorithm strength is primarily based on key size, which relates directly to the size of the search space for an exhaustive attack on the key. Let's first look at a 40-bit RC4 key. RC4 is an algorithm developed by Ron Rivest at MIT. Since a bit is a binary value and has only two possible values, there are $2^{40} = 1,099,511,627,776$, or approximately 1 trillion, possible keys. This is a much larger search space than an 8-character password! The simplest form of an exhaustive key search is a known plaintext attack, where the adversary has a sample cleartext and ciphertext. The attack is to try all possible keys until the right key is found. Assuming that we can try 1000 keys per second, it would take a billion seconds, or about 35 years, to search the key space. This sounds fairly strong.

Now let's look at a 56-bit DES key. DES is the Data Encryption Standard originally developed by IBM in the early 1970s and jointly modified by NIST and the NSA. There are 2^{56}, or about 72 quadrillion, possible keys. Recall that for every bit added to the key size, the key space doubles in size. Assuming that we can try 1 million keys per second, it would still require over 2000 years to search the key space. This sounds really strong! However, recognize that the possible key space is known, it is simply all the numbers between 0 and the maximum number $2^{56}-1$, so the keys can be searched using more than one computer. At the RSA Security Conference in January 1999, 100,000 workstations loosely connected via the Internet by *distributed.net* and a specialized computer called Deep Crack developed by the Electronic Freedom Frontier (EFF) searched 25 percent of the DES key space and discovered the correct DES key in an unprecedented 23 hours.

The advent of the Internet, fast computer speeds, and cheaper computer memory has prompted the National Institute of Standards and Technology (NIST) to launch the Advanced Encryption Standards (AES). AES is expected to announce a new symmetric algorithm sometime in the year 2000. AES strength begins at 128-bit keys, which is certainly beyond the reach of computing ability in the near future. The discussion of symmetric cryptographic strength related to key size makes the assumption that all symmetric algorithms are equivalent and have no other weaknesses. This is simply not the case. Part of the AES research is to determine the overall security of the new algorithms.

Asymmetric Algorithms

Asymmetric algorithm strength is a more complex topic than symmetric algorithms. Today, the underlying strength of asymmetric algorithms is based on what is referred to as "hard" mathematical problems. The two most common "hard" problems are the factoring of large numbers and discrete logarithms. The RSA algorithm, named for its three inventors Ron Rivest, Adi Shamir, and Len Adleman, relies on the difficulty of factoring large numbers that are a product (multiplication) of two primes. Other algorithms, such as the Digital Signature Algorithm (DSA), Diffie-Helman, and Elliptic Curve Cryptography (ECC), are based on the difficulty of determining a discrete log.

All of these asymmetric algorithms employ various key sizes of large lengths. For example, the X9 financial standards limit the minimum size of asymmetric keys, such as 1024-bit keys for RSA, and 163-bit keys for ECC. The size of these keys effectively prevents an exhaustive key search; therefore, more efficient mathematical attacks are used, such as factoring algorithms and finding discrete logs.

CHAPTER 5

Certificate and Validation Authorities

Digital certificates were described in Chapter 2, "What's in a PKI?" and the importance of key management was reinforced in Chapter 4, "Key Management." Simply stated, a certificate authority (CA) is an independent trusted third party that issues and maintains digital certificates.

Moreover, just as a brick-and-mortar business needs a clearinghouse to confirm that a credit card is valid and not over its limit, online business transactions also require quick and reliable confirmation that a certificate is valid, that it was issued to the appropriate entity, and that it grants permissions appropriate to the application. Only then can a certificate be accepted with confidence. A validation authority (VA) can perform these functions. More details are provided on validation authorities in the next section.

Similarly, exact functional descriptions and boundaries of a CA are still a contested and debated topic that's undergoing constant definition and understanding. This is primarily due to the fact that any aspect of the CA can also be outsourced, and therefore should be treated as a separate entity, which changes the trust relationship.

Figure 5.1 attempts to show the interaction between the various roles that comprise a certificate authority and its relationship to the PKI. Instead of trying to define what a CA is and isn't, let's describe these functional roles of a certificate authority.

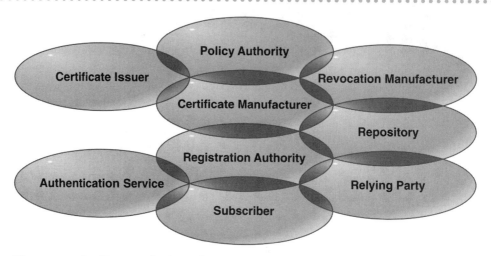

Figure 5.1 Certificate authority and PKI.

Functional Roles

The following roles present a logical division of the functions required within a CA and the overall PKI. These partitions represent a combination of theoretical and real-world business models that exist and are emerging in the marketplace.

Policy Authority

The *policy authority* is responsible for establishing, distributing, maintaining, promoting, and enforcing the policies and procedures for all of the functional entities. Consequently, the policy authority is responsible for the authorization or accreditation of entities to perform a functional role under the established policies. Specifications for the content and intended usage of certificates by relying parties, for the registration process for the subject of certificates, for the certificate revocation process, and for managing the root and all subordinate CA certificates fall under the auspices of the policy authority. Hence, the policy authority is chartered to resolve or enable resolution of disputes related to the policies and procedures, and therefore must remain current regarding potential security threats, policy inadequacies, and regulatory requirements.

Certificate Issuer

The *certificate issuer* distributes the certificates generated by the certificate manufacturer, and in so doing, manages the brand name associated with the certificate. This includes providing a means for subscribers to request certificate revocation, granting and revoking certificates, and managing the certificate revocation list.

Certificate Manufacturer

The *certificate manufacturer* generates and manages the certificate signature asymmetric key pairs consistent with the policies and procedures provided by the policy authority. Therefore, the certificate manufacturer may also distribute the root public key(s) and do the actual signing of certificates. Furthermore, the certificate manufacturer provides the out-of-band notification to a subscriber that a certificate has been generated. If more than one certificate issuer is hosted, the certificate manufacturer establishes and maintains separation between the different issuers.

Revocation Manufacturer

The *revocation manufacturer* generates and manages the revocation signature asymmetric key pairs consistent with the policies and procedures provided by the policy authority. Therefore, the revocation manufacturer may also distribute the root public key(s). Furthermore, the revocation manufacturer provides the out-of-band notification to a subscriber that a revocation has been generated. If more than one certificate issuer is hosted, the revocation manufacturer establishes and maintains separation between the different issuers.

Registration Authority

The *registration authority*, sometimes referred to as a *registrar*, is essentially the front end for the subscriber to all of the other functional entities, providing certificate registration, certificate status, and revocation services. The registration authority obtains a public key from the subscriber or, optionally, if non-repudiation is not intended, generates an asymmetric key pair on behalf of the subscriber. Before the registration authority forwards the certificate request to the certificate manufacturer, the subscriber is authenticated according to the policy and procedures established by the policy authority. The registration authority determines that the subscriber holds the public key's corresponding asymmetric private key.

Authentication Service

The *authentication service* validates a subscriber's credentials for the registration authority prior to the registration authority submitting the subscriber's public key and identity to the certificate manufacturer. The subscriber's credentials are presented to the registration authority and validated by the authentication service in accordance to the policies and procedures established by the policy authority. Credentials can range from anything as simplistic as an e-mail address to photo identification (e.g., driver's license, passport) and letters of introduction on company letterhead signed by an officer of that company.

Repository

The *repository* is an online database storing and distributing all public key certificates, information on certificate status (such as CRLs), and other PKI-related information (e.g., certificate policy). In some instances, the repository also maintains regulatory and financial information about each functional role.

Related Roles

Although not directly related to the CA functional roles, other responsible parties are certainly part of the overall PKI and directly related to the certificate authority.

Subscriber

The *subscriber* is the subject of the certificate, whose identity and public key are implicitly bound together in the public key certificate. Although the subscriber is not part of the certificate authority, the subscriber is part of the PKI and is responsible for generating asymmetric key pairs, and managing the proper access controls over the private key in accordance with the policy and procedures established by the policy authority. Any incidence of known or suspected compromise of the private key results in immediate notification of the registration authority.

Relying Party

The *relying party* is any entity using a subscriber's certificate, and whose trust of that certificate depends largely on the policies and procedures established by the policy authority. Although the relying party is not part of the certificate authority, the relying party is part of the PKI by using the public key in the subscriber's certificate for authorized business applications and appropriate cryptographic functions (e.g., digital signature verification, key exchange, etc.) in compliance with policies and procedures established by the policy authority.

Applications

There is a significant distinction between technology applications (e.g., electronic mail) and business applications. Technology applications are software products whose functions enable a business to operate. For example, the telephone is a technology application that enables sales agents to contact their customers. Thus, business applications are comprised of technology applications, people, and transactions.

In a PKI, the relationship to the certificate authority and a business application is that the PKI-enabled technology applications used by the business application rely on the certificate authority to manage public key certificates. The importance of access controls over the asymmetric private key, as discussed in Chapter 4, cannot be overly emphasized.

Cross-Certification

Clearly, all of the certificates for the population of the planet Earth, not to mention all of the technology applications, cannot and would not be issued by a single certificate authority. Multiple CAs do and must exist. The real question is, what are the business and technology relationships between multiple certificate authorities? Let's look at three typical CAs depicted in Figure 5.2, identified as CA1, CA2, and CA3.

Further assume that each CA has issued some number of certificates to subscribers, labeled as S1 through Sn. Each CA has no direct relationship with another CA. Therefore, in order to validate a certificate issued from any CA, each relying party would need to have the public key of all three certificate authorities. Other CA models aid in the interoperability for relying parties.

Hierarchy Model

The CA hierarchy model is shown in Figure 5.3. CA1 and CA2 have submitted their public keys to a common CA referred to as a root CA. The root CA can be defined as the highest-level CA whose public key is usually contained in a self-signed certificate. CA1 and CA2 by definition are designated as subordinate CAs. Self-signed certificates provide data integrity, but cannot provide authentication. The root CA public certificate is distributed to all relying parties.

This model requires that CA1 and CA2 establish a business relationship with the root CA, and consequently a trust relationship that can be used by the subscribers and relying parties. The existence of the root CA places a burden and reliance on maintaining the security over the root CA private key and its corresponding public key. Thus, the root CA represents a potential single point of failure. If the root CA private key is compromised, all certificates issued by any and all subordinate CAs are suspect, and must therefore be revoked and reissued.

As the level of complexity increases, the dependency on the root CA and higher-level subordinate CAs becomes critical. Therefore, the security policies and practices imposed by the root CA must address the roles and responsibilities of the subordi-

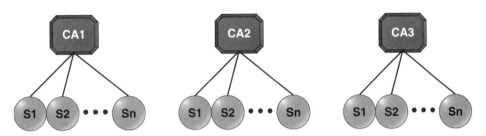

Figure 5.2 Certificate authority.

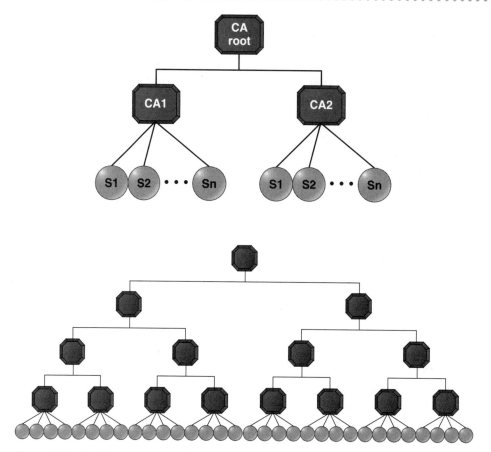

Figure 5.3 Certificate authority hierarchy.

nate CAs. Thus, each subordinate is said to inherit the policy and practices of the higher-level CA. However, a root CA hierarchy is not the only means by which interoperability can be achieved.

Peer-to-Peer Model

Where certificate authorities operate on an equal basis, one or more CAs can cross-certify each other in a peer-to-peer relationship. Each pair of CAs mutually exchanges public keys and issues a certificate to each other. This enables a relying party to verify a subscriber's certificate issued from any CA that has been cross-certified with the CA for which the relying party holds and trusts that CA's public key.

Figure 5.4 shows the three certificate authorities CA1, CA2, and CA3, where the pairs CA1 and CA2, and CA2 and CA3 have cross-certified. Thus, CA1 issues a certificate to CA2, containing CA2's public key, and signed by CA1's private key. Likewise, CA2

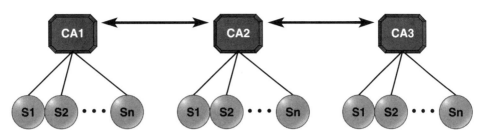

Figure 5.4 Peer-to-peer certificate authority.

issues a certificate to CA1, containing CA1's public key, and signed by CA2's private key. Similarly, CA2 and CA3 have cross-certified.

In this model, each CA is essentially a root CA; however, no highest-level root CA actually exists. Therefore, no burden is placed on a single point of failure. Each CA is responsible for its subscribers and for providing trust to its relying parties. Interestingly, the policy and practices of each CA are relatively independent of each other, and therefore as each cross-certification is established, the policy and practices must be reviewed to ensure compatible operating rules.

Bridge Model

An alternative model has been proposed by the Federal PKI Technical Working Group and endorsed by the Federal PKI Steering Committee. The hierarchical model was seen as too restrictive, and no one government agency could satisfactorily fulfill the role of a root CA for all other civil and defense agencies. Furthermore, a simple cross-certification model is prohibited by the sheer number of agencies, as this creates what is referred to as the N^2 (n-squared) problem.

For N certificate authorities, it requires $\dfrac{N^2-N}{2}$ cross-certifications. So, for 300 CAs, it would require 44,850 certificates just between all of the CAs. Figure 5.5 shows a cross-certification scheme using a central peer-to-peer CA, where CA1 and CA3 cross-certify with just the bridge CA. So, for 300 CAs, it would only require 300 cross certificates, or in general N cross certificates, a number substantially smaller than the so-called N^2 problem.

However, similar to the cross-certification model, the policies and practices of each CA cross-certifying with the bridge CA would need to be harmonized. Minimal policies and practices should be established, implemented, and verified.

Validation Authorities

A validation authority (VA) can help provide *ubiquitous trust*. It can perform an important role within a PKI by confirming the trust status of an electronic credential

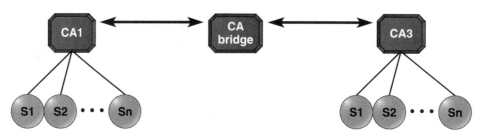

Figure 5.5 Bridge certificate authority.

regardless of application, the certificate authority (CA) that issued the credential, or the physical location of the parties to the transaction. In effect, it can act as a clearing-house to validate eBusiness transactions.

eBusiness Transactions Require Validation

Today, Web servers are increasingly being used for e-commerce and software distribution. E-mail, virtual private networks (VPNs), and extranets carry contracts, bids, and proprietary financial information. Valuable and sensitive information that was once accessible to a limited number of people over private networks must now be protected on a network that is used by the whole world.

As companies embrace the Internet for business transactions, they need stronger, more flexible security for this more open environment. Companies need to keep a new array of potential perpetrators out of their business, while insuring that authorized users—who may be employees, partners, suppliers, or customers—can access the systems and information they need.

Digital certificates are emerging as the preferred enablers of strong Internet security.

Examples of certificate-enabled applications are many. For instance, a company may use certificates internally to control access to sensitive data. Partner organizations may use certificates as "passports" allowing access to an extranet. Or an e-commerce server may present a certificate to a consumer, to satisfy the consumer that the server is authentic and not an impostor set up to steal credit card numbers.

In deploying certificates on an enterprise scale, three major functional elements should be considered:

➤ The *certificate authority* (CA). To check the identity of a person, program, or service, and issue a certificate.

➤ The *validation authority* (VA). To validate individual transactions involving certificates, verify that the certificate is still in force, and that it was issued to the appropriate entity.

➤ The *directory*. To allow users and programs to store, search for, and retrieve objects, including encryption keys, certificates, usernames, and passwords.

These three elements help to provide a scalable solution for businesses rolling out enterprise applications that use digital certificates. They also allow Internet Service Providers (ISP), Application Service Providers (ASP), and web-hosting companies to provide strong, flexible security to their customers.

As shown in Figure 5.6, a regulatory body, such as a Big Five accounting firm, may audit both the CA and the VA.

In Figure 5.6, a PKI provides a basis of trust for eBusiness transactions. The CA issues certificates to subscribers. Subscribers present certificates to relying parties. Relying parties verify the validity of certificates through the services of a VA. The VA also maintains a registry of CAs that relying parties can consult. A regulatory body, such as a Big Five accounting firm, may audit both the CA and the VA.

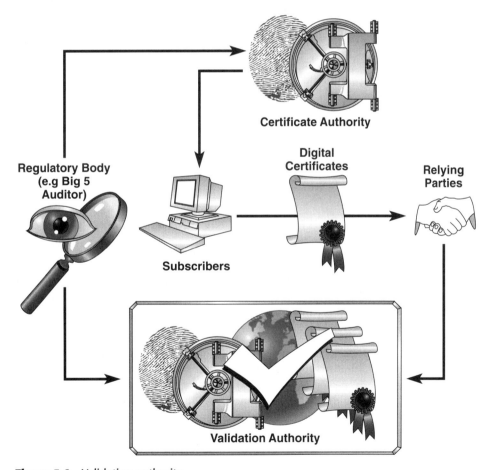

Figure 5.6 Validation authority.
Source: ValiCert.

It is certainly possible to deploy a CA without a VA. However, by using certificates, organizations create expectations that transactions are secure and liability could become an issue when customers, partners, and suppliers literally put their assets on the line based on a false sense of security. Without proper validation, any certificate-based security system is fundamentally incomplete and insecure. As the number of certificate-based transactions rises, and the average value of transactions goes up, the risk increases.

The Validation Authority

The VA essentially performs three main functions, each of which helps the relying party (which has been presented with the certificate) to decide whether to accept this particular certificate for this particular transaction:

1. The VA ensures that a certificate has not *expired* or been *revoked*. Revocation may occur when an employee leaves a company, for instance, or when the computer containing the certificate is stolen. Revoked certificates are listed in a certificate revocation list (CRL).

2. The VA can check for *permissions* associated with a certificate. For example, is the certificate valid for a transaction that involves a payment or funds transfer of a certain amount? For a transaction that involves accessing a particular dataset?

3. Lastly, the VA can *audit* a CA's processes and *maintain a registry* of CAs, which users can consult to determine what level of trust to place in a particular CA. This auditing and registry function may become increasingly important as CAs proliferate.

Certificate Revocation Lists

A certificate revocation list (CRL) is a list of revoked certificates with the time of revocation. The CRL is also digitally signed by the CA that issued the certificates, so it is tamper-proof.

CRLs from large, active CAs also have a tendency to get very large. This is mainly because revoked certificates remain on the list until they expire, which can be a number of years. The list can grow quite rapidly in active organizations with any reasonably sized deployment.

When a client has been presented with a certificate, it may require the client to download and search through a large CRL to determine whether the certificate has been revoked It is quite common today to simply not to check the CRL. However, there are better ways to address this problem. One is to use the Online Client Status Protocol (OCSP), which allows a client to submit a certificate serial number to an OCSP server and get a "valid/invalid" response that takes into account the certificate's revocation status. The server may need to consult a CRL, but that may be much less onerous than forcing every client to download the full CRL.

The task of searching through the CRL can be facilitated by organizing the CRL into an efficient data structure, such as a binary tree. Downloading the CRL may still be required, but the search should go faster.

It's also possible to set up CRL Distribution Points (DPs), which are CRLs that have been partitioned into more manageable, smaller pieces. Instead of trying to download a massive CRL to check individual certificates, clients get small, manageable updates that allow them to have a definitive copy of the CRL at all times.

Stages of Validation

The validation authority plays a critical role at several points in an eBusiness transaction:

➤ Before trust is established

➤ Prior to each transaction

➤ During and after the transaction

Before Trust Is Established

Before trust is established, subscribers and relying parties need reliable information about CAs, in order to make informed decisions about where to buy certificates and which certificates to accept.

CAs can easily proliferate in proportion to the growth of eBusiness itself, and may increase considerably as deployment of Microsoft Windows 2000, which comes bundled with CA software, accelerates. As such, the question of which CAs are acceptable to the company becomes more important. Companies considering buying or accepting certificates from a CA need a central registry of trust information, where they can get the information needed to determine the trustworthiness of that CA.

Prior to Each Transaction

Issuing certificates establishes trust between subscribers and relying parties, based on the relying parties' trust in the CA. After trust is established, the certificate needs to be validated prior to each transaction. The responsibility for insuring that the certificate is valid falls on the relying party. A relying party that accepts an expired, revoked, or otherwise invalid certificate will generally have no legal recourse against the CA, in the event that the compromised credential resulted in damage or fraud. The VA can provide this necessary certificate validation service.

During and After Each Transaction

Finally, high-value transactions require that an audit trail be maintained during the transaction, and stored after the transaction for future dispute resolution. The VA may act as a neutral, trusted third party involved in the transaction, and maintain an audit trail.

VA Planning, Evaluation, and Implementation

There are a number of different approaches to providing the validation function. For instance, companies can outsource the function or implement it in-house. The CA and VA functions can be combined or provided separately. The VA can be implemented during the piloting stage, or left until production deployment. In all cases, however, careful planning is the key to successful VA deployment.

Planning

The difficulty of deploying a VA depends on the general sophistication of the network, the number of applications that need to be enabled, the number of sites to be connected, and the complexity of the specific policies to be implemented.

Deploying a VA is not necessarily a huge undertaking. A software developer could relatively provide a VA as a turnkey system. Implementing a VA for a single application at a single site may only take a matter of days. Generally speaking, VA deployment may represent just a small investment of time relative to the entire PKI.

Nevertheless, careful planning is always advisable. The two most important areas to consider are protocols and hardware requirements.

The organization needs to map out all of the applications and CAs that will interact with the VA, and understand the protocols associated with each application and CA. For example, certain applications support OCSP for validation, where others support CRLs or CRL DPs. Ensuring a test plan that covers all of these areas in detail will save time in later stages of deployment.

Hardware planning includes not only determining the required processing power, but also the necessary network bandwidth. Additionally, hardware devices used for accelerating the digital signature process in a VA should be strongly considered up front. Chapter 8, "Hardware Mechanisms," provides additional information on this topic. Planners should also be aware that bandwidth requirements for a VA are dramatically higher than for a CA, because the VA usually handles more transactions and becomes a much more time-critical function than a CA. Since VA traffic may vary significantly over time, organizations should give serious consideration to network services that provide bandwidth on demand. Similarly, it is very important to be able to scale the system hardware. Organizations should start with a high-end platform with ample room for expansion. If digital signatures are going to be used, plan for an appropriate number and configuration of hardware signing modules as well.

Outsourcing the VA

A fundamental question is whether to outsource the VA function or implement it in-house. An enterprise-level VA can easily become a complex, specialized function that may require labor-intensive maintenance, such as auditing the CA, for example. There may be substantial liabilities associated with mistakes or oversights. Still, for deployments with a limited scope (e.g., single application, single CA), many organizations may be able to validate in-house. At the enterprise level, where multiple applications or multiple CAs are involved, considerations of staffing, expertise, and liability may call for outsourcing the VA function. Exceptions may include companies in certain sectors, such as the financial or government arenas, which have the expertise and staff to implement enterprise-level VAs.

A Combined CA/VA?

An important question, when outsourcing, is whether the VA should be independent of the CA, or if the CA can provide both functions. There are a number of reasons for a separate, independent VA:

Independent auditing. An independent VA can provide independent auditing for CAs.

Objective testimony. An independent VA can be a source of legally binding evidence that a credential was validated. Thus, the VA can provide a means of resolving disputes, such as a customer at an auction site claiming that he never made a bid that has been attributed to him.

Core competencies. It may also make sense to separate the CA and the VA functions since they utilize different core competencies. The CA is analogous to a bank that issues a credit card. The VA is analogous to the clearinghouse that validates credit card transactions. CAs, like banks, do not have to be available 24 × 7. They don't have to be global in scale. Nor is speed of service vital. In contrast, certificate validation, like credit card validation, must be available immediately, anywhere and any time. This is especially true for high-value, real-time transactions such as funds transfers. Due to such differing requirements, CAs and VAs are evolving into separate functions.

CA independence. An independent VA can check certificates from any number of CAs. This is much easier than going to each CA to check certificates issued by that CA. Unfortunately, most CAs today cannot "cross-validate"; that is, provide validation for one another's certificates. VA independence also makes it much easier to change CAs, since the procedures for validating individual transactions do not have to change.

Interoperability and compatibility. Finally, organizations that run eBusiness applications from several vendors, or transact business online with several different organizations, generally find that separating the VA makes more sense from the standpoint of a technical architecture. In these cases, the VA provides compatibility with the various CAs used by different organizations, and the various protocols used by different applications. It could be more efficient to provide broad interoperability centrally at the VA rather than require every CA, organization, or application to duplicate this very demanding capability.

Evaluating a VA

A number of criteria come into play when evaluating a VA product or service. In the case of a VA service offering, many of these elements should be specified in a contract or service level agreement (SLA).

Important criteria for evaluating an enterprise-level VA include:

Application independence. The VA should work with all certificate-based applications and it should not be tightly bound to a single application, or to applications from a single vendor. Ask what level of compatibility testing has been done with various applications.

CA independence. Similar to applications, ask what level of compatibility testing has been done with various CAs.

Location independence. Can the VA effectively validate transactions anywhere in the world?

Availability. Is the VA available 24 × 7, with 99+ percent uptime.

Online and batch validation. Does the VA offer both online and offline/batch methods of validating transactions? For instance, a user may read secure e-mail on a laptop in disconnected mode. In that case, the user may need to download critical security data such as certification revocation lists (CRLs) in advance, so that certificates can be validated offline.

Reliability. Does the VA provide fail-over and disaster recovery mechanisms to ensure continuous service during foreseeable failures or natural disasters?

Protocol support. Is the VA able to support all protocols in use throughout the enterprise for eBusiness transactions?

Performance. Is the VA able to validate transactions quickly, even under maximum load?

Scalability. Is the VA able to scale to meet increasing demands?

Replication. Is a robust data replication scheme incorporated to ensure scalability and reliability?

Assumption of liability. In the case of an outsourced service offering, does the service provider assume an appropriate level of liability if something goes wrong? It's certainly possible to negotiate different levels of liability assumption, depending on the user organization's tolerance for risk.

Customer support. Does the service provider provide a customer support function that is available whenever it is needed, and that responds to inquiries within an acceptable timeframe?

Hardware acceleration for digital signing. Does the enterprise VA support hardware acceleration technologies for performance and scalability?

Lastly, a VA that is brought in later during production deployment can certainly risk being the weak link in the security chain. For best results, the VA function should be tested during pilot deployments, along with the rest of the system.

CHAPTER 6

Directories

• •

D irectory Services and PKI often get mentioned in the same breath. Most experts advise companies that are planning for PKI to integrate it with an enterprise directory initiative. For companies embarking on a major directory services rollout, the experts counsel, "don't forget to build in support for PKI." Why do these two technologies keep getting mentioned together? They are not dependent on each other to function. They are, however, extremely compatible, and when used in combination as part of a complete solution, they provide a level of business value that is greater than either can provide independently.

The protocols and products for directory services have matured in the past few years and are poised to become critical enablers of PKI. eBusiness is driving directory services implementations, and recent directory offerings from high-profile companies such as Microsoft (Active Directory Services with Windows 2000), Novell (Novell Directory Services), and Netscape (Netscape Directory Server) have generated a lot of corporate interest in the use of directories.

However, implementation of either a directory service or a PKI is not to be taken lightly. Both initiatives require a thorough understanding of the business problem to be solved, and a coherent and reasonable implementation strategy. With that in mind, the first order of business is to help clarify the Directory Service/PKI synergy. To do so, this chapter provides an introduction to the basic services and technologies in common directories. It explains what a business can expect to gain when adding PKI to the directory service, reviews services provided by a directory, identifies integration considerations when linking the PKI to single and multiple enterprise directories, and finally, builds a business case for getting the most out of the Directory Services/PKI power pair.

What Are Directories?

Directories are repositories of information, organized in a logical order to facilitate quick and easy lookup. In the non-digital world, the Yellow Pages is a directory that everyone is familiar with; it contains business listings with addresses and telephone numbers categorized into logical groups. In the digital world—which is the world we're discussing in this book—directories can hold information about systems, network services, or users. Directories can range from the very simple, such as a username/password file on a mail server, to the very complex, such as a linked hierarchy of user attributes and access rights across an enterprise.

Simple or complex, all directories provide the basic service of making information available in a coherent and searchable manner. Systems and applications rely on the information in these directories to function. For example, an operating system may rely on a directory of available printers to let a user know which one to print to. The print server, in turn, will probably check a directory to make sure that the user is valid and authenticated, and that he has appropriate access rights to use the printer. In this same vein, directory service information can extend far beyond control of printing rights to include control of access to privileged applications and highly sensitive and valuable data.

Directories in the Enterprise

Two key security services are required to establish who a user is, and whether that user can conduct a given transaction. First is the combined service of identification and authentication. Second is the authorization service. Directories and directory services provide a way to store and manage the information needed to make these services work. They provide a framework to link and manage distributed, enterprise-scale directories, consolidate user and resource management, and expand accessibility to information. This functionality allows organizations to build and manage complex eBusiness relationships.

Historically, enterprise network applications have been developed as individual entities, and each system or application has had its own user authentication database and access control attributes. For example, many legacy-based systems use a host-based security model such as Resource Access Control Facility (RACF), Access Control Facility/2 (ACF/2), or TopSecret. Depending on the size of the company, there may be hundreds of atomic applications, both homegrown and packaged, each with its own directory.

In such an environment, multiple directories must be maintained and updated independently, resulting in wasted time and costly administrative overhead. This can lead to a dangerous lack of data integrity, because the information is not synchronized across directories in any way. For example, if an employee leaves a company, his access rights should be revoked from all the directories in which he was listed. However, if he was listed in 20 different directories managed by 20 different administrators, there's a good chance that one or more of his accounts will not be revoked. More than a few people have been shocked to discover that they can still access a system weeks or months after leaving the company.

Corporations know that this distributed model for administration of directory information is risky, messy, and inefficient. Some companies think that moving to a single, consolidated directory is the solution. While this is appealing from an administrative perspective, it is probably not feasible for most companies, especially those with large, heterogeneous environments. In order to participate in a directory, every application, resource, and service needs to be directory aware and able to support common directory standards. More realistic, perhaps, is the move toward a reduced number of directories and the implementation of synchronization services.

Looking beyond the enterprise, the power of directories becomes even more interesting.

As Internet convergence drives organizations together in virtual trading communities, the importance of reliable, secure directory information increases considerably. In a trading community, a centralized directory can provide single sign-on support by storing information about all of the users and resources that exist in the community, and the types of transactions they are authorized to conduct. Single sign-on is appealing to administrators and users because it means that a user logs in once to a network or portal to gain access to multiple resources without having to repeat the login process or remember multiple passwords. In order for a single sign-on solution of this type to work, all applications and resources need to be directory enabled. It will take time and planning before enterprises can support a completely directory-aware network.

Database or Directory?

Directories are basically databases. The first big difference is that database information is changed frequently, usually in complex ways. Think of large, complex queries that result in updates to thousands of records at a time. Databases supporting these types of complex transactions require two-phase commit, rollback, and transaction-monitoring services to maintain data integrity. Many times, during the completion of a transaction, something interferes with the process. This can result in a loss of data integrity. To prevent mishaps, many systems implement a two-phase commit for transaction processing. A transaction monitor or manager oversees the transaction process in two phases. First, the monitor issues transaction requests to resources; next, the monitor receives ready-to-commit responses from those resources. If the resources are not ready for the commit, the transaction request is rolled back; if the resources are ready, the transaction is committed. In contrast, directory information is read far more than it is changed.

Another difference between directories and databases is that, because of the nature of the data involved, absolute data integrity is required in a database environment; in a directory services environment, slight lags in data consistency are tolerable. Think of it this way: If a user who leaves a company continues to have mail access for four hours, that is of far less concern than if a manufacturer places an emergency order believing that a component is in stock, only to find out later that the inventory shown on the screen did not reflect the inventory in the warehouse.

A third difference between databases and directories is that copies of databases exist only for backup purposes. Directories, however, are often replicated and made available on many servers in order to maintain high availability for users in large, highly distributed environments. This does mean that each replication of the directory could receive updates at a slightly different time. However, this is OK, since, as mentioned earlier, directories can tolerate slight lags in data consistency.

Role of Directories in PKI

Alright, so a directory is an information repository, but how does that aid in the deployment of PKI?

First, many of the most critical components of the PKI require organized storage and easy accessibility. Directories can make PKI deployment easier and more manageable by providing the means to store PKI information, organize it, and make it widely available. Accessibility and manageability are the cornerstones of a successful PKI, and directories are the perfect technology for those tasks. Although directories are not the only way to store PKI information, they are an attractive option for companies with directory solutions already in place, as well as for those companies that are moving toward a directory implementation. For example:

> As organizations continue the migration to Internet-based eBusiness communities, a publicly available directory of certificates is indispensable. Certificates stored in a directory can be made readily available to other users and applications.

> Directories can be used to store certificate validation information in the form of certificate revocation lists (CRLs).

> For organizations that require key recovery, the directory can become the repository of encrypted private keys.

The concept of key recovery can be expanded to support mobile users by allowing them access to their private keys from any computer or terminal. Traditionally, the private key is stored on a user's hard drive, which does not easily support mobile users. By allowing users to remotely access their private key from a directory store, organizations can make their PKI truly mobile.

Second, directories are designed using commonly available Internet standards, linking a PKI to the open standards of a directory broadens the certificate base of the PKI.

Third, PKI-enabled directory services allow a company to increase the strength of legacy application authentication. Legacy applications can be extended to check for a certificate in the directory to support two-factor authentication.

Fourth, in business-to-business communities, PKI-enabled directories can provide a scalable, manageable method for creating user accounts. Users in possession of valid certificates from trusted third-party CAs can auto-register for user accounts with partner organizations.

In order to work with a PKI, the directory needs to meet two common criteria. First, the directory must support certificate storage of X.509 v3 certificates and CRLs. Second, the directory must support the Lightweight Directory Access Protocol (LDAP), the de facto standard for accessing directory information (more on LDAP later). This increases the PKI's reach well beyond PKI-enabled solutions.

Some PKIs require a directory in order to function. These PKIs are directory dependent. With directory-dependent PKIs, it's important to examine the underlying schema requirements. If the PKI's schema is not extensible, you'll have a hard time integrating it with your company's overall directory strategy.

Other PKIs, like VeriSign's OnSite, are not directory dependent. They can work in conjunction with an external directory, but do not require one. For PKIs that are not directory dependent, make sure they come with an automated method of exporting certificates into your directory. Without this kind of integration tool, the PKI and directory could easily grow out of sync, causing security risks and creating administrative difficulties.

Directory Access Protocols

To understand directories, it is critical to understand a little about the two basic directory access protocols: X.500 and LDAP.

X.500

This is the granddaddy of the directory service models. X.500 defines both the Directory Access Protocol (DAP)—the protocol used to access directory information—and the information model that defines how data is stored and managed. The original X.500 project had ambitious objectives. One prominent objective was to define a single public directory infrastructure with multiple independently managed directories that coexisted in a single, navigable namespace. The X.500 standard was issued by the International Standards Organization (ISO) in 1988. Since 1988, it has been through a number of revisions that expanded it to include support for access control and schema management.

Because the initial purpose of X.500 was to support a single directory infrastructure, it is well suited to large organizations. X.500 allows users and applications to access directories that they may not be aware of by using distributed directory servers, directory system agents (DSAs), directory information bases (DIBs), and hierarchical directory entries. This hierarchical scheme allows for massive distribution of information accessibility without sacrificing control of federated data. In other words, while each administrator retains control over her domain, the information in the domain is accessible across the entire infrastructure.

X.500 failed to become the de facto Internet standard for a few reasons. The major drawback of the X.500 directory access protocol is that it is complex and resource intensive. There was never an agreed-upon method for registering names, which held back its ability to deploy. Finally, it was hampered by the fact that it runs over the Open Systems Interconnection (OSI) network protocol stack, so it is not as easily supportable on the Internet.

LDAP

To address the need for Internet access to directories, the Lightweight Directory Access Protocol (LDAP) was created at the University of Michigan. In 1997, the Internet Engineering Task Force (IETF) proposed LDAP v3 as Internet standard Request for Comments (RFC) 2251. LDAP runs over standard TCP/IP and is far less resource hungry than X.500. LDAP has quickly become the de facto standard for directory access. Companies that are reviewing directory products should demand that the directory support LDAP.

A word of LDAP caution is in order, however. What makes LDAP light and flexible can also make it a little more difficult to implement in large installations. First, the LDAP specification only defines the external client interface; it does not define internal directory behavior. This means that there are no formal LDAP standards on how certain directory behaviors should be implemented. For example, a valuable directory function is chaining. Chaining allows a DSA that is not able to perform an operation itself, such as data lookup, to pass the request to another DSA for execution. This in turn allows DSAs to work together to complete directory service functions. Although an LDAP directory can implement chaining support itself, without a formal standard to adhere to, one LDAP directory's chaining function runs the risk of being incompatible with another's.

This lack of standardization also holds true for replication, partitioning, and federation. This lack of a defined replication standard means that organizations attempting to link directory servers from different vendors may find that one server does not support the others' replication methods. This could result in an inability to replicate data across multiple servers and a serious lack of data integrity within the directory information. An IETF working group, LDAP Duplication/Replication/Update Protocols (LDUP), is currently working on ways to standardize replication in LDAP.

The result is that the directory servers offered by various vendors have their own unique solution to address certain internal directory functions. For organizations that implement multiple directory servers, this means that the servers might not be compatible. Therefore, eBusiness must be careful to review interoperability cross vendors and select a directory server that meets their needs for distributed access and compatibility.

Schema Considerations

Any data repository needs some kind of mechanism for controlling data integrity. Without rules about what types of data are allowed and where data can be placed, the directory could quickly turn into a toxic-waste dump of garbage data. The schema is a set of rules that defines what data types and forms are acceptable to the directory in an attempt to keep the data store relatively clean. Schema design is sometimes referred to as data modeling.

Directories hold data in entries in the Directory Information Tree (DIT). These entries are created using attributes, and attributes are types that have one or more associated values. Every entry is required to have an attribute that specifies the object classes, known as the Object Class attribute. A class definition is a named bundle of attributes. Attributes can be defined as mandatory or optional (see Figure 6.1).

The attribute type is defined using a descriptive name and an object identifier (OID). Usually, the schema asserts what attributes are supported and required (such as country, common name, telephone). The attribute syntax determines what the value associated with that attribute looks like (e.g., country must be a two-letter code), and the attribute type asserts how the value data is stored and used (a certificate is stored in X.509 certificate format). Directories use matching rules to determine if the data entered is compliant with the directory's schema.

Since the schema is such a powerful part of the directory service, an organization needs to plan it carefully. Some directories support subschemas, allowing different administrators to federate the directory schema. This can be very useful in large enterprise directory solutions that portion off different parts of the directory to functional business groups.

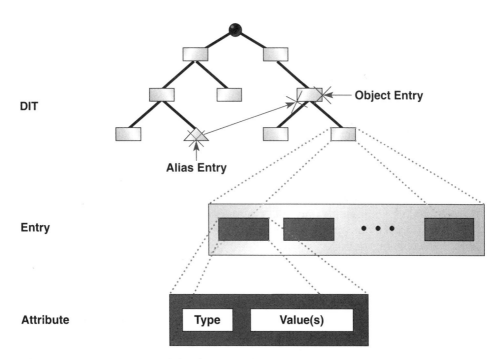

Figure 6.1 Components of the directory information tree.
Source: ITU-T X.500.

The schema needs to be open and extensible so it can be changed as needed as the company grows and changes. Another reason the schema needs to be extensible is so that it can interoperate with other directories belonging to different areas of the organization and to external business partners.

Directory Services Offerings

Directories are great ways to provide business-to-business authentication and authorization and extend the reach of your PKI. But which directories should a company consider? There are a number of viable directory services offerings, but for brevity's sake, we're going to concentrate on a couple of the key players: Microsoft's Active Directory Service and Novell's Novell Directory Services (NDS) eDirectory.

Microsoft AD

Shipping with Windows 2000, the Active Directory (AD) is Microsoft's directory service. Active Directory was around prior to the release of Windows 2000, but it has yet to go through years of production use in large enterprises.

Active Directory is very Windows-centric. Cisco has announced plans to support Active Directory on Solaris, but it is not available yet. For now, Active Directory only runs on the Windows platform. Active Directory depends on a process called the directory system agent (DSA) that accesses stored information. The DSA also manages replication and synchronization. LDAP clients connect to Active Directory via the DSA using standard LDAP. Active Directory supports storage of X.509v3 certificates and SSL.

Because the Active Directory grew out of the Windows NT Domains model, it shares some of the same limitations. Although Active Directory allows multiple domains to be organized into a hierarchical namespace that supports automated and transitive trusts, there is limited portability of objects between domains. This means that an object in one domain cannot be linked directly to one in another. The lack of ability to provide such linkage makes administration complicated, because it means that a manager cannot create a group in one domain and then populate it with users from another (or many other) domain. To accomplish this, Active Directory requires that administrators create universal groups that are stored in the global catalog (GC) instead of a domain. This limits the ability to distribute administrative ownership to the domain controllers.

Perhaps the most important consideration when assessing Active Directory is that it uses static inheritance. In a directory, access control properties on an object can be inherited from parent objects. This inheritance can be done dynamically or statically. Dynamic inheritance means that the access control on any object is calculated at the time of access. Therefore, each time an object is accessed, the access control is calculated in real time. Static inheritance means that whenever a parent object is updated, all of the children below it are updated at the same time. All objects in the directory must carry their access control attributes with them at all times, even when replicating, which can lead to engorgement of the directory. Active Directory's use of static inheritance can lead to inefficiencies of scale in directories with thousands of child objects.

Novell NDS eDirectory

NDS eDirectory has been in corporate use for years. Novell has concentrated on developing a directory that integrates with a large variety of platforms. NDS runs on Windows 2000, NT 4.0, Solaris 2.6, RedHat Linux 5.2, and NetWare 5. The corporate edition features a redirection function that imports remote objects and turns them into NDS objects, allowing companies to manage a heterogeneous environment through a single interface. NDS is robust and has been proven to scale to up to a billion objects.

NDS eDirectory supports storage of X.509v3 certificates for integration into a PKI solution. Novell offers a certificate server solution for companies that do not want to invest in a full-scale PKI. Because NDS eDirectory supports SSL, communications to and from the server can be encrypted for added security in transport.

Meta-Directories

Due to space constraints, we've covered just two of the popular directories. There are many more available in the market, Netscape being a notable standout, not to mention the large number of older directories and home-grown directory databases that many large organizations have to contend with in their existing infrastructures.

To help consolidate multiple, heterogeneous directories, the concept of directory gateways and meta-directories was born and initially held great promise, but is quickly becoming something of a legacy concept. A meta-directory attempts to solve the problem of having multiple directories that are incompatible with each other by storing information in a single, consolidated directory. This allows the organization to reap the benefits of LDAP directory services for centralized support of PKI without throwing away their old systems.

In 1999, Microsoft purchased premier meta-directory vendor Zoomit to increase Active Directory's ability to integrate with directories from other vendors. Critical-Path's Meta-Connect (formerly Isocor) is the other big meta-directory provider.

While meta-directories do solve some problems of integration, they are not one-size-fits-all solutions. Very often, organizations find that they need to invest heavily in customization of the meta-directory APIs in order to access their legacy directories. Customization costs may continue to be a factor if and when updates to legacy directories result in a need to update the meta-directory API connector.

Overall, the industry appears to be moving toward creating a common language to support multivendor directory interoperability. An example of this trend is the Directory Service Markup Language (DSML) effort led by BowStreet and Novell's DirXML. The basis of these approaches is to use the power and flexibility of a shared language to reduce the cost and effort of integrating directories.

Considerations when Choosing a Directory

The choice of which directory or directories to integrate into an organization is a complicated one. We've mentioned some considerations throughout this chapter that companies need to review, such as powerful centralized management tools, extensibility, schema flexibility, multiplatform support, adherence to open standards for access such as LDAP, and application support via open APIs.

The specific considerations that lead a company to select one solution over another will be unique to that organization. However, all organizations should research the performance and scalability of any solution before adopting and implementing it.

Performance refers to the speed with which the directory can return an answer to a query. Performance can be tested in two ways:

➤ Directories should be tested on different types of queries, including simple queries and "contains" searches. Testing performance on "contains" searches forces the directory to search across sub-trees, which can greatly affect performance.

➤ The ability to support multiple concurrent users should also be tested. If a directory returns queries fast in a small user environment, but bogs down under heavy loads, it may not be able to support your entire enterprise.

Scalability is related, in part, to performance. However, it extends beyond the ability to perform well under high loads to include several other issues:

➤ Reliability issues such as fault tolerance and backup availability in distributed environments must be considered.

➤ The directory's method of storing data should also be considered. If a massive directory becomes a storage hog, enterprises may find themselves running out of disk space quickly as the directory grows.

➤ How a directory handles the processes of referrals and chaining directly relates to how it will scale. Referrals and chaining are different ways that directories can provide a single, logical view to a partitioned directory. (see Figure 6.2).

Chaining, on the other hand, depends on server knowledge to find the partitioned information the client is looking for. Because chaining depends on server knowledge, it can be difficult to implement successfully across multivendor directory solutions that support different trust models (see Figure 6.3).

When this happens, the directory must be able to query, or pass the query to, a directory that does have the information. Note that before LDAP v.3, referrals were not supported.

Efficiency of replication schemes in wide area networks will affect directory availability. Replication pertains to how copies of information are stored in distributed locations, and the rules surrounding the replication process. Distributing replicas of the directory information to local servers increases the overall efficiency of the directory.

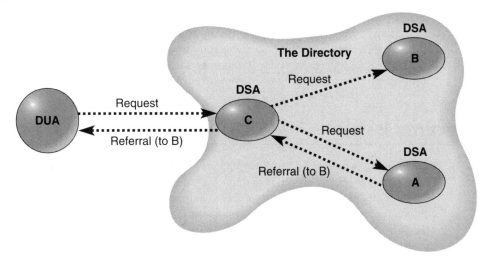

Figure 6.2   How referrals work.
Source: ITU-T X.500.

Since not all local servers may need all portions of a directory, the ability to choose which parts of the directory to replicate can make updates quicker and less wasteful. This is of extreme concern for large PKI installations where the ability to search large CRLs in a timely manner is crucial to the success of the PKI.

X.500 has a defined replication protocol as part of its standard, but LDAP does not. The current LDAP v3 does not support a multi-master replication scheme. Rather, it depends on a master/slave model that is less scalable and puts the enterprise at risk, since the

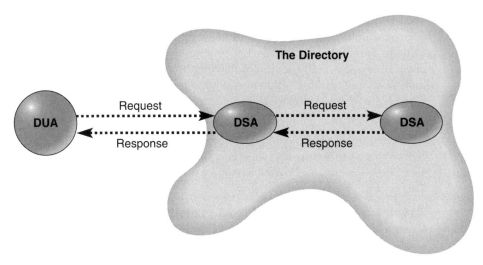

Figure 6.3   Chaining.
Source: ITU-T X.500.

master directory becomes a single point of failure. Due to LDAP's replication shortcomings, many of the directory vendors use proprietary methods of replication, so be sure to examine their replication process to ascertain whether it is compatible with other directories and your enterprise policy requirements. Replication management should be flexible enough to support delegated authority and configurable scheduling.

Security Issues

Information is power, and well-populated directories can house a lot of power and intellectual property. This makes them juicy single-point targets for attack. While many companies integrate their PKI into a directory structure to increase security for clients and applications, securing the directory might be done only as an afterthought. To ensure the security of the directory-supported PKI, companies need to protect the security of the directory itself.

Transport Layer Security (TLS) such as SSL can and should be used to protect the confidentiality of queries and responses to and from the directory. LDAP (v.3 and up) supports SSL. Client access to the directory can be protected with standard user ID and password, or strengthened by implementation of two-factor authentication. Here, certificates have an ideal role to play in the increased security of the directory solution. Although client-side certificates are not required as part of a directory authentication scheme, for those instances where queries to the directory require strong authentication, client-side authentication can be implemented to restrict access.

The ability to delegate authority over certain portions of the directory will greatly improve management capability of the enterprise directory. In a very large, complex installation, line of business controllers and partners can be assigned authority over appropriate portions of the directory.

The ability to partition the directory contributes greatly to its overall security. In a partitioned directory, users can only see certain portions of the directory or the data. Without the ability to boundary information in the directory, it would be possible for any authorized user of the system to access all the directory data. Whenever a directory must provide information to anonymous requestors—a common requirement in many Internet applications—be certain to partition the directory appropriately so that only non-sensitive data can be accessed by the world at large.

Access control is implemented with access control lists (ACLs) set by the directory administrator(s). Setting up properly restrictive ACLs is mandatory for directory security. ACLs can also be used to control who can change and delete information. This control promotes data integrity.

As with any server, physical protection of the directory server and standard perimeter security such as firewalling and a hardened operating system (OS) should be put in place. Since directories need to be available, a monitoring mechanism for denial-of-service attacks (DOS) is recommended. And don't forget auditing. Be sure to log access, especially change access, to the directory information so that discrepancies and possible attacks can be audited and tracked.

Summary

Directory services and PKI are strong, complementary technologies. Integrating a PKI solution into an organization's overall directory strategy increases the business value of both solutions. The PKI becomes accessible via the open standard of LDAP, and the directory supports the layered security of PKI.

The fact that they work so well together as supporting technologies does not necessarily mean that a company should leap into purchasing an integrated directory service and PKI solution. Both technologies are complex and require extensive strategic planning before a successful implementation can take place. Take a careful look at the type of directory or directories that the company will use, and then make sure it supports the enterprise needs in terms of flexibility, interoperability, scalability, and security. A directory that doesn't meet business needs runs the risk of restricting or holding back the success of the PKI initiative. A strong, secure directory solution will expand the reach and value of the PKI. A PKI will strengthen the security of a directory services initiative. When PKI and directory services are deployed correctly, in a coherent, strategic fashion, it translates to a win/win situation for all involved.

CHAPTER 7

Time Stamps

I n digital transaction processing, or computing in general, time stamps provide control and evidentiary standing for a transaction's control and audit process. The time stamp can be used to control specific policy for firewalls as a trigger event, and can also be used as an evidentiary token to represent that some event did in fact actually happen in Cyberspace. In the practical world, all transmission of time over a network is done in the form of time stamping.

Primitive time stamps have long been used inside commercial database systems for triggering payment or inventory control, so the use of time stamps controlling real-world events is already common practice, just not one that is talked about in the terms of the time stamps. Factory and industrial automation have long used time-based stamping as token-level control for their real-world activities In the emerging world of eBusiness, the time stamp is used to secure digital transactions and perform a vital piece of the assurance requirements of data integrity.

Quite obviously, since time stamp answers one of the critical questions concerning any digitally recorded event, "when" did it happen? For the time stamp to provide a reliable answer to that question, the time stamp's data structure must be cryptographically sound. If the time stamp is to be made comparable to any other outside time stamps, then additionally, the time upon which it is based must be provably derived from a trusted source.

From an evidentiary context, a time stamp that is based upon an unreliable or arbitrary time, or cannot prove the authoritative source from which it drew the time for the stamps it has created, cannot in the end be relied upon as a true indicator of "when" an event transpired.

Trustworthy time stamps require the system performing the time stamps to use a provable or audited time source as the source of its time data. Back in the real world, this is analogous to that anyone can tell you the time, but how does he prove that if ever required to? In other words, where did they get the time? Once the time that is used in the system can be proven to be trusted, cryptographically speaking it is a relatively easy matter to determine whether the time stamps are trustworthy. However, a system that cannot prove the source for the time it is using is a system whose time stamps cannot be trusted, no matter how cryptographically secure they might be.

A standardized time base like Coordinated Universal Time (UTC) and nationally authorized providers of that time base such as the Time and Frequency Division of the National Institute of Standards (NIST), Canadian National Research Council (NRC), and the Mexican Centro Nacional de Metrología (CENAM) in North America, as well as other agencies of governments throughout the world, are in place. A robust PKI implementation must supplement the "who" assured by certificates with the "when" answered by time stamps by using just such a trusted time base to validate the time stamps.

Enterprises implementing time stamps on a wide scale would be well served to be able to use them directly in the database as a native element instead of their having to be "bolted on." This will require a standardized and interoperable time-stamping token to facilitate inter-enterprise time-stamp data exchange. Unfortunately, the industry has not yet settled upon a time-stamping token standard. This means that the enterprise must either use an existing time-stamping format and hope that it becomes the standard, or create one of its own. In either case, the enterprise would be better off if a standard were in place. As things currently stand, the enterprise must settle on a format and hope, if the enterprise chooses incorrectly, that it doesn't cost too much to convert when the dust settles and a standard time-stamping token standard emerges.

In contrast with the definition given by the NRC, we assert here that what is critical is not that the time stamp be certified by "some authority" to prove its validity, but rather that the time upon which the time stamp is based be derived from a certifiable time source. That is, if the time base in a system can be shown to have been derived from and synchronized with a recognized time source over a specific period of time, then any time stamps created by that system during that specific period of time can be trusted. In fact, "shown" may require an independent audit to prove the time in the system is trustworthy. That audit should then be repeated on a regular basis to *show* that the trust value of the time base is ongoing and continuous from a fixed starting point, through this review until the next review.

The first critical factor is that the time base in use be provably shown to have come from a recognized time source, such that the clock in question is now using a time base that is coordinated with an absolute time base. The second part, determining the cryptographic validity of any trusted time stamps created thereafter, is a technical matter best accomplished by referring to experts in cryptographic procedures.

Mechanical Value

A time stamp must be secure enough such that it can be reviewed or audited long after its moment of creation and not be considered suspect cryptographically. In short, it must have a long enough hash to preclude any brute-force attacks in the near term.

Properly deployed time stamps using trusted mechanisms make it impossible to retroactively change recorded data. A good time stamp, like digital signatures, assures *data integrity* of the object stamped, and can be used to determine whether the object represented is the same now as that which was recorded when the stamp was created. Policies should be in place such that changes to data previously time stamped require new time stamps to be applied to the new data configuration. For example, digital images that are time stamped upon image creation should be preserved with the original image, while any time stamps created with any enhanced image created later should be preserved with the new enhanced image. To preserve data integrity, time stamps should never be altered.

An evidentiary time stamp can be used in transaction processing to *defeat a replay attack*, one of the foremost cryptographic and information security purposes behind instituting time stamps as a requirement in the process. Anytime a computer applies time data to anything, it is generically referred to as time stamping. However, see the following paragraph for one example of how time is used in evidentiary and control models in PKI based transaction processing:

> Alice digitally signs a negotiable instrument for Bob. Bob takes it to Alice's Bank. At the Bank, it is validated for payment because Alice's certificate is valid and the Bank relies upon her digital signature in the instrument to enable them to recover payment from Alice, which the Bank does. The Bank debits Alice's account, and credits the funds to Bob's. Some time passes, and Bob goes back to Alice's Bank seeking payment again on the same instrument. In this model, since Alice's certificate is valid, the signature is trusted, and the instrument is validated. Bob's account would be credited again, and possibly again and again until Alice's certificate expired. So without the use of provable time data in the transaction, Bob can continue to seek payment as long as Alice's certificate is valid.

Because the "is valid" attack exploits a hypothetical signing and reliance process that does not use time to bound the validity period, the transaction can be repeated ad infinitum. Bob can continue this attack as long as Alice's certificate is valid. In a similar attack where time stamping is required, the validating of a digital signature after the certificate is expired, or has been revoked, will look to the operational period of the certificate *to determine whether the signature was reliable at the time it was bound* to the signed object. This may seem to make it possible for Bob to continue his attack forever, assuming that Alice digitally signed during the operational period of her certificate. In fact the time stamp precludes this because it links the signed instrument and its redemption in a database, and any attempted repetition is discoverable. Thus the time stamp is used to support the making of digital decisions and is evidentiary content in and of itself.

By employing time stamps for all transactions, the Bank can defeat Bob's efforts. When Alice signs the instrument, a time stamp is associated with her digital signature. When Bob goes to the Bank to redeem the instrument, a time stamp is associated with that event. When Bob goes to the Bank to cash the same instrument in the future, it is now possible to determine that he is attempting to get payment a second time, and the transaction will be stopped.

Time stamps can also be used to assert *non-repudiation*. To achieve non-repudiation, time stamps must be generated from a trusted time source. Before we can discuss a trusted time source, however, it is necessary to review how trust is inserted into systems, and then how a system clock can be set using trusted time.

Human versus Machine-Based Trust Models

Time stamps are not new—the paper-based transaction-tracking world has employed them for ages through the services of the notary. Date/time stamps are commonly employed every day: Brokers use them to imprint date/time data on paperwork to validate trades, workers punch in and out by the millions by placing the timecard into the time clock on entry and again on departure to record and "prove" time spent on the job, postmarks are used to cancel postage stamps, and practically every cash register receipt of any sophistication includes date/time stamps. Notarial seals, data imprinted on paperwork, postmarks, timecards, and receipts all reflect a very simple trust model: people telling machines, "Record this transaction as taking place now."

What is required for digital acts to rise to the same level of trust accorded paper-based time-stamping mechanisms that has built up over hundreds and even thousands of years? That is, what will make it possible for a person to empower a machine to act on that person's behalf, such that the machine can from that moment forward act without human intervention in a trusted manner, and that the actions of the machine will be attributed to that person?

A key requirement of such an act is that people not be involved in the system any further, to minimize potential security breaches. A second is that the person the machine's actions are attributed to be identified, most likely through the use of a digital certificate, and that the party identifying that person for the certificate be held accountable for that identity certificate. A third is that the time in use in the system be trusted, such that the date/time stamps it generates can always be trusted.

So, the requirements for trusted time stamps are as follows:

➢ Trust requires that the systems generating them and the time stamps be secured as to "who" and "when," such that non-repudiation is possible, and preferably a standardized time-stamping token should be available to facilitate interoperability.

➢ Trust needs to be self-contained within the machine. That is, human witnesses cannot be the foundation of trust—*the machine must be able to prove itself* as a trusted provider through the processes and policies in place that control its actions. These policies and processes must be audited and verified, but they should not require human intervention once the system is up and running.

In electronic commerce, and especially in a robust PKI where the idea is to automate trust, it is computers that must be trusted to manage most, if not all, elements of a transaction. Turning all the "paperwork" into digital processes that can be called up and verified possibly long after the event, requires a considerable amount of trust in the system when the records are created and over time while the records are archived and accessed. Before trusting the machine, first to perform and then to keep track of everything it does, all in a trusted manner, questions arise that require satisfaction before the machine can be relied upon. How did the person empower the machine to act on the person's behalf? Was agency established? Were there witnesses? Were they physically present or virtual? What policies are in place that determine whether that empowerment may go forward, or must be curtailed? At what point in the process, if any, must the human interact with the machine to keep the process online, or to revoke it? These are just some of the questions that have to be worked through when placing trust in machines. Answers to such questions must come from the policies put in place by the enterprise.

What Is Trusted Time, and Why Is It Needed for Time Stamps?

The ability to keep time accurately must be distinguished from the ability to tell what time it really is. Many solutions exist to help the enterprise *keep* the time on the desktop and across the enterprise. Enterprise synchronization can be extremely useful.

However, before trusting the system it is essential to know how the time that is being used got into the system in the first place, and whether it can be proven that the time in use by the system derived from an acknowledged standard time source. And once it was introduced to the system, did the system actually use it? And can all of this be proven to the satisfaction of an independent auditor, such that the enterprise can declare itself to be operating in a trusted environment?

It might be helpful to first examine the methods in use today to get time into the system, and determine what each offers and what each lacks with regard to an end-to-end solution to trusted time. It should be noted that most of the methods in place are designed to keep time accurately, and do so with precision and accuracy. However, it is very difficult to initialize a system with time from a trusted source and to later prove that to be the case in a satisfactory manner. Evidentiary proof of time sourcing requires an unbroken chain of custody of time from the source to the enterprise.

Traditional Time-Sourcing Methods— Why They Cannot Be Trusted

Global positioning systems (GPS), mechanical clocks, and timeservers accessed on the Internet are the most frequent methods used to instill time in the enterprise. These sources can provide very accurate time, and can be used for time-keeping purposes without any concern. That is, if all the enterprise requires is to keep the time it has accurately, like the referee of a football game, then there is no need to worry about where these methods got their time. However, the time signals these methods deliver cannot in any provable manner guarantee either their own accuracy or that they were not modified in delivery.

GPS users cannot prove the satellite from which its time data is received. It is not possible to request time data from a specific satellite, and therefore it is not possible later to offer acceptable evidence as to the source of the time derived from satellites. Even if one could request time data from a specific satellite, GPS is operated by the United States Air Force, and the USAF is not an official source of time. And finally, the USAF could choose to alter or turn GPS time sources off in times of national emergency—if time data is mission critical, relying on GPS would be a very questionable move on the part of the enterprise. GPS is also very susceptible to antenna location problems, and requires line-of-sight to its satellites in order to work. GPS is also easily spoofed, and so provides an unreasonable security liability for most risk models.

Mechanical clocks, or atomic clocks, are extremely accurate, but offer no proof of not having been tampered with or re-set since synchronization with an acknowledged time data standard. On their own, standalone clocks cannot be relied upon for trusted time. However, when combined with a practice providing a certifiable way of initializing them, the locally run atomic clocks provide a strong and reliable source of time. The key to using them is the audit model that manages their setting and recertification on a regular basis.

Timeservers on the Internet cannot deliver reliable time, because the Network Time Protocol (NTP) request path will not mirror the time data's return path, and NTP always assumes a symmetric network to compensate for the latency in the arrival of the request. On the Internet, the mere availability of any timeserver is always an issue. Also, the public time servers are unsecured and have no operable audit practice currently available, so there are technical problems with the data transport model and also at the service level. How many business owners would rely on a time server run by a university somewhere with no liability as to the validity of the time or security to enforce its existence?

In the final analysis, an enterprise relying on time stamping that needs to make its digital audit data transportable will need to be able to prove the source of the time used in its system. Since none of the methods detailed here can establish a chain-of-custody or document their source, they offer no provable time source, rendering an audit or reliable record-keeping impossible.

Evidentiary Grade Time—
Time Sourcing for Trusted Time Stamps

To implant trusted time within a system requires the following:

➤ An unbroken chain of custody of time data over a symmetric network (either a private network, a VPN, or a telephone line)

➤ From an acknowledged time data standard to the target system

➤ That sets the time in the system

➤ Monitors the system clock to keep it synchronized with the acknowledged time standard

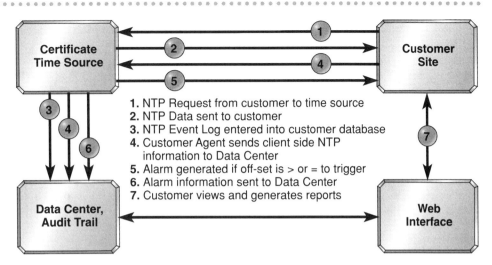

Figure 7.1   Network time protocol time setting request and fulfillment.
Source: CertifiedTime.

> Maintains a time-stamped log recording every time data and timing event on the network

To establish a trusted time stamp, the user must submit requests to a trusted time source from an accepted time standard, prove a chain of custody over the time data from the source to the device making the request, and then log that data securely for as long as is commercially reasonable (see Figure 7.1).

The frequency with which a system should be monitored and re-set is as often as is required by the operating policies with which the enterprise must comply. For example, NASD brokers must stay within three seconds of UTC in their system clocks. Assuming some system clocks may drift by as much as one second per hour, it would be enough to have the system clock monitored and synchronized automatically every hour.

Operating Policy Advantages of a Trusted Time Base

Using a standard (absolute) time base and trusted time creates a side benefit for the enterprise. By setting the time base properly with a trusted source, and thereby enabling trusted time stamps, it becomes possible for machines in distinct enterprises to trust each other. By operating on the same time base, machines can interact and exchange data without having to receive an "okay" from human hands. All that needs to be done is to set the machine up to respond and interact only with other machines that are on the same time base. For machines on different time bases, each of which can be trusted, an offset table relating the two time bases over time will be required. The automated interactions of machines will be facilitated by the speedy acceptance of a standardized time-stamping token (see Figure 7.2).

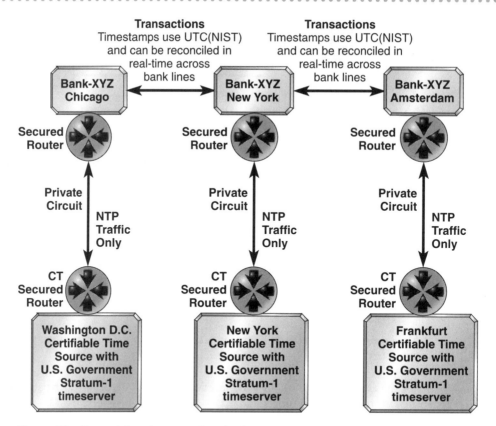

Figure 7.2   Trusted time-base synchronization.
Source: CertifiedTime.

By using the same time base, banks across the globe can time stamp transactions and trades, which can then immediately be reconciled by other banks, eliminating the heavy costs of proving transactions.

Portability in Trust Models

The next step in the use of time stamps is removing them from the machine. Employing a trusted time base creates time-stamp tokens that are comparable to any other token created using the same time base. This will allow standardized time-stamp tokens to be broken off on disks, zip drives, or smart cards. In short, time-stamping tokens based on absolute time can be transported out of the machine and still be trusted. Trust becomes portable. This is possible because the time-stamping token is cryptographically secure, and the time base used in the time stamp is universally recognized.

Summary

Time stamps can serve as a control service, or can be used for evidentiary purposes to pinpoint "when" a digital event transpired. Before a time stamp can be trusted, the system deploying the time stamps must be able to prove that the time base in use was set using time data from one of a number of nationally recognized time sources. Once a system can prove that its time base can be trusted, and therefore that the time stamps it creates are trustworthy, some very interesting possibilities are created for the use of such time stamps. One example would be that diverse systems using the same time base can begin to "speak" to one another through policy management tools, because events in each will be synchronized. Another example would be the acceptance and transference of time-stamping tokens offline—portability will permit low- and high-level offline token transactions, from frequent-flier miles to cash. This will depend, of course, on just how much people actually do trust the systems creating the time stamps.

What we refer to as time stamping is a critical part of auditing, and the technology that companies such as CertifiedTime are working on is an evidentiary grade method of mechanically demonstrating "some thing"; in other words, a person, place, or whatever, frozen in a reliable instant in time. Think of time stamping as a mechanical process of creating and evaluating time stamps.

The real issue here is the establishment of evidentiary models that can be machine interpreted, so that control and financial systems can be made to run autonomously—especially ones that are accepted internationally.

From a mechanical standpoint, there are likely two key issues to address in the creating of a national standard for this watermarking or the time stamping of events.

The first of these two components would be a recommendation for the definition of the data structures themselves, a statement of how they are to be evaluated, and their use models. Essentially, this statement would be analogous to the defining of the etching in U.S. currency and the statement of its use, the redemption or exchange rules for the completed currency itself.

The second is the statement setting the bar height for the quality of data (QoD) used in the structure itself; this is particular to information like time and location data that is used to anchor the trust model (nee "Trust Anchors"). This is analogous to defining the type of paper and ink used in the printing of currency.

Structures built on best practices will have to address both of these issues.

8

Hardware Mechanisms

• •

Like other application vendors, PKI solution providers offer their applications on popular platforms such as generic Windows NT or Unix systems in order to make deployment as easy and cost effective as possible for their customers. However, there exist two public key cryptography issues with which generic systems may need some help: the risk of potential key loss in software, and the compute-intensive nature of cryptographic processing.

First, the most sensitive component of any PKI is the private key. Many experts feel that storing private keys in software increases the risk of theft, and employ hardware modules as storage devices for private keys. The highest security applications can require that authorization for private key use be divided across multiple people with their own hardware devices.

The second issue is not a function of the public key infrastructure, per se, but of the processing it requires. The public key algorithm uses a great deal of a CPU. The essence of its ability to disguise data consumes an inordinate amount of a computer's available cycle time, thereby rendering it unavailable for other tasks. Thus, special hardware can accelerate the cryptography when server performance is important.

Secure Private Key Management

As mentioned previously, the private key is the most sensitive component of public key cryptography. Theft of your private key means you can be impersonated in electronic communications, documents, or transactions. This could obviously be disastrous for enterprises conducting high-value electronic transactions validated with digital certificates. Besides the risk of fraud, there is the cost of recovery. If the private key of a CA were lost or stolen, all the certificates in a hierarchy that have been signed by that CA are invalid and would need to be reissued. In a large PKI, this can be an onerous task, and the security of a private key is paramount.

To mitigate this risk, a PKI hardware device called a Hardware Storage Module (HSM) secures cryptographic keys by keeping them on the device and off the potentially more accessible server when being used in cryptographic operations. HSMs come in various form factors: peripherals, modules, PCMCIA cards, and smart cards. In all cases, a private key is generated on the HSM and, in most designs, never leaves the HSM unencrypted. Data requiring signature, encryption, or decryption is passed to the HSM using a standard interface, and all the cryptographic processing based on the key is done on the HSM. The result of the processing is then passed back to the server. The sensitive key is never downloaded unencrypted to the server software.

Key-Finding Lunchtime Attacks

While there has been general agreement that storing a key in software on the server is inherently risky, a specific attack against a private key stored in software had not been demonstrated until Adi Shamir and Nicko van Someren published their research on key finding (van Someren and Shamir, 1998). The researchers stated that private keys stored on a hard drive are characterized by a more random pattern of bits than other data on the drive, and that searching for this randomness can result in the discovery of the key.

One common counterpoint to the announcement of this attack was that privileged access was required to search the memory and file system for a key, and that granting this kind of access to anyone other than trusted system administrators is very poor system management (Brown, 2000—Talkback). While there still have not been any notable reports of serious loss as a result of this "lunchtime attack" (it could be foisted upon your PC while you are out at lunch), the generally accepted risk of software key storage has now been demonstrated, and applications that will certainly benefit from HSMs include Web servers, CAs, and VAs.

Sharing Key Responsibility

Besides keeping the key off the server, another important security feature of some HSMs is the ability to spread the responsibility for key operations across multiple individuals and, in so doing, greatly reduce the risk of key compromise. Critical key operations, such as signing or recovery, require the authorization of several people, and the risk of multiple people agreeing to misuse the key is much less than the risk of an individual misusing it either accidentally or intentionally.

This feature of an HSM goes by many names, such as secret splitting, key sharing, and "m of n" secret splitting, but at a high level it always involves splitting the approval of key operation across multiple individuals with some configurable subset of those appointed approvers required to authorize key operation. Vendors supporting this advanced feature include Chrysalis-ITS and nCipher.

FIPS 140-1

Just how secure is an HSM? The U.S. government, specifically NIST, has developed a standard against which cryptographic modules can be measured for security. This standard, Federal Information Processing Standard (FIPS) 140-1, specifies requirements for 11 aspects of HSM design to rate a module at one of four security levels. Levels 1 and 2 are commonly achieved by HSMs.

Security Level 1

Security Level 1 provides the lowest level of security. It specifies basic security requirements for a cryptographic module (e.g., the encryption algorithm shall be an Approved algorithm (Section 2)), but it differs from the higher levels of security in several aspects. For example, no physical security mechanisms are required in the cryptographic module beyond the requirement for production-grade equipment. An example of a Security Level 1 system is a personal computer (PC) encryption board.

Security Level 1 allows software cryptographic functions to be performed in a general-purpose PC. Such implementations may be appropriate for low-level security applications. The implementation of PC cryptographic software may be more cost-effective than hardware-based mechanisms. This will enable organizations to select from alternative cryptographic solutions to meet lower-level security requirements.

Security Level 2

Security Level 2 improves the physical security of a Security Level 1 cryptographic module by adding the requirement for tamper-evident coatings or seals or for pick-resistant locks. Tamper-evident coatings or seals are placed on a cryptographic module so that the coating or seal would have to be broken in order to attain physical access to the plaintext cryptographic keys and other critical security parameters (CSPs) within the module. Tamper-evident seals or pick-resistant locks are placed on covers or doors to protect against unauthorized physical access.

Security Level 2 requires, at a minimum, role-based authentication in which a cryptographic module authenticates the authorization of an operator to assume a specific role and perform a corresponding set of services. Furthermore, Security Level 2 allows software cryptography in multiuser timeshared systems when used with an operating system that:

➤ Meets the functional requirements specified in the Common Criteria (CC) Controlled Access Protection Profile (CAPP)

➤ Is evaluated at the CC evaluation assurance level EAL2 (or higher)

An equivalent evaluated trusted operating system may be used. A trusted operating system is needed in order for software cryptography to be implemented with a level of trust comparable to hardware cryptography.

Security Level 3

Modules that achieve level-3 validation are highly secure. In addition to the tamper-evident security requirements of Security Level 2, Security Level 3 attempts to prevent the intruder from gaining access to CSPs held within the cryptographic module. For example, a multiple-chip embedded cryptographic module must be contained in a strong enclosure and, if a removable cover is removed or a door is opened, any unprotected CSPs are zeroized.

Security Level 3 requires identity-based authentication, which is stronger than the role-based authentication specified for Security Level 2. A cryptographic module authenticates the identity of an operator and verifies that the identified operator is authorized to assume a specific role and perform a corresponding set of services.

Security Level 3 requires the data ports used for entering and outputting CSPs to be physically separated from other data ports. Furthermore, the parameters are either entered into or output from the cryptographic module in encrypted form (in which case, they may travel through enclosing or intervening systems), or are directly entered into or output from the module (without passing through enclosing or intervening systems) using split knowledge procedures.

Security Level 3 allows software cryptography in multiuser timeshared systems when used with an operating system that:

➤ Meets the functional requirements specified in the CAPP with the additional functional requirement of a Trusted Path (FTP_TRP.1)

➤ Is evaluated at the CC evaluation assurance level EAL3 (or higher) with the additional assurance requirement of an Informal Target of Evaluation (TOE) Security Policy Model (ADV_SPM.1)

An equivalent evaluated trusted operating system may be used. The trusted path has the capability to protect cryptographic software and CSPs from other untrusted software that may run on the system. Such a system prevents plaintext from being mixed with ciphertext, and it prevents the unintentional transmission of plaintext keys.

Security Level 4

Security Level 4 provides the highest level of security. At this level, physical security provides an envelope of protection around the cryptographic module with the intent of detecting a penetration from any direction. For example, an attempt to cut through the enclosure of the cryptographic module is detected and all CSPs are zeroized. Security Level 4 cryptographic modules are useful for operation in physically unprotected environments.

Security Level 4 also protects a cryptographic module against a compromise of its security due to environmental conditions or fluctuations outside of the module's normal operating ranges for voltage and temperature. Intentional excursions beyond the normal operating ranges may be used by an attacker to thwart a cryptographic module's defense during an attack. A cryptographic module is required to either include special environmental protection features designed to detect fluctuations and zeroize CSPs, or to undergo rigorous environmental failure testing in order to provide a reasonable assurance that the module will not be affected by fluctuations outside of the normal operating range in a manner that can compromise the security of the module.

Security Level 4 allows software cryptography in multiuser timeshared systems when used with an operating system that:

➤ Meets the functional requirements specified for Security Level 3

➤ Is evaluated at the Common Criteria evaluation assurance level EAL4 (or higher) with the additional assurance requirements of Formal TOE Security Policy Modeling, Covert Channel Analysis, and Modularity

An equivalent evaluated trusted operating system may be used. An operating system evaluated at EAL4 with the additional listed requirements provides assurances of the correct operation of the security features of the operating system.

If key security is important to you, check the list of validated products at NIST's Web site *(www.itl.nist.gov/fipspubs/fip140-1.htm)* for two reasons: First, the terminology is very specific. You should be wary of phrases in marketing literature such as "designed for level 3" or "level-3 complaint," as these do not mean the same thing as "validated." A vendor may use the term "level 3" in its literature because it designed a module with the intention of achieving level-3 validation. However, it may not actually achieve *overall* level-3 validation, because one or more of the components only validated at levels 1 or 2. The NIST Web site will tell you exactly what the validation level is. Second, it may be that although the overall validation is level 2, the components that achieve level 3 validation are those that are important to your application. If this is true, your security requirements will be met much more economically, since vendors charge a hefty premium for a FIPS 140-1 level-3 validated product. Again, the NIST site will tell you the component validation levels

Offline Storage: Hardware or Software?

HSM designs also differ in how the key is stored when the CA, VA, or Web server is not in operation. One common approach is to keep the key stored on the HSM when it is not in use, as exemplified by the Chrysalis-ITS Luna family of HSMs. The nCipher nShield, on the other hand, keeps the key on the HSM during use, but when not in use, the key is stored in software on a server, encrypted and protected by other keys on smart cards in what nCipher calls a *security world*.

On the one hand, nCipher states that with the security world concept, the private key is stored in an encrypted *blob* on the server, and that makes key backup easy—you just include it in the normal production backup schedule. It also eliminates the need for creating duplicate keys that might get lost or stolen. Those who keep the key stored in hardware, on the other hand, maintain that key security is tighter if it never leaves the hardware. Key backup in this case is done by generating a backup copy of the key at "keygen"—when the public/private key pair is created—securely transferring it to another HSM, and storing it in a very secure location such as a safe deposit box. Both approaches are quite secure, and it becomes a matter of policy or preference. Even in cases where policy dictates that the key be stored in hardware for the top-level CAs and VAs in a PKI, it is likely that this remains a point of open discussion due to the high security encryption affords.

Smart Cards: An Enabling Form Factor

While it may be viewed as just another form factor for an HSM, the smart card deserves special mention precisely because of its form factor. It is a credit card look-alike with a familiar look and feel and compact size, and it probably has the best chance of bringing secure HSM benefits to the masses. Unlike credit cards, however, it does not have a magnetic strip to house information on the owner. Rather, it has a microprocessor, a small amount of memory, and gold contact pads for I/O. Like its heftier HSM cousins, a smart card designed for PKI applications contains a cryptographic engine supporting both asymmetric and symmetric encryption algorithms, cryptographic keys, and multiple certificates. Important interface standards for smart cards are PKCS #11, PKCS #15, Microsoft CryptoAPI, ISO 7816, and the PC/SC standard (see the section *Interface Standards* later in this chapter).

Smart card applications are growing rapidly and include secure Web browser authentication, wireless communications, secure application authentication (such as CA signing approvals), and access control. While all the smart card application efforts and vendor initiatives could probably fill a separate chapter, a small sampling—far from a comprehensive list—is offered:

Baltimore Technologies Telepathy Program. Unites smart card, PKI and wireless vendors to bring secure, public key authentication to wireless communications.

Certicom SC400/500 card. Implements elliptic curve cryptographic algorithms on smart cards.

Litronic three-factor authentication. A demonstration of technology combining digital signatures, iris biometrics, smart cards, and smart card readers with potential for FIPS 140-1 level-3 validation.

Spyrus Rosetta Smart Card and Personal Access Reader 2 (PAR 2). Enhances smart card usability with a reader that, according to Spyrus, will fit in your purse or pocket.

A final comment on the smart card made noteworthy by the recent approval of the Electronic Signatures in Global and National Commerce Act: It can potentially place highly secure authentication technology in the hands of the masses, so it must be accompanied by a modicum of education on associated security practices. For example, many smart cards are protected by passwords, and users need to understand that selecting your spouse's name, your birth date, or your dog's name as a password—as Bill Clinton recently did when signing the Electronic Signatures in Global and National Commerce Act using his smart card—greatly degrades the security of any HSM.

Public Key Performance Improvement

While not directly related to the "I" in PKI today, a performance bottleneck is another issue that hardware has always been a potential solution for, and public key cryptography happens to be a very, very compute-intensive operation. Specifically, public key operations are significantly more costly than symmetric key operations in terms of CPU utilization. If PKI and certificate status checking becomes fundamental to all significant e-commerce transactions as expected, the spotlight focuses on this public key performance issue.

The popular protocol used by secure Web servers is the Secure Sockets Layer (SSL) from Netscape, also available as OpenSSL from RSA Security. SSL is a protocol based on the RSA algorithms. Every time a user initiates an SSL session with a secure Web server, the server authenticates itself to the user's client system and an RSA public key operation is executed. Once authentication is complete and a session key is exchanged, SSL switches to a less-costly symmetric key algorithm such as DES. However, the initial authentication process puts a significant load on a server.

Applications or tasks requiring these public key calculations are growing and include certificate authentication, SSL session setup, transaction and document signing, authentication of parties setting up a virtual private network (VPN), and secret session key exchange for a VPN. To date, however, the application that has attracted the most attention is the moment of secure session authentication on an SSL Web server.

Under normal conditions, most commercial Web servers can handle the SSL authentication load without significant impact on perceived response time or quality of service. However, if you have ever tried to connect to an online stock brokerage system during a period of heavy trading, for example, you probably experienced a frustrating increase in server response time and, perhaps, even a "server busy" response. At peak activity periods such as these, the server's processor becomes overly consumed by the cryptographic processing in the SSL authentication, or *handshake*. This is the nightmare scenario of every Chief Technology Officer (CTO) of a Web-enabled business, and nearly every article on cryptographic acceleration starts with its own spin on it. There is always a business-critical Web server that is not responding to customer connection requests due to burdensome crypto overhead.

Web server software passes the cryptographic calculations off to a special peripheral device in order to keep the system CPU from being overloaded. Web servers and other applications pass the necessary data to the cryptographic device using a standard interface defined in the Public Key Cryptographic Standard (PKCS) #11, simply referred to as just PKCS #11.

The enhanced performance achieved with accelerators has been clearly demonstrated in recent tests by two leading journals. In a *Network Computing* review, the nCipher nForce SCSI 300 walked away with Editor's Choice honors, while *Network World* chose the Rainbow CryptoSwift 600 for its Blue Ribbon Award. While actual results vary with platform and accelerator used, the testing showed that adding one of these leading hardware acceleration devices boosts the secure transactions per second by about 10 times. With respect to response time, the *Network Computing* testing demonstrated a four-fold improvement in average response time with a drop from 1.36 seconds to .33 second.

Add an Accelerator or a Web Server?

For anyone who needs increased server throughput and responsiveness by mitigating the cryptographic bottleneck, there are two options: add a Web server or add a cryptographic accelerator. In both cases, the computing resources available for the public key operations are increased, but there are differences that can move you in one direction or the other.

One obvious difference is cost. The first option, adding a Web server, involves the purchase of a complete system with all the hardware and software necessary to clone the original, bogged-down Web server and relieve it of SSL load. Server costs vary widely depending upon processor and options, but for a PC server configured to offer commercial-quality functionality, capacity, and performance, the initial capital investment can easily be $15,000 to $20,000 with significant annual maintenance costs. The two Web servers—the new server and existing server—can share connection requests to the same URL using round-robin DNS. Or, a Web traffic load-balancing appliance from Cisco, HydraWeb, Radware, F5, and others can be added to the mix for an additional cost of over $5000 for an entry-level end product.

Typical accelerator prices vary by promised performance and generally range from $5000 to $12,000. Likewise, HSMs prices tend to increase with the level of FIPS 140-1 validation promised, and can exceed $25,000 for a device with level-3 validation. So, if you are interested in high-performance SSL only, the capital cost of an accelerator is less than that of an additional Web server. However, if the highest level of FIPS validation is also important to you, the cost of an HSM approaches that of an additional Web server.

The financial analysis should not stop here. A comparison must be made between the alternatives of equal performance, and to achieve 200–300 SSL connections per second at times of peak demand, you would need at least three Pentium Web servers, or two additional servers. Thus, the Web server alternative is really twice as costly, even with a FIPS 140-1 level-3 HSM.

For the accelerator/HSM alternative, justifying the cost is relatively straightforward. The benefit of the additional resource is cryptographic-specific, so a metric such as cost per incremental SSL connection is appropriate. You could simply divide the total incremental annual cost in each case by the total number of SSL connections achieved with the single accelerator-assisted Web server. For the incremental Web server alternative, however, other benefits may be realized, since the additional computing resource is available for running other applications during the non-peak load periods when there is no cryptographic bottleneck. Thus, the cost can be spread across multiple applications, and an appropriate mixed-use cost per transaction should be devised to help justify the additional cost.

Simply put, the question is whether you only need to address the cryptographic performance or if you can use an additional Web server with other applications. In most cases, a business-critical public Web server would probably be dedicated to the revenue-generating application, and the accelerator option would be easily cost-justified in the absence of other applications. However, a careful financial accounting for all costs and all benefits should make the choice between accelerator and server clear.

Not to confuse the analysis, but several vendors offer both secure private key storage and cryptographic acceleration with the same product. The financial impact of a lost private key includes not only the potential fraud damages but also the cost to generate a new public/private key pair and distribute the new certificates to all those with the old, invalid public key. Thus, the financial justification of private key security is based on avoiding disaster rather than saving operational costs, pumping up productivity, or increasing revenue. This means it is more difficult to quantify. Nevertheless, the potential cost of a compromised private key needs to be considered along with the acceleration benefit with products that do double duty.

Interface Standards

Besides security standards such as FIPS, other important standards address the interface to HSMs. While some HSMs offer a proprietary interface, interoperability with other PKI components such as Web servers, CAs, and VAs requires a standard interface. The two interface standards that HSMs generally comply with are PKCS #11 and the Microsoft CryptoAPI. These standards specify an interface through which an application can request cryptographic services, such as data encryption/decryption and public key signing, from cryptographic modules.

The development of PKCS is spearheaded by RSA Security. PKCS #11 specifically addresses a common application programming interface (API) for cryptographic hardware. Likewise, Microsoft's CryptoAPI also provides application developers with an API for adding cryptographic functions to Win32-based applications.

In the realm of smart cards, ISO 7816 defines smart card standards for basic architectural and functional characteristics, such as location of contacts, physical card characteristics, electronic signals, and transmissions. Another standard, the Personal Computer/Smart Card (PC/SC) standard, strives to build on ISO 7816 with additional interface standards in an effort to improve the integration of smart card devices with PCs, and to advance interoperability between products from various vendors. Participants in the PC/SC effort include smart card manufacturers such as Gemplus, Schlumberger, and Infinion, and computer manufacturers Apple, Bull, HP, Microsoft, Sun, and Toshiba.

Products

Assuming you have done a comparative analysis and have decided your needs are best met with a cryptographic accelerator or HSM, let's look briefly at some of the available products. Table 8.1 presents a sample of hardware devices available on the market; it is not intended to be comprehensive. The reader should do his or her own research into all the available alternatives, a task made easy by the Web.

Table 8.1 Sampling of PKI Hardware Vendors

VENDOR	PRODUCT	FORM FACTOR	BEST PERFORMANCE[1] AND/OR FIPS VALIDATION[2]	WEB SITE
Baltimore Technologies	Keyper	Peripheral	FIPS 140-1 validation in process	www.baltimore.com
Baltimore Technologies	Runner	Module	Performance not available yet	www.baltimore.com
Chrysalis-ITS	Luna-CA3	PCMCIA	FIPS 140-1 Level 3	www.chrysalis-its.com
Compaq	SignMaster ISP	Storage	Not validated	www.tandem.com
Compaq	AXL200 PCI Accelerator Card		236 SSL/s	www.tandem.com
Gemplus	GemXplore Trust smart card	Smart card	Not validated	www.gemplus.com
HP	Praesidium SpeedCard[3]	Module	200 SSL/s	www.hp.com
IBM	4758 PCI Crypto Coprocessor	Module	Performance not available; FIPS 140-1 Level 3	www.ibm.com
Intel	NetStructure 7110 e-Commerce Accelerator[4]	Rack mount appliance	200 SSL/s	www.intel.com
Litronic	Forte Smart Card	Smart Card	FIPS 140-1 validation in process	www.litronic.com
NCipher	nShield 300	Module, drive, peripheral	FIPS 140-1 Level 3 300 SSL/s	www.ncipher.com
Rainbow	CryptoSwift	Module	Not validated 200 SSL/s	www.rainbow.com
Spyrus	Rosetta Smart Card	Smart card	FIPS 140-1 Level 2	www.spyrus.com
Spyrus	LYNKS Privacy Card	PCMCIA	FIPS 140-1 Level 2 732 msec for a 1024 bit RSA key signing	www.spyrus.com

1. SSL/s = Highest number of SSL connections per second as advertised by vendor for a single module or processor.

2. *Overall* validation level as listed on NIST validation list at http://csrc.ncsl.nist.gov/cryptval/140-1/1401val.htm. Some product components may be validated at a higher level.

3. Based on Rainbow Technologies' FastMAP cryptographic engine.

4. Includes network failover when second device is added.

Hardware Technology to Watch

While the 64-bit Alpha processor from Compaq has been around for several years, and while IBM recently announced the RS/6000 Model H70 64-bit Web server pushing over 11,000 Web hits per second, PKI hardware watchers should keep an eye on Itanium, Intel's 64-bit processor. According to Intel, Itanium has built-in cryptographic functions, and a prototype executed 650 RSA 1024-bit signings per second. Intel projects that the production version should surpass the 1000 signings per second mark without any additional hardware acceleration. Contrast that with today's benchmark of 300 signings per second with a hardware accelerator.

It sounds fantastic, but there are potential downsides to be aware of. First, there is cost. While the price of an Itanium processor alone will not come close to the price of an accelerator, its initial appearance on high-end (read *expensive*) servers is likely. Thus, it will be an expensive alternative from a total system cost perspective. Second, add-on accelerators free up CPU cycles by offloading cryptographic processing. To achieve the results RSA signature performance advertised, it is likely that that the Itanium CPU was 100 percent dedicated to the RSA calculations. Therefore, available CPU resources are still an issue during peak SSL processing times, unless Intel markets an Itanium cryptographic co-processor on the motherboard or on a separate module. Finally, there is the 64-bit application issue. While Intel says a 64-bit version of Linux will run on Itanium, the lack of high-performance 64-bit applications was the reason for the slow penetration of DEC's Alpha into mainstream computing. If native 64-bit Web servers, CAs, and VAs are not available, the advertised optimal performance may not be realized, as 32-bit executables must be translated while running on a 64-bit processor.

PART THREE

PKI and Business Issues

Getting Certificates

In this chapter, the attempt is to provide a simple, yet effective tutorial for obtaining a personal use digital certificate. Installing a digital certificate on your personal computer will help you understand several basic issues, functions, and limitations much more than just reading about it. By actually using a certificate, you find that no technology is perfect, and that it is often difficult for users to figure out. Users want the benefit of security that certificates can provide, not the hassles of learning all about it. For that reason, transparency to users should be on the top of your requirements list for your PKI so users not just accept but also use certificates.

Introduction

Before getting into the actual steps, some key points must be understood about this particular procedure:

It is just one example. The products, features, and functionality illustrated here are only an example of what can be used. They are neither the only choices nor representative of the full functionality and benefits of certificates. While the example cited in this chapter uses Microsoft Outlook, similar applications such as Netscape and Eudora are also capable of utilizing certificates. Similarly, the certificate we'll be obtaining from VeriSign is also available from some other vendors.

It does not provide true authentication as written. It's worth noting that while this certificate will provide you with the capability to send and receive e-mail with confidentiality and integrity, it does not offer true authentication and non-repudiation. Because there's no requirement for presenting any identity credentials to obtain the certificate other than an e-mail address, you and others should ascribe much less assurance and trust to this type of certificate. Of course, you can always increase the level of trust by performing what's called an *out-of-band verification*. By using another means of communication, such as a telephone call, you could verify the serial number and fingerprint of the certificate to ensure its validity.

It uses the latest versions of Outlook, and Microsoft's or Netscape's Browser. To ensure that you have all the features, functionality, and security available, you should have the latest version of software and related update patches installed on your personal computer. Since implementations of software do change, if one of the following steps does not appear or does not make sense, something has probably changed since this was written. Additional information for your particular application is also available via the Help menu.

It may differ from your organization's procedure. If you are in an organization that is using certificates, or will be using them, the following steps may differ considerably, and you should consult with the appropriate responsible individuals. Again, this tutorial is intended to get you acquainted with installing and using a certificate strictly for your personal use and learning.

Two certificates are required. To be able to take advantage of sending and receiving encrypted and signed e-mail, both you and the other party need to have a certificate installed. Since you are going to be a pioneer in your organization, I'll later show you how to locate other certificate holders, like myself, so you'll be able to test your new capability.

Copying yourself on encrypted e-mail is recommended. Be *very* careful about sending encrypted e-mail only to the recipient(s). If you need to keep a copy for yourself that you can access later, you may need to include yourself as a recipient as well. This is because the message you send is encrypted using the recipient's public key, and only the recipient's private key can decrypt it. More on this later.

Procedure

While all steps in this procedure need to be completed, the procedure can be logically subdivided into three main tasks:

1. Applying for a certificate—the longest part, taking about 10 minutes.
2. Receiving and installing the certificate—the simplest task, but may be either 2 minutes or 30, depending on VeriSign's speed in issuing your new certificate.
3. Testing your certificate—the most gratifying task, taking 5 minutes.

The entire procedure will take roughly 15 to 30 minutes, depending on how quickly VeriSign issues your certificate; so let's get started.

Applying for a Certificate

The first major task is to apply for a certificate:

1. Open Microsoft Outlook.

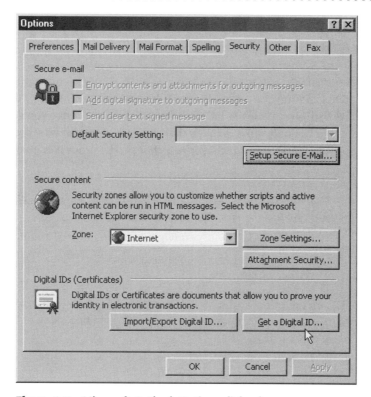

Figure 9.1   Microsoft Outlook Options dialog box.

2. From the Tools menu, click Options, and then select the Security tab.

   You should now see the window that appears in Figure 9.1. Notice that the upper section under Secure, e-mail is grayed out. Once you have your certificate installed, you are able to adjust these settings according to your preference.

3. Click "Get a Digital ID."

   This will take you to the Microsoft Web site.

4. Choose the appropriate country.

   You are redirected to another Web page that lists a choice of vendors, such as VeriSign, GlobalSign, British Telecommunications, and Thawte.

5. For this exercise, click VeriSign.

   You should now be at VeriSign's Digital ID Center Web page as shown in Figure 9.2. Take a few minutes to read about the Class 1 Digital ID that VeriSign offers.

6. Select one of the following:

   a. The 60-day free trial certificate,

or

b. The certificate that is good for one year.

Be aware that you cannot revoke a trial ID once it has been issued. That is, the certificate is listed on VeriSign's Web site indefinitely. Consequently, once you start using certificates, you not only must manage their lifecycle, but also how they are going to be listed in the directory. Whichever you choose, the process is going to be the same.

7. Type in your personal information into the Enrollment Form as seen in Figures 9.3 and 9.4.

8. Type your name and e-mail address as you want it shown on your certificate.

Once the certificate is issued, others will be able to search the Digital ID directory based on the information you provide.

9. Choosing No about including additional information is recommended, as there is no need to share any more information about yourself than necessary.

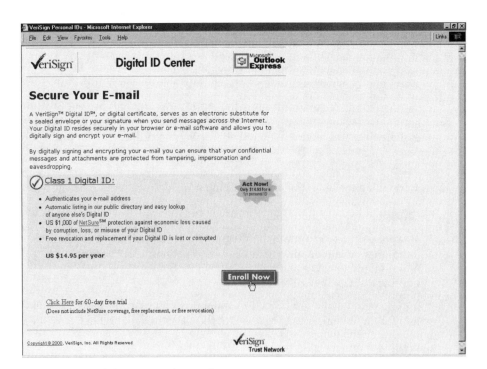

Figure 9.2 VeriSign Personal ID Web page.

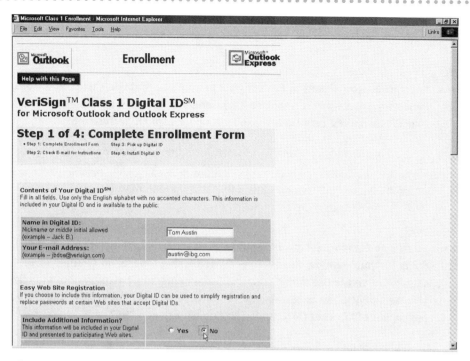

Figure 9.3 VeriSign Class 1 Enrollment Web page.

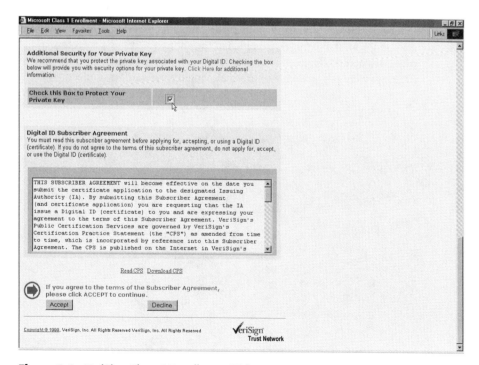

Figure 9.4 VeriSign Class 1 Enrollment Web page.

10. Check the box indicated to protect your private key for added security for your certificate.

Specifically, you'll want to protect your private key that will reside in the system registry. Your private key is accessed each time you use your certificate, is yours alone to use, and should only be accessed with your explicit permission.

11. Download and read VeriSign's Certificate Practice Statement (CPS).

You'll also be able to access it later if you would like. Given the length and depth of the document, you may want to put it aside to read later.

Be sure to compare what VeriSign has done with its CPS, what you're planning on doing for your own organization, and what we've covered in Chapter 11 on Certificate Policy and Certification Practices Statements. In particular, note the terms concerning liability. This is certainly not a document to be taken lightly. When you deploy your PKI, what do you plan to publish as your CPS?

12. Click Accept.
13. Click Set Security Level, as shown in Figure 9.5.
14. For your best protection, choose High, as shown in Figure 9.6.

With this setting, whenever your certificate is accessed, it requires the password you assign it. It's somewhat ironic isn't it, that you can be protecting a higher level of security identification with a less than secure password. Of course, there are other ways of protecting the certificate, including hardware mechanisms such as smart cards. For more information, refer to the appropriate chapters in this book.

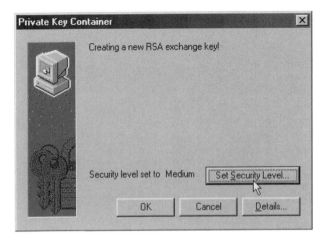

Figure 9.5 Private Key Container dialog box.

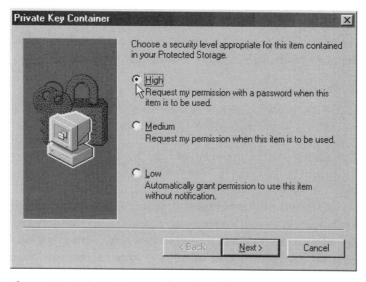

Figure 9.6 Private Key Container dialog box–security level selection.

15. If you've done the right thing and elected to use good security, type in a password or a passphrase with numbers, as shown in Figure 9.7.

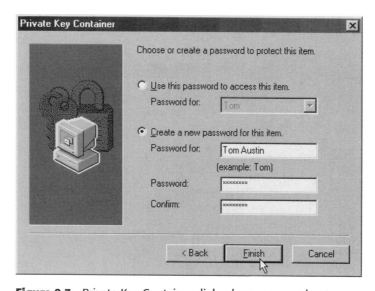

Figure 9.7 Private Key Container dialog box–password entry.

A passphrase or saying such as "love94harleys" is not easy for others to guess, is easy for you to remember, and offers more security than a password.

16. Click Finish.

The Private Key Container dialog box in Figure 9.8 now appears, and your browser creates the key pair needed for your certificate.

17. Type in the password or passphrase you just created, and then click OK.

Selecting "Remember password" is not recommended. It may sound convenient, but if anyone else gains access to your system, you're giving up any security you have. There's nothing wrong in writing down the passphrase you created; just leave it in a safe place. Obviously, this should not be on a Post-It note on your monitor, under your keyboard, or in an unlocked desk drawer.

18. Enter in your passphrase once more, do not select "Remember password," and then click OK.

Again, enter in your passphrase once more, do not select "Remember password," and then click OK (see Figure 9.9).

The VeriSign page shown in Figure 9.10 appears and says you are on Step 2 of 4, but you are really almost done. At this point, you probably have a lot of windows open on your screen. It's safe to close all the ones this process just created.

Because it is going to take several minutes before VeriSign e-mails you the next step, it may be time to go get that cup of coffee. You can even shut the system down at this point and come back at a later time to finish.

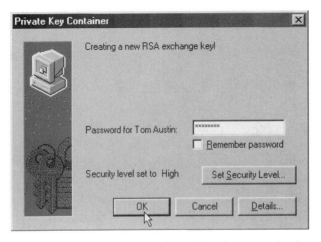

Figure 9.8 Private Key Container dialog box—creating key.

Figure 9.9 Private Key Container dialog box—signing data.

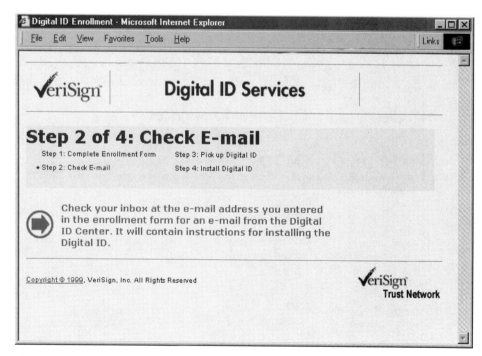

Figure 9.10 Digital ID Enrollment page—Step 2 of 4.

Receiving and Installing Your Certificate

Okay! Now it's time to check your e-mail inbox. If all has gone according to plan, you should now have an e-mail similar to Figure 9.11.

1. Click Continue.

You should now see Step 4 of 4 in your Web browser appear just like in Figure 9.12.

2. Click INSTALL.

NOTE

As stated in Figure 9.13, if you're using Outlook Express or Outlook 98, you can follow the instructions given on the VeriSign web site for your particular e-mail application from this point. Once you've completed the steps indicated, go to the next section, Testing Your Certificate.

3. For Outlook 2000 users, open Outlook.
4. On the Tools menu, click Options, and then select the Security tab.
5. Click Setup Secure E-Mail as shown in Figure 9.14.

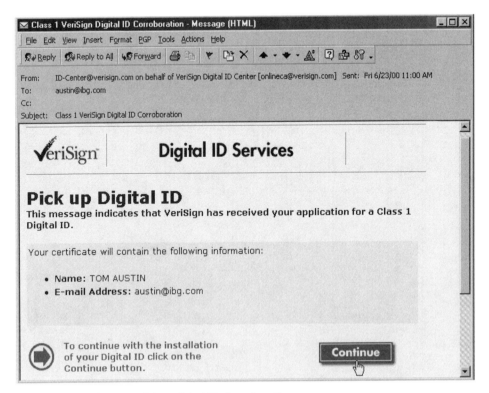

Figure 9.11   Class 1 VeriSign Digital ID Corroboration message.

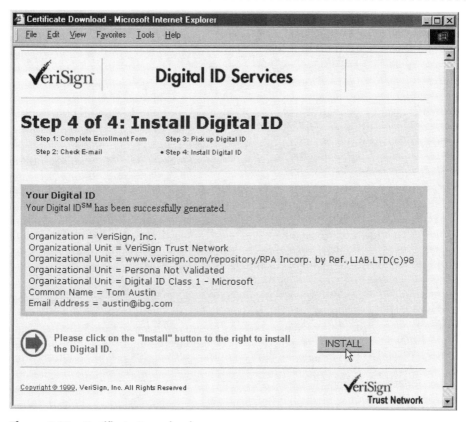

Figure 9.12   Certificate Download page.

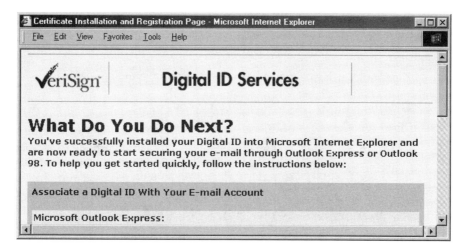

Figure 9.13   Certificate Installation and Registration page.

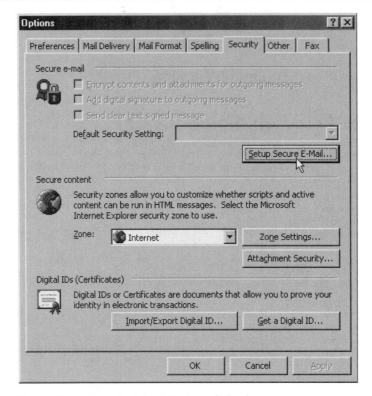

Figure 9.14   Security tab of Options dialog box

The Change Security Settings dialog box appears, as shown in Figure 9.15.

You should see your certificate listed. The check marks for the default security setting and sending certificates with signed messages are okay to leave checked. Actually, sending your certificate will help you and others import it into Microsoft's contact list to enable you to send and receive secure e-mail.

6. Click Choose (for signing certificate).

    The Select Certificate dialog box appears as shown in Figure 9.16.

7. Click the certificate listed to highlight it, and select your certificate.

8. Click View Certificate.

    As shown in Figure 9.17, you can finally see the actual certificate. By selecting any of the tabs, you see the details, the certification path back to the certificate authority that issued this and other certificates, along with the level of trust you are willing to assign this certificate. By clicking on the Issuer Statement, you view a page displaying VeriSign's Relying Party Agreement.

9. Click OK to close the windows of Figures 9.16 and 9.17, and return to the Options window shown in Figure 9.18.

Figure 9.15   Change Security Settings dialog box.

Note the changes now in the Security tab of the Options dialog box. First, the Change Settings button has replaced the Setup Secure E-mail button. Second, the previously grayed out area for Secure e-mail is now enabled allowing you to set your preferences.

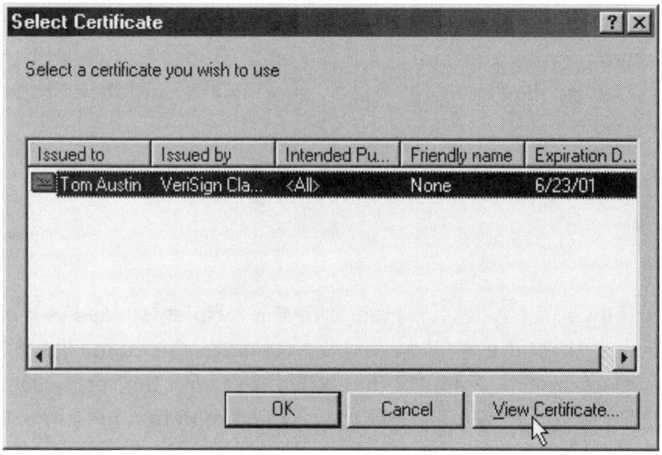

Figure 9.16   Select Certificate dialog box.

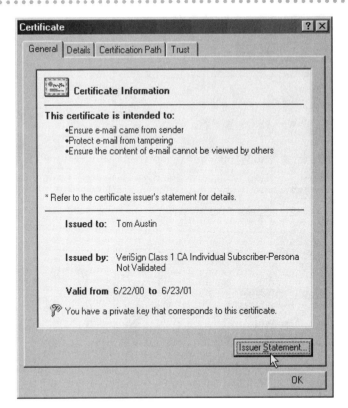

Figure 9.17   Certificate window.

TIP

Be careful in choosing what you want to check here as defaults. Is every message you send out really confidential so that it requires encryption? In any case, it's best to leave these defaults unchecked, since you can later choose to sign and encrypt anytime you create a new mail message just by clicking File, and then Properties.

10. Click OK.

Congratulations! You are now ready to use your certificate.

CAUTION

Remember that when you encrypt an e-mail, only the recipients listed will be able to read it. Otherwise, you'll get the window and the message shown in Figure 9.19. The benefit of secure, or encrypted, e-mail is that only those with the certificate and the privilege to use that certificate will be able to view and read that message. It cannot be opened and read without authorization from the certificate. That's why it's important to safeguard the passphrase to use the certificate.

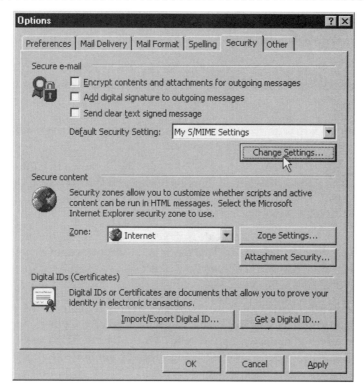

Figure 9.18 Options dialog box.

Testing Your Certificate

As you may recall, one of the key points I mentioned at the beginning of this chapter was to copy yourself when you send out encrypted e-mail. Now that you've completed this installation, you should e-mail yourself a message so that you'll be able to easily add your name to the contact list.

1. Open a new e-mail message and address it to yourself.

2. If you did not choose to sign all e-mail by default, click Options on the toolbar, and then select "Add digital signature to outgoing message."

Figure 9.19 Microsoft Outlook message box.

3. Send yourself the e-mail.

4. Open the message when received, and then right-click in the From box.

   This action adds your certificate, as well as others you may receive later, to the contact list. For more details, open Microsoft Help and type in the word *certificate*. You'll find this and other helpful hints about how to use certificates and secure e-mail.

5. While the e-mail you sent yourself is still open, double-click on the ribbon icon in the upper right-hand corner of the message.

   This will open up the Digital Signature Valid window as shown in Figure 9.20, where you'll be able to view any senders certificate and learn if it is still valid.

6. Click OK to close the window.

Looking for someone? Having a certificate isn't very useful if you're the only one with one. So, how do you find others? That's where the importance of a directory comes into play. For more information on how directories work, refer to Chapter 6, "Directories."

Another key point is managing all those certificates. Who's going to do the registering, issuing, validating, revoking, replacing, renewing, and all the other operational aspects that are involved in deploying your PKI? Will you have Help Desk capability to answer questions and problem issues? Things do get complicated rather quickly, especially as the number of certificates increases. And just like credit cards, many

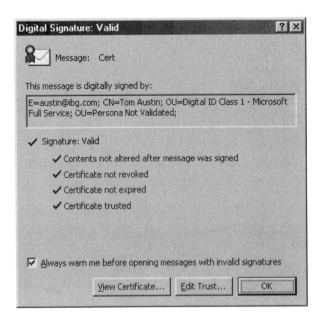

Figure 9.20   Digital Signature Valid window.

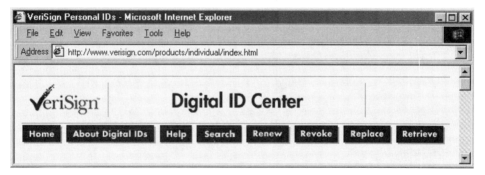

Figure 9.21 VeriSign personal IDs page.

people may have more than one certificate to use for varying purposes, depending on the certificate policy. Refer to Chapter 4 and Chapter 11 on Certificate Practice Statements for more insight to help you strategize and plan for your PKI.

In the meantime, where we acquired a certificate that's readily available from VeriSign, let's go back to their Web site to their Digital ID Center as shown in Figure 9.21.

7. Open you browser and type www.verisign.com/products/individual/index.html in the Address box.

8. Use the Search tool and find others like me (austin@ibg.com) to test your certificate and send secure e-mail.

You'll also be able to set preferences for your certificate here too, as well as a considerable wealth of information regarding secure e-mail. Good luck!

Acquiring a PKI

O nce you've done the basic research and reading about what PKI is and the security services that it provides, you'll soon be talking with vendors about what they have to offer and how they can satisfy your requirements. How do you pick which vendors to talk to, what factors should you take into consideration, and how do you measure what they have to offer in order to select the best vendor for you?

Qualifying Vendors

Let's start with your requirements. Before qualifying any vendor, you need to quantify what you need, what your resources are, and who the vendors are, and recognize their respective operational business model. No doubt, before you even have the time to put your list together, most likely you'll be having informational meetings. Sometimes these get-togethers can be beneficial in formulating your strategy and in getting a sense about the company and the people you may eventually be working with to implement your PKI. I say *working with* because in all likelihood you're going to need some level of support from the vendor as you plan, deploy, and operate your PKI.

Whatever criteria you decide to measure vendors on, all should be measurable. Whether the criteria are tangible or intangible, the importance that you allocate to any one factor depends on what's important to your organization in successfully getting the PKI up and running. After all, if a vendor is typically slow or doesn't respond when you need them to, what's the cumulative impact going to be on your implementation schedule? What's their reaction to your questions during product and technology briefings? Are they providing you with insightful and helpful information? Are your e-mails and telephone inquiries responded to promptly and adequately? Can someone easily be reached that will help you when you need him or her, or do you just get voicemail? These are just a few of the intangibles that will quickly add to or detract from the goals you need to achieve. First, let's consider your business requirements.

Your requirements should be based on an overall vision of where the business is going and what security services are going to be needed to support the ongoing operations of the business. The overarching question to ask is "Where do you want to be?" Management support and budget are the outcome of a commonly shared and agreed upon vision, established and written goals, and explicit business requirements. All the successful deployments of PKI covered in the accompanying case studies include these fundamental and essential elements.

Note that above all else, your requirements originate from vision and goals (see Figure 10.1). When others ask "Why PKI?" be prepared to demonstrate that while other technologies may be available, only PKI provides the security services necessary to move beyond simple file and disk encryption for confidentiality and signing for integrity. Of course, if that's all that's required, you need to justify the business case for making the decision to pursue PKI over passwords, tokens, and other applications.

While many PKI vendors would like you to think that they can provide for all your needs, some simply cannot. As you think about your requirements, you can begin to position vendors across the bottom of Figure 10.1 as to where their product technology is today. While some vendors talk PKI, do they provide more than just a certificate server? You'll find that only a few select vendors actually offer the products,

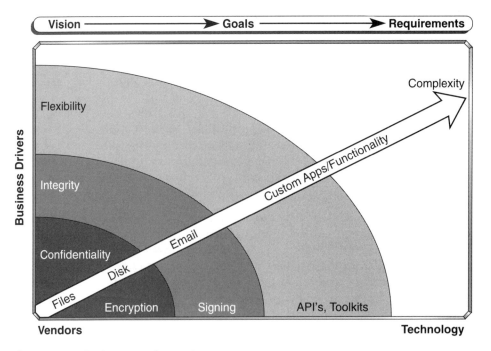

Figure 10.1 Business requirements.

services, and necessary application toolkits to support your operation as either an internal or outsourced solution. These particular vendors also have marked differences in management, strategy, and implementation support capability.

Your available resources will also impact which vendors you concentrate your discussions with and the quality of those meetings. Given that management has allocated a sufficient budget to proceed (see the section *Cost of Ownership* for more details), the biggest gating factor to your success will probably be the people you have available and their skill set to evaluate, procure, implement, and manage an ongoing PKI operation. As the saying goes, good people are hard to find. When it comes to security services and implementing PKI, attracting and retaining competent people to fulfill the business mission is an exceptionally difficult issue to satisfy. Having the right staff will impact your capability to design, build, deploy, and maintain a PKI solution internally or you may have to look to outsourcing some of it.

What premium do you place in sharing or not sharing control over the technology and processes that will enable access to your electronic business assets and your intellectual property? How trustworthy and reliable will that vendor be in handling this part of your business operation? How much risk are you willing to assume or assign to that organization? Answers to these questions will help you set the direction for the type of deployment you need to pursue and will make it somewhat easier in selecting the appropriate vendor to support your business operation.

Factors to Consider

While the following list is far from complete, it's intended to get you thinking about the vendors you'll be talking to and to begin compiling a list of questions that are meaningful to you. All vendors are different in how they began, what their culture is like, and how they view and treat their customers. How ethical and trustworthy is the vendor? The last thing you want to see is their name appearing on the front page of the *Wall Street Journal* for unethical or questionable business practices. As part your fiduciary responsibility to your constituency, take the time to perform the research on these companies as a matter of due diligence. That way, you'll be sure you'll be dealing with a company that you know will serve you well.

Management team. What is the makeup of the executive team leading the company? How involved are they in the operations of the company and how accessible are they to you? What's their background and experience? Are they thrusting the company forward on the technology front to support your current and future requirements? How are they managing the assets of the company and what's their growth strategy?

Market strategy. What direction is the company headed in? What's their track record? Are they gaining or losing market share to competing companies in their space or to alternative technology companies? Why?

Technology strategy. What's their core mission? Do they live and breathe the technology or is it just another part of their overall portfolio? Where is the architecture headed? How will this affect what you're buying into today? Will it support your business process or will your business process need to change to accommodate the technology?

Financial strength. Does this company have staying power? Do they have the financial backing and resources to grow and acquire other companies and technologies or will it become a target for acquisition? You certainly do not want to buy into a vendor's architecture only to find that someone else bought the company and will be discarding technology that you considered critical.

Team support. What's the caliber and quality of the people the vendor employs to support you? What are the sales, systems and technical support people like in responding to you? Are you comfortable and confident in what they tell you? Moreover, the number of employees a vendor has to directly support you is much more important than the total number it has. Although a vendor may have 1,000 employees, what's the actual number it has in the functional areas that are critical to you? Don't be surprised later to find only a handful of people supports their entire customer base, you included, and that one sales representative and his support person are always out because they cover large territories. Remember, vendors are drawing from much of the same talent pool as you do for staffing. Picking the right vendor means you're picking their team. These people will be an important part of your team and will make you or break you. This should be a *major* factor in your decision process.

Now that we've highlighted several factors to consider, let's expand our list hypothetically and begin to quantify them. Undoubtedly, the points and the weight percentages that you assign to them, along with which factors to include, will depend completely upon you and your particular situation. For best results, a dedicated team should work together to establish the critical success factors, score the vendors as they individually see them, and then combine their assessments as shown in the Vendor Evaluation Matrix (see Table 10.1).

Of course, adding more depth to this higher-level evaluation is the next logical step. Now, you'll want to review the vendor product architecture in more detail. For this, let's take a look at what the U.S. Patent and Trademark Office (USPTO) did in their preliminary PKI market survey. The survey was done to evaluate several vendors against the PKI requirements they established in terms of characteristics, features, and functions (see Table 10.2).

To begin with, the USPTO felt that the sensitivity of the information it handled left it no choice but to have full control over their PKI. Faced with uncertain legal and liability issues the USPTO further convinced them that outsourcing was not an option. Reaching that conclusion, the USPTO looked for vendors to meet these certain security services requirements such as:

➣ Interoperability with other government agencies

➣ Full key and certificate lifecycle management

➣ Transparency to users

➣ Separate public key pairs for digital signatures and encryption

Table 10.1 Sample Vendor Evaluation Matrix Summary

REQUIREMENTS	WEIGHT	VENDOR A	VENDOR B	VENDOR C
BUSINESS				
Market leadership	3	0	2	3
Technology focus	5	2	4	5
Standards adherence	3	3	2	3
Technology partners	2	0	2	2
Financial condition	5	3	4	4
Depth of experience	5	5	4	4
Outsourcing capability	2	1	2	2
Terms & conditions	5	4	4	3
Indemnification	5	2	2	2
Meet deadlines	10	7	6	5
Subtotal	**45%**	**27**	**32**	**33**
SUPPORT				
Legacy applications	10	8	5	7
Technical support	10	7	6	7
Help desk	5	3	4	3
Training	5	3	4	4
Subtotal	**30%**	**21**	**19**	**21**
COSTS	**25%**	**20**	**15**	**23**
More details on costs follow in the section, Cost of Ownership.				
TOTAL	**100%**	**68**	**66**	**77**

➢ Backup and recovery services for encryption keys to support non-repudiation
➢ Digital signatures and encryption for Web based and internal workflow applications
➢ Support for selected encryption, signature standards
➢ Flexibility to accommodate future selected encryption, signature standards
➢ Ability to issue X.509 v3 certificates to support selected functionality
➢ Software toolkits to support selected functionality
➢ Scalability to support more than 10,000 users
➢ Proven product that's been successfully deployed in a production application

Table 10.2   PKI Requirements to Product Features Comparison

	PKI PRODUCTS AND SERVICES							
USPTO PKI Requirements	Entrust	Baltimore	CertCo	GTE Cybertrust	Microsoft NT 5.0	Netscape	VeriSign	Xcert
Product* (In-house) or Service (Outsource) CA	Product	Product	Product	Product	Product Note 4	Product Note 5 Cur/New	Service	Product
Cross-certification*	Yes	Yes	No	Yes	Yes (NT)	No/No	No	No
Applications Supported (digital sign/encryption)								
•Extranet (browser)*	Yes	Yes	Yes					
•Internal workflow*	Yes	Yes						
•E-mail/attachments*	Yes	Yes						
•File*	Yes	Yes	No			No/No		No
•Other: VPN	Yes							
Remote access	Yes							
Single Sign-on	Yes							
Certificates Supported:								
•Identity*	Yes	Yes	Yes	Yes	Yes	Yes/Yes	Yes	Yes
•Key exchange* (different from above)	Yes	No				No/Yes		
•Attribute								
•Transactional								
•Timestamp*	Yes					No/No		
FIPS 140-1 Validated								
•CA Rt Key Level 3*	Yes	No	Yes (H/W)	Yes (H/W)		No/Yes	No	No
•Client: Level 1/2* (Win NT, 95/98)	Yes	No				No/No	No	No
Client Software		Browser	Browser	Browser	Win98/NT	Browser	Browser	
•Key protection	Yes	No	No	No	Yes	No/No	No	
•Hardware supported	Yes							
API/Toolkit Provided	Yes	Yes	No					
Key Management								
•Backup/recovery*	Yes	No	No	No	Partial	No/Yes		
•Update (automated)	Yes					No/Yes		
•Histories	Yes					No/No		
Standards Supported:								
•Digital signature: RSA and DSS* Encryption: DES, 3DES*	Yes Yes	Yes	RSA only	RSA only		No/Yes No/No		
•S/MIME	Yes	Yes						
•SET	Yes	Yes						
•Ipsec	Yes	Yes				No/Yes		
•PKCS#7	Yes	Yes				No/Yes		
Interoperability Commitments:		Partial						
PKIX	Yes							
MISPC	Yes							
NSA/SPOCK	Yes							
CommerceNet	Yes							
NACHA	Yes							

Notes:
1. An asterisk (*) denotes an essential USPTO requirement; a vendor's offering must provide the characteristic, function or feature listed.
2. A "blank" cell denotes no information obtained; it does not necessarily mean the requirement cannot be met.
3. All products except Entrust fail to meet all essential (*) USPTO requirements.
4. Microsoft NT 5.0 has not been released; information is provided for background purposes only.
5. Netscape information is based on the currently available Certificate Server 1.0 (listed under "Cur") and Certificate Management System (CMS) 4.0, expected release: April 15, 1999 or later (listed under "New.") Many of the new features of the CMS 4.0 product will require implementation of the new Netscape browser, Communicator Pro 5.0, which is not expected to be available until the 3rd or 4th quarter of 1999.
6. A Gartner Group analysis describes Entrust and VeriSign as the "leaders" in the PKI space with Entrust having exceeded all vendors regarding "completeness of vision."
7. A report by The Burton Group indicates "Entrust's products have a feature lead over most competitive efforts, providing key management features essential to effective PKI implementations."
8. A report by Hambrecht and Quist Research Group indicates "Entrust supplies software that enables a corporation to deploy a CA that scales from departmental to enterprise-wide."

Moving Forward

Once you've completed your list of requirements and reviewed vendor product architectures, features, and functions, you should start meeting with the companies that best match your needs if you haven't already done so. Depending on the procedures your organization follows, you need to determine what the appropriate mechanism is to move forward with the vendor selection. Will you be required to write a formal request for proposal? If so, what should you include and how should it be written? Determine the timeframe for the following:

➤ Getting the proposal out to the appropriate internal people for review

➤ Sending the RFP to the vendors

➤ Responding to vendor request for clarifications

➤ Obtaining the vendor's response

➤ Evaluating the vendor's response

➤ Following-up with any questions you have

➤ Getting necessary management approvals

To help you get started with this endeavor, there's a sample RFP in the appendix that you can use as a starting template. I would further suggest that you ask vendors to refrain from including any marketing hype or language in their response. Request that they succinctly answer your questions, preferably in a format you provide,which will enable you to easily compare their proposals. A simple rule would be for vendors to include a table of contents, and to consecutively number all pages. A good procurement professional on your team will contribute immensely to streamlining the process and to ensure you're covering all the necessary issues. You'd be amazed with the responses some vendors will send you. What should be a straightforward response can easily turn into 25 to 50 pages of text for you to wallow in.

Lastly, while PKI may be a complex technology to deploy, qualifying and selecting a vendor to work with should not be as difficult a task. In essence, choosing a PKI vendor should not be that much different than any other system or technology vendor. Consider the company's long term vision, technology architecture, capability, reliability, support, and service. These factors, along with a sound understanding of your business, delivery, and support requirements will go a long way in getting you started on your request for proposals.

Above all, don't just take the vendor's word for it. Talk to reference accounts, other groups within your organization, make some calls yourself, and visit the vendor's premises. Since your business will ultimately depend on the continuous operation of the PKI, a good working relationship with your vendor for business continuity is critical. Get everything in writing by establishing a Level of Service Agreement and be sure to test it periodically. After all, when emergencies come up, and they will, it just may fall on your shoulders to get it resolved. Based on the requirements you establish, take the time and effort upfront to pick the right vendor.

Cost of Ownership

Whenever the topic of PKI comes up, the first questions to crop up are, "what's the cost, how are we going to pay for it, and do we really need it?" To answer these questions, you first need to step back and assess where you are regarding the state of security. The cost of deploying an infrastructure (that the "I" in PKI denotes) depends a great deal on the structure and organizational culture you have in place today. For instance, many government defense agencies are long accustomed to security policies, procedures, and the disciplined nature they require to implement and execute them consistently and faithfully. If you don't have a basic security environment to start with, then that's the first item on the agenda that needs to be addressed before embarking on the road to PKI. As a precaution, obtain a copy of the latest security assessment to determine the strong and weak points that will need to be addressed. For more information on what's involved to achieve basic security, refer to Chapter 3.

The next major question to ask is, "what is the management mindset toward security services in general?" How much attention and budget are devoted to ensure that the necessary precautions are taken to minimize risk to electronic assets and intellectual property? If the organizational culture is such that closes the barn door after the horses have left, you have little chance of successfully implementing a PKI. Without a doubt, you need to have full executive management support to foster a favorable environment for security and to fund the budget necessary to fulfill these requirements.

What the case studies in this book reveal is that a PKI deployment generally requires significant funding and ongoing commitment from management. Whether a suitable environment is readily in place to proceed also has a considerable impact on the time and cost of deployment. Indeed, the time required to design, develop, and deploy a PKI usually covers several fiscal quarters over a period of two to three fiscal years.

Table 10.3 presents a cursory, high-level summary of "typical" deployment costs. As you can see, the numbers don't really tell you the whole story. No one number fits all or reveals what's involved or has been done. You need to take into account several of the factors we've mentioned, assess your particular needs, and work from there. These organizations have disparate environments and very different business and security requirements that needed to be addressed. To understand this, refer to Part Four, "Case Studies," for the details behind the numbers.

Table 10.3   Deployment Costs

CASE STUDY	BUDGET	PERIOD	CERTIFICATES
Bank of Bermuda	$750K	3 years	10,000
Idaho National Environment & Engineering Labs	$ 1.5M	3 years	275
Perot Systems	$ 2.M+	2 years	6000
Ruesch	$ 100K	6 months	2500
U.S. Patent & Trademark Office	$ 4.M	15 months	10,000

Remember, we're talking about costs here, not return on investment. Costs can be deceiving when viewed out of context. For example, you need to look at the U.S. Patent & Trademark Office (USPTO) as making a significant investment, not making a major expenditure. The return on investment for USPTO, not to mention the major changes they're accomplishing in their business processes, will deliver excellent results. It's the same for all of these organizations—PKI is regarded as an investment.

In 1998, Giga Information Group conducted a fairly comprehensive analysis of two vendors by interviewing four customers from each vendor. In his report, Ira Machefsky noted that *"a public key infrastructure (PKI) is probably the most critical enterprise security investment a company will make in the next three years."* The analysis went further than just simple cost of ownership to what Giga refers to as a Total Economic Impact model. Using this model, Giga contends that organizations move away from a cost center focus to one that helps evaluate project decisions in terms of goals and into more of a value proposition.

Through in-depth interviews, Giga chose three PKI deployment scenarios, each ranging from 5000 to 20,000 users. The first scenario was the lowest cost, using certificates simply for user authentication in a Web environment. Costs were calculated at $669K at the low end to $1.7M at the high end. The second scenario went a step further and included life-cycle management. Not surprisingly, costs were now somewhat higher and ranged from $951K to $2M. The third and last scenario added two enterprise security applications, secure mail and desktop file encryption, with the costs going from $2.8M up to $12.4M.

Interestingly enough, the report cited that while cost may be a common differentiator, the more important issues dealt with the perceived benefits, flexibility, and risks. It emphasized that *"it is interesting to note that not a single customer we interviewed for this study cited cost as the most important element in their choice of a PKI."* The case studies for this book, performed almost two years later, confirm this finding.

Let's conclude by finishing the Sample Vendor Matrix we began with in the earlier section, *Qualifying Vendors*. Not surprisingly, in Tables 10.4 through 10.6, you can see that the cost to deploy vendor A's solution appears out of the question compared to vendors B and C. Or is it? What's not evident here are other significant costs regarding who controls and manages the PKI and the key management operation. What requirements are

Table 10.4 Sample Vendor Evaluation Matrix Summary

COSTS	VENDOR A	VENDOR B	VENDOR C
Weight – 25%			
Start-up			
Hardware	0	0	0
Software	9000	0	0
Consulting services	5000	19,000	0
Other	0	49,950	0
Non-recurring start-up	0	0	80,000
Subtotal	**14,000**	**68,950**	**80,000**

Table 10.5 Sample Vendor Evaluation Matrix Summary

	VENDOR A	VENDOR B	VENDOR C
Pilot & rollout			
Cost per certificate	11	2	2
Initial pilot (500 users)	5,500	1,000	1,000
Rollout #1 (14,500 users)	159,500	19,000	29,000
Total $ outlay—Year 1	**165,000**	**88,950**	**110,000**
Total cost per user—Year 1	**11.93**	**5.93**	**7.33**

Table 10.6 Sample Vendor Evaluation Matrix Summary

	VENDOR A	VENDOR B	VENDOR C
Rollout			
Year Two			
Software maintenance	5,000	6,145	0
Rollout #2 (100,000 users)	1,100,000	200,000	200,000
Total $ outlay—Year 2	**1,105,000**	**206,145**	**200,000**
Total cost per user—Year 2	**11.05**	**2.06**	**2.00**
Average cost per user for 2 years	**11.04**	**2.57**	**2.69**

we looking to satisfy? What type of certificate is being issued? Is it a simple Web certificate, or does it offer more capability? Understand what you're asking the vendor to provide and what the product features and functions will actually accomplish for you. In other words, know what you're getting. If you're simply looking to replace passwords with certificates, then a certificate server and a couple of administrative staff may be all that's necessary. However, for business contracts and financial transactions where the risk of non-repudiation exists, simple Web certificates may not be sufficient.

Independent of which vendor you select, consider what additional costs need to be allocated for systems hardware, secure office space, new or transferred staff, help desk, as well as ongoing training on procedure and systems operations. More importantly, you'll need to investigate the cost to integrate whatever legacy applications are in place to take advantage of PKI. For more information, see Chapter 13.

What's the bottom line? The numbers could be as low or as high as those shown in the matrix. Only a Request for Proposal (RFP) will effectively answer the question. Remember that it's only after you assess and understand your environment, establish your criteria, and communicate with various vendors for your RFP that you'll fully understand the PKI cost factor. Once you know the cost, weigh that against the current cost of doing business and how effective you are in serving your customers. PKI is truly an e-commerce enabler. Your competitors certainly will be thinking strategically about this as investment—you should too!

Certificate Policy and Certification Practices Statement

W hen a prospective PKI owner, operator, or installer sees a model Certificate Policy (CP), a model Certification Practices Statement (CPS), the reaction is one of awe, and a lot of questions pop up. The first question that pops up is, "why do I have to do this? If a PKI binds the identity of a user to the public key, why do I have to answer all these questions?" The answer to the question is simple. In order to ensure the security of the PKI, some fundamental security needs at the various PKI components must be addressed. The key security requirements include the following:

➤ Private keys must be kept confidential.

➤ Private keys must only be used by the owners of the keys.

➤ Public keys' integrity must be assured.

➤ Initial authentication of the subscriber (private key holder and the subject of the public key certificate) must be strong so that identity theft does not occur at the point of certificate application.

In addition to the security requirements, in order to facilitate electronic commerce, the PKI must address obligations of all parties, and liabilities in case of dispute. Furthermore, in order to facilitate global electronic commerce, the PKIs must be able to cross-certify each other. The cross-certification is based on the degree of trust one PKI can place in another one. This trust is what is basically articulated in a CP or a CPS.

Lack of well-formed CP and CPS can give rise to lack of security in the PKI, compromise of electronic transaction, and liability claims. If an organization does not properly address the CP and CPS, or does not address the security, liability, and other aspects of CP and CPS, it is not likely to be a candidate for cross-certification by other PKIs. This will impede the organization's ability to conduct secure global electronic commerce. A poorly run PKI is also likely to lose subscribers and lose the trust of relying parties, and hence lose its ability to carry out electronic commerce.

There are several very well-written CPs and CPSs. They form a very good start and can be used by an organization to draft its own CP and CPS. A CP or CPS can be formulated using these other CPs and CPSs within one week of staff time spread over a calendar month or less. An organization should involve the following personnel in drafting the CP and CPS:

➤ IT department (for security of network and PKI computer systems and applications)

➤ PKI owner (for cryptographic security and coordination)

➤ Application owners (for degree of security required)

➤ Legal staff (for obligations, notice, liability, etc.)

➤ Security and badging office (for physical security, personnel security, and subscriber initial authentication)

A public-key certificate (hereinafter called simply "certificate") binds a public-key value to information that identifies the entity (such as person, organization, account, or site) in control of the corresponding private key (that entity is known as the subject of the certificate or a subscriber). A certificate is used by a certificate user (hereinafter called "relying party") for the accuracy of the binding of the public key to the certificate's subject (herein called "subscriber"). The relying party (after verifying the digital signature on the certificate) can trust the subscriber public key and use it for the applicable purpose of digital signature verification or for the purpose of encryption.

The degree to which a relying party can trust the binding embodied in a certificate depends on several factors. These factors include:

➤ The practices followed by the Certification Authority (CA)[1] in authenticating the subscriber; the CA's operating policy, procedures, and security controls.

➤ The subscriber's obligations (for example, in protecting the private key); and the stated undertakings and legal obligations of the CA (for example, warranties and limitations on liability).

Figure 11.1 illustrates the central governing role they play in the operation of a Public Key Infrastructure (PKI).

An X.509 Version 3 certificate may contain a field declaring that one or more specific certificate policies apply to that certificate. According to X.509, a certificate policy (CP) is "a named set of rules that indicates the applicability of a certificate to a particular community and/or class of application with common security requirements." A certificate policy may be used by a certificate user to decide whether a certificate, and the binding therein, is sufficiently trustworthy for a particular application. The certificate policy concept is an outgrowth of the policy statement concept developed for Internet Privacy Enhanced Mail.

---

[1] CA that is issuing the public key certificates.

Certification Authority

A trusted entity that:
- Is centraly located
- Operated under control of Security Officer(s)
- Generates Public Key Certificates
- Revokes Public Key Certificates
- Publishes Public Key Certificates and Certificate Revocation Lists in Directory Servers
- Archives Public Key Certificates and Certificate Revocation Lists in Archive

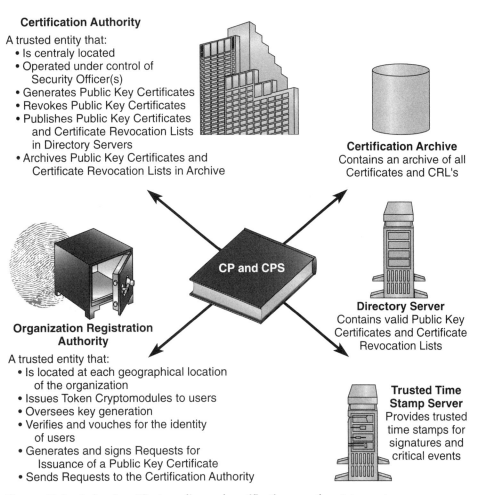

Certification Archive
Contains an archive of all Certificates and CRL's

Organization Registration Authority

A trusted entity that:
- Is located at each geographical location of the organization
- Issues Token Cryptomodules to users
- Oversees key generation
- Verifies and vouches for the identity of users
- Generates and signs Requests for Issuance of a Public Key Certificate
- Sends Requests to the Certification Authority

Directory Server
Contains valid Public Key Certificates and Certificate Revocation Lists

Trusted Time Stamp Server
Provides trusted time stamps for signatures and critical events

Figure 11.1   Role of certificate policy and certification practice statement.

A more detailed description of the practices followed by a CA in issuing and otherwise managing certificates may be contained in a Certification Practice Statement (CPS) published by or referenced by the CA. According to the American Bar Association Digital Signature Guidelines (hereinafter "ABA Guidelines"), "a CPS is a statement of the practices which a certification authority employs in issuing certificates."

Concepts

This section explains the concepts of certificate policy and CPS, and describes their relationship. Other related concepts are also described. Some of the material covered in this section and in some other sections is specific to certificate policies extensions as defined in X.509 version 3. Except for those sections, the ideas presented in this chapter are intended to be adaptable to other certificate formats (such as PGP, SDSI, etc.) that may come into use.

Certificate Policy

When a certification authority issues a certificate, it is providing a statement to a relying party that a particular public key is bound to a particular entity (the certificate subject). However, the extent to which the relying party should rely on that statement by the CA needs to be assessed by the certificate user. Different certificates are issued following different practices and procedures, and may be suitable for different applications and/or purposes.

A certificate policy, which needs to be recognized by both the issuing CA and the relying party, is represented in a certificate by a unique, registered Object Identifier. The registration process follows the procedures specified in ISO/IEC and ITU standards. The party that registers the Object Identifier also publishes a textual specification of the certificate policy, for examination by the relying parties. By asserting one or more policies in a certificate, a CA is making a statement that the certificate is issued in compliance with the asserted policy(s).

Certificate policies also constitute a basis for accreditation of CAs. Each CA is accredited against one or more certificate policies which it is recognized as implementing. When one CA issues a CA-certificate for another CA, the issuing CA must assess the set of certificate policies for which it trusts the subject CA (such assessment may be based upon accreditation with respect to the certificate policies involved). The assessed set of certificate policies is then indicated by the issuing CA in the CA-certificate. The X.509 certification path processing logic uses these certificate policies in determining policies for which a given chain of certificates is acceptable.

Certificate Policy Examples

Suppose that IATA (International Air Transport Association) undertakes to define some certificate policies for use throughout the airline industry, in a public-key infrastructure operated by IATA in combination with public-key infrastructures operated by individual airlines. Two certificate policies are defined: the IATA General-Purpose policy and the IATA Commercial-Grade policy.

The IATA General-Purpose policy is intended for use by industry personnel for protecting routine information (e.g., casual electronic mail) and for authenticating connections from World Wide Web browsers to servers for general information retrieval purposes. The key pairs may be generated, stored, and managed using low-cost, software-based systems, such as commercial browsers. Under this policy, a certificate may be automatically issued to anybody listed as an employee in the corporate directory of IATA or any member airline who submits a signed certificate request form to a network administrator in his or her organization.

The IATA Commercial-Grade policy is used to protect financial transactions or binding contractual exchanges between airlines. Under this policy, IATA requires that certified key pairs be generated and stored in approved cryptographic hardware tokens. Certificates and tokens are provided to airline employees with disbursement authority. These authorized individuals are required to present themselves to the corporate security office, show a valid identification badge, and sign an undertaking to protect the token and use it only for authorized purposes, before a token and a certificate are issued.

X.509 Certificate Fields

The following extension fields in an X.509 certificate are used to support certificate policies:

➢ Certificate Policies extension

➢ Policy Mappings extension

➢ Policy Constraints extension

Certificate Policies Extension

The Certificate Policies extension contains certificate policies that the certification authority declares are applicable. When processing a certification path, an intersection of this extension is computed for all the certificates in the path to determine the certificate policy(s) the certificate path is valid for:

valid policies = $\cap_{i=1,n}$ certificatePolicies (certificate$_i$)

Policy Mappings Extension

The Policy Mappings extension may only be used in CA certificates. This field allows a CA to indicate that certain policies in its own domain can be considered equivalent to certain other policies in the subject CA's domain.

For example, suppose the ACE Corporation establishes an agreement with the ABC Corporation to cross-certify each others' public-key infrastructures for the purposes of mutually protecting electronic data interchange (EDI). Further, suppose that both companies have preexisting financial transaction protection policies called ace-e-commerce and abc-e-commerce, respectively. One can see that simply generating cross certificates between the two domains will not provide the necessary interoperability, as the two companies' applications are configured with and employee certificates are populated with their respective certificate policies. One possible solution is to reconfigure all of the financial applications to require either policy and to reissue all the certificates with both policies. Another solution, which may be easier to administer, uses the Policy Mapping field. If this field is included in a cross-certificate for the ABC Corporation certification authority issued by the ACE Corporation certification authority, it can provide a statement that the ABC's financial transaction protection policy (i.e., abc-e-commerce) can be considered equivalent to that of the ACE Corporation (i.e., ace-e-commerce).

Policy Constraints Extension

The Policy Constraints extension supports two optional features. The first is the ability for a CA to assert whether a certification path must be valid for a certificate policy. The other optional feature in the Policy Constraints field is the ability for a CA to disable policy mapping by subsequent CAs in a certification path. It may be prudent to disable policy mapping when certifying outside the domain. This can assist in controlling risks due to transitive trust; e.g., domain A trusts domain B, domain B trusts domain C, but domain A does not want to be forced to trust domain C.

Policy Qualifiers

The Certificate Policies extension has a provision for conveying, along with each certificate policy identifier, additional policy-dependent information in a qualifier field. The X.509 standard does not mandate the purpose for which this field is to be used, nor does it prescribe the syntax for this field. Policy qualifier types can be registered by any organization. The intent of the qualifiers was to support the definition of generic, or parameterized, certificate policies; e.g., a single financial policy with qualifiers of different maximum, or different national currency unit, etc. However, in practice, the policy qualifiers are not being used much.

The following policy qualifier types are defined in the Internet RFC 2459:

➢ The CPS Pointer qualifier contains a pointer to a Certification Practice Statement (CPS) published by the CA. The pointer is in the form of a uniform resource identifier (URI).

➢ The User Notice qualifier contains a text string that is to be displayed to the relying party prior to the use of the certificate.

Certification Practice Statement

The term *certification practice statement* (CPS) is defined by the ABA Guidelines as: "A statement of the practices which a certification authority employs in issuing certificates." In the 1995 draft of the ABA guidelines, the ABA expands this definition with the following comments:

"A certification practice statement may take the form of a declaration by the certification authority of the details of its trustworthy system and the practices it employs in its operations and in support of issuance of a certificate, or it may be a statute or regulation applicable to the certification authority and covering similar subject matter. It may also be part of the contract between the certification authority and the subscriber. A certification practice statement may also be comprised of multiple documents, a combination of public law, private contract, and/or declaration."

Certain forms for legally implementing certification practice statements lend themselves to particular relationships. For example, when the legal relationship between a

CA and subscriber is consensual, a contract would ordinarily be the means of giving effect to a CPS. The CA's duties to a relying party are generally based on the CA's representations, which may include a CPS.

Whether a CPS is binding on a relying person depends on whether the relying party has knowledge or notice of the certification practice statement. A relying party has knowledge or at least notice of the contents of the certificate used by the relying party to verify a digital signature, including documents incorporated into the certificate by reference. It is therefore advisable to incorporate a CPS into a certificate by reference.

As much as possible, a CPS should indicate any of the widely recognized standards to which the CA's practices conform. Reference to widely recognized standards may indicate concisely the suitability of the CA's practices for another person's (or entity's) purposes, as well as the potential technological compatibility of the certificates issued by the CA with repositories and other systems.

Relationship between Certificate Policy and Certification Practice Statement

The concepts of certificate policy and CPS come from different sources and were developed for different reasons. However, their interrelationship is important.

A CPS is a detailed statement by a CA as to its practices, that potentially needs to be understood and consulted by subscribers and relying parties. Although the level of detail may vary among CPSs, they will generally be more detailed than CPs. Indeed, CPSs may be quite comprehensive, robust documents providing a description of the precise service offerings, detailed procedures of the life-cycle management of certificates, and more—a level of detail which weds the CPS to a particular (proprietary) implementation of a service offering.

Although such detail may be indispensable to adequately disclose, and to make a full assessment of trustworthiness in the absence of accreditation or other recognized quality metrics, a detailed CPS does not form a suitable basis for interoperability between CAs operated by different organizations. Rather, CPs best serve as the vehicle on which to base common interoperability standards and common assurance criteria on an industry-wide (or possibly more global) basis. A CA with a single CPS may support multiple CPs (used for different application purposes and/or by different certificate user communities). Also, multiple different CAs, with non-identical CPSs, may support the same CP.

For example, the Federal Government might define a government-wide certificate policy for handling confidential human resources information. The certificate policy definition will be a broad statement of the general characteristics of that certificate policy, and an indication of the types of applications for which it is suitable for use. Different departments or agencies that operate certification authorities with different certification practice statements might support this certificate policy. At the same time, such certification authorities may support other certificate policies.

The main difference between certificate policy and CPS can therefore be summarized as follows:

➤ Most organizations that operate public or inter-organizational certification authorities will document their own practices in CPSs or similar statements. The CPS is one of the organization's means of protecting itself and positioning its business relationships with subscribers and other entities.

➤ There is strong incentive, on the other hand, for a certificate policy to apply more broadly than to just a single organization. If a particular certificate policy is widely recognized and imitated, it has great potential as the basis of automated certificate acceptance in many systems, including unmanned systems and systems that are manned by people not independently empowered to determine the acceptability of different presented certificates.

➤ A CP is generally a specification of the policy objectives, whereas a CPS is detailed implementation specifics of how the objectives are achieved.

In addition to populating the certificate policies field with the certificate policy identifier, a certification authority may include, in certificates it issues, a reference to its certification practice statement. A standard way to do this, using a certificate policy qualifier, is described above in *Policy Qualifiers*.

Contents of CP or CPS

A Certificate Policy and Certification Practices Statement Framework has been developed to assist the writers of certificate policies and/or certification practices statements. The Framework provides a comprehensive list of topics that potentially, at the CP and CPS writer's discretion, need to be covered in a CP or CPS. At the highest level, the topics to be considered include:

➤ Introduction
➤ General Provisions
➤ Identification and Authentication
➤ Operational Requirements
➤ Physical, Procedural, and Personnel Security Controls
➤ Technical Security Controls
➤ Certificate and CRL Profile
➤ Specification Administration

Figure 11.2 illustrates the organization of a CP or CPS.

These requirements must be specified for all the PKI components, as applicable, not just to the CAs. In other words CAs, RAs, subscribers, relying parties, and repositories should all be considered for each of these requirements.

The best way to write a CP or CPS is to consult documents such as the Digital Signature and Confidentiality Policy for the Government of Canada PKI.

Figure 11.2   Organization of certificate policy and certification practice statement.

Components can be further divided into subcomponents, and a subcomponent may comprise multiple elements. The following subsections expand upon the contents of a practices and policy specification.

It is not necessary for a certificate policy or a CPS to include a concrete statement for every such topic. Rather, a particular certificate policy or CPS may state "no stipulation" for a component, subcomponent, or element on which the particular certificate policy or CPS imposes no requirements. In this sense, the list of topics can be considered a checklist of topics for consideration by the certificate policy or CPS writer. It is recommended that every component and subcomponent be included in a certificate policy or CPS, even if there is "no stipulation"; this will indicate to the reader that a conscious decision was made to include or exclude that topic. This avoids inadvertent omission of topics, while facilitating comparison of different certificate policies or CPSs; e.g., when making policy mapping decisions.

It is generally a good idea to develop a CP first, to use the CP as a tool to select and configure the PKI, and to develop the CPS for the specific installation.

Introduction

This component identifies and introduces the CP or CPS, and indicates the types of entities and applications for which the specification is targeted. This component has the following subcomponents:

➣ Overview
➣ Identification
➣ Community and Applicability
➣ Contact Details

General Provisions

This component specifies any applicable presumptions on a range of legal and general practices topics. This component contains the following subcomponents:

> Liability

> Obligations

> Financial Responsibility

> Interpretation and Enforcement

> Fee

> Publication and Repositories

> Compliance Audit

> Confidentiality

> Intellectual Property Rights

Identification and Authentication

This component describes the procedures used to authenticate a certificate applicant to a CA or RA prior to certificate issuance. It also describes how parties requesting rekey or revocation are authenticated. This component also addresses naming practices, including name ownership recognition and name dispute resolution. This component has the following subcomponents:

> Initial Registration

> Routine Rekey

> Rekey After Revocation

> Revocation Request

Operational Requirements

This component is used to specify requirements imposed upon issuing CA, subject CAs, RAs, or end entities with respect to various operational activities. This component consists of the following subcomponents:

> Certificate Application

> Certificate Issuance

> Certificate Acceptance

> Certificate Suspension and Revocation

> Security Audit Procedures

> Records Archival

➤ Key Changeover

➤ Compromise and Disaster Recovery

➤ CA Termination

Physical, Procedural, and Personnel Security Controls

This component describes non-technical security controls (that is, physical, procedural, and personnel controls) used by the various PKI entities to perform securely the functions of key generation, subscriber authentication, certificate issuance, certificate revocation, audit, and archiving.

Technical Security Controls

This component is used to define the security measures taken by the PKI components. This component has the following subcomponents:

➤ Key Pair Generation and Installation

➤ Private Key Protection

➤ Other Aspects of Key Pair Management

➤ Activation Data

➤ Computer Security Controls

➤ Life-Cycle Security Controls

➤ Network Security Controls

➤ Cryptographic Module Engineering Controls

Certificate and CRL Profiles

This component is used to specify the certificate format and, if CRLs are used, the CRL format. Assuming use of the X.509 certificate and CRL formats, this includes information on profiles, versions, and extensions used.

Specification Administration

This component is used to specify how this particular practices and policy specification will be maintained. It contains the following subcomponents:

➤ Specification Change Procedures

➤ Publication and Notification Procedures

➤ CPS Approval Procedures

Major Consideration

The preceding section, *Contents of CP or CPS*, has provided just a glimpse of the requirements. Actually, subcomponents are further divided into elements. Thus, crafting a CP or a CPS could be daunting task for some one. Needless to say, not all of these requirement elements are equally important. The following is a list of topics that should be paid special attention to during the development of a CP or CPS:

➤ Obligations of the various parties, including the CA, RA, subscriber, and the relying party

➤ Limitations on liability

➤ Subscriber authentication requirements during initial registration

➤ Revocation notification procedures (to the relying parties)

➤ Secure audit and secure archive requirements

➤ Physical, procedural, and personnel security controls at the CA and at the RA

➤ Technical security controls at the CA, RA, subscribers, especially in the areas of cryptographic module, computer security and network security, and cryptographic token and private key protection

Future

If the world was suddenly perfect, it would be great to see:

➤ There is a need for fewer policies. The organizations based on vertical markets and horizontal functions in public as well as private sectors, should use a common set of policies. This will make cross certification and policy equivalency a lot easier.

➤ The PKI products vendors, especially the application tool kit vendors, need to provide full policy processing capability in accordance with the X.509 standard.

➤ A tool developed that takes the CP and CPS framework, takes some of the more popular CPs and CPSs, and allows one to craft a new CP or CPS.

➤ A tool that can take a CP and assist in crafting a CPS.

➤ Policy processing be more real and automated in X.509 standard and standard compliant software. Currently, X.509 does not really process the actual policy. It allows one to determine if an abstract tag (called object identifier) is present or not.

➤ Automation in comparing policies asserted in a certificate. This can be achieved by codifying the policy elements of the framework for automated processing.

CHAPTER 12

Auditing a PKI

About Audits

Traditionally, auditors are often thought of as professional bean counters, complete with the requisite green visor and ink-stained fingers, pouring over dusty general ledgers. Although financial audits are still very much a part of due diligence and prudent business practices, technology continues to advance into our everyday lives, and therefore it has become practical to audit the systems and the security of those systems.

The term *audit* is often misused as a generic label referring to a security assessment of a PKI implementation based on established evaluation criteria. An audit taken in its proper context is actually a report by a licensed practitioner attesting to the existence and adherence of proper security controls over a PKI implementation. The difference, albeit a bit subtle, is the reliability of the audit based upon the licensing of the practitioner or the licensing of the professional practitioner's employer. For example, in the United States, only a Certified Public Accountant (CPA), and in Canada, only a Chartered Accountant (CA) can sign an audit report. In the United States, the American Institute of Certified Public Accounts (AICPA) is the official certification body, and in Canada, it is the Canadian Institute of Chartered Accountants (CICA).

So, how does that relate to an organization that has implemented a PKI? If that organization offers services to employees, customers, or business partners, and those services use PKI-enabled applications or rely on PKI technology, then having an assessment or an audit provides a level of assurance that the services are reliable. In general, there are three types of audit models:

> ➣ An *internal audit with an internal practitioner* is where the organization performs a self-assessment of its PKI. The assessment must have proper evaluation criteria in order

to verify the reliability, maintainability, availability, and security of the PKI. However, self-assessments are only valuable to the organization itself, and should not be relied upon by external parties, such as customers and business partners. Otherwise, this would be equivalent to a company claiming "hey, my stuff is safe, *trust* me."

➤ An *internal audit with an external practitioner* is where the organization outsources the assessment of its PKI. Again, the assessment must use proper evaluation criteria. The results of the assessment are valuable to the organization, and depending upon its relationship, may be shared with its business partners. In this scenario, the value of the assessment can be increased by the use of an external practitioner, if the practitioner is qualified.

➤ An *external audit with an external practitioner* is where the organization builds trust with its employees, customers, and business partners via an independent third-party audit firm. In this case, the third party must be licensed, and the evaluation criteria must be established as agreed-upon procedures between the organization and the audit firm.

SAS 70

Let's take a closer look at audits. Probably the most familiar audit is the Statement on Auditing Standards (SAS) 70. SAS 70 was first issued in April 1992, and the focus of SAS 70 is auditor-to-auditor communication in the circumstance where an entity outsources its responsibility for:

➤ Executing transactions and maintaining the related accountability

➤ Recording transactions and processing related data

The auditor-to-auditor focus evolved around the needs of an auditor of financial statements to understand procedures and controls pertaining to the outsourced activity. Other users were anticipated, but were not the primary focus of the expected reports. SAS 70 provides a framework for reporting the results of the audit procedures performed, but it does not specify the minimum control objectives, control procedures, or test procedures. Control objectives and the related procedures to be tested are determined jointly by the auditee and the auditor, based upon an expectation of the needs of the relying (user) auditor. Accordingly, no minimum control procedures are specified in SAS 70. SAS 70 engagements come in two varieties: Type 1 and Type 2 reports.

SAS 70 Type 1 reports include a description of the application audited and control objectives specified by the service provider (with the agreement of the auditor) that are thought to be relevant to the needs of the users of the services provided. The conclusion in a Type 1 report is that the accompanying description of the application presents fairly, in all material respects, the relevant aspects of the service provider's policies and procedures that have been placed in operation *as of a specific date*, and that the policies and procedures, as described, are suitably designed to provide reasonable assurance that the specified control objectives would be achieved if the described policies and procedures were complied with satisfactorily.

SAS 70 Type 2 reports include all that is in a Type 1 report, plus:

➤ A description of policies and procedures for which tests of operating effectiveness were performed, the control objectives the policies and procedures were intended to achieve, the *tests applied* and the *results* of those tests.

➤ That the policies and procedures that were tested were operating with sufficient effectiveness to provide reasonable, but not absolute, assurance that the control objectives specified were achieved *during a specific period from [start date] to [end date]*.

The key points for the SAS 70 reports are:

➤ No minimum control procedures are specified (and, therefore, there is no consistency in one report to the next in its usability).

➤ Type 1 is point in time vs. Type 2, which is for a period of time.

SAS 70 reports are intended for distribution to both users and user auditors (who combined are the relying parties). As to the question of audit frequency, there is no minimum or maximum time period specified, although the common time period is annually. Also, the level of specificity of the controls tested is often quite high, and therefore of limited real value to the relying parties.

SSAE No.1

A less familiar, however just as important, audit is the Statement on Standards for Attestation Engagements (SSAE) Number 1. SSAE No.1 provides an alternative way to report on policies and procedures. Using this reporting model, an audited entity makes a written assertion regarding the reasonable effectiveness of specific control procedures based upon specified criteria. Then the auditor, after performing appropriate test procedures, reports that the assertion of management is fairly stated. The criteria used to measure the controls must be:

Objective. The evaluation criteria should be free from bias.

Measurable. The evaluation criteria should permit reasonably consistent measurements, qualitative or quantitative.

Complete. The evaluation criteria should be sufficiently complete so those relevant factors that would alter a conclusion about them are not omitted.

Relevant. The evaluation criteria should be relevant to the controls.

Reports on assertions as to compliance with specific criteria that meet the preceding conditions and are suitable for a broad number of users, or are developed by groups of experts who follow due process procedures, including the exposure of the proposed criteria for public comment, are eligible for broad distribution. In such instances, the evaluation criteria must be provided with the report, unless developed by a public due process, in which instance the evaluation criteria already exist in the public purview.

SSAE No.1 reports that are issued are often posted on a Web site. Because of the way in which the criteria are written, the trade secrets of an organization, or the way in which it achieves a specific criteria, do not need to be publicly disclosed, although the auditor must be allowed knowledge so as to evaluate whether the criteria have been met.

CA Trust

PKI evaluation criteria can be developed internally by an organization for any of the audit models; however, the completeness and appropriateness of such criteria is difficult to develop due to the complexity and intricacies of PKI technology. Let's face it, if PKI were that easy, this book would not be necessary. Only evaluation criteria developed by professionals and reviewed via public comment should be considered for the assessment or audit of a PKI. So, where does such material exist, and how does this fit into the audit models?

The X9 Committee, accredited by the American National Standards Institute (ANSI), has developed the new ANSI standard X9.79 *PKI Practices and Policies*, which includes the Certification Authority Control Objectives. These control objectives are the evaluation criteria for performing assessments or audits of CAs within a PKI.

Furthermore, the American Institute of Certified Public Accounts (AICPA) and the Canadian Institute of Chartered Accounts (CICA) jointly formed the *Electronic Commerce Assurance Task Force* to develop *WebTrust for Certification Authorities* (CA Trust). CA Trust is an audit standard for certification authorities based upon the Certification Authority Control Objectives contained in the ANSI standard X9.79 *PKI Practices and Policy*. CA Trust is an adaptation of the SSAE No.1 reporting model for which the criteria have been subjected to public due process; therefore, the reports resulting there from are available for general (public) distribution and do not require that all the specific criteria be disclosed. The criteria generally focus on business practice disclosures, transaction integrity, security, and privacy issues. More importantly, because the Web-Trust services provide a specific minimum set of required principles and criteria that must be met for each type, there is a better/broader understanding of the implications of such an audit report, because the criteria have been standardized.

13

Enabling Legacy Applications

W ill PKI impact your existing system? Many organizations use legacy systems, which are badly prepared for implementation of the key features of PKI, such as certificate-based access control, use of digital signatures in their transaction systems, and revocation control. Throughout this chapter, the idea is to educate the reader in how and what approach to take when building a PKI into an existing legacy system. While other solutions may exist, this example uses a solution from CeloCom.

PKI Solutions for Legacy Applications

Many of the challenges of PKI-enabling legacy applications can be addressed with thorough planning, testing, and adherence to standards. Some, such as reliability, also require some "burning in" in production situations. Unfortunately, time-to-market considerations may work against long planning, testing, and burn-in cycles. Buying rather than building PKI solutions for legacy applications may shorten these cycles.

The most successful approach to PKI-enabling legacy applications that has been proven over time is: Don't change the existing infrastructure, and move with flexible implementation within open standards in order to deploy clients in an Internet environment.

The vital components that need to be integrated in the PKI, moving from client to server, include:

➢ Browsers

➢ Plug-ins

➢ Web servers

➢ Access control

➤ Single sign-on

➤ Revocation

➤ Digital signature verification servers

All of the preceding components will be discussed throughout this chapter, with the intention of providing a better understanding of the tasks involved when implementing a full-blown PKI. The last section of the chapter will discuss the importance of open PKI standards, and provide some guidance for starting up your PKI.

What Needs to Be Done?

Once the PKI infrastructure is chosen, the organization faces the task of integrating applications with the PKI of choice. PKI enabling brand-new applications is often quite straightforward, because the applications can be designed from the ground up with PKI support in mind, using the features of modern tools and Web servers that are ready to use.

Browsers

The browser is the closest thing to a universal, standard client interface available today. By implementing browser-based access to applications, organizations insure the widest possible accessibility to these functions, while minimizing user training. Clearly, this is critical for e-commerce, where end-user access equates to sales. However, the browser is also typically the most convenient and cost-effective end-user interface for intranet applications.

A browser used for e-commerce or secure intranet applications typically requires support for a PKI, certificates, a unified digital-signing capability across different types of browsers, and often strong client authentication technology, such as smart cards. In reality, the majority of distributed browsers lack good PKI support.

Web Browsers

In many discussions about PKI, the statement, "the Web browser will support that" is often used. This is roughly akin to describing Windows and Mac as being the same. The two leading browser brands, Microsoft Internet Explorer, and Netscape Navigator, have a long and winding path from the first version more than five years ago to the present, spread on the millions of PCs and Macs out there. Even if most systems are fairly modern, recent surveys show that the average user seldom upgrades his browser to every new version out there. This means that the level of PKI support is over the complete spectrum, from none to the latest available.

Support means the capability to:

➤ Generate keys and store a certificate

➤ Support for different storage; for example, smart cards, USB tokens, soft certificates

➤ The ability to use the certificate and keys for generating digital signatures and client authentication over SSL

➤ The support for other applications via the used storage; for example, e-mail, remote access, thin clients, and Java

Openness in access methods includes supporting a variety of browsers. This can be challenging, due to the vast number of browser versions and implementations. The main requirement for any solution in this area is easy installation on the client, which eases support problems for intranets and maximizes the number of potential customers for e-commerce. There are two common approaches to this problem:

1. Don't install anything additional on the client. Trust the browser.

   The risk is that differences in the way browsers implement PKI functions or registration procedures may cause difficulties for users, and users may not adopt the solution. Thus, time will be lost waiting for the installed base of browsers to unify sufficiently.

2. Install security software on the client.

   This solution provides the same PKI functions and registration procedures for all browsers. It is thus more likely to provide the required openness in a timely fashion. However, the application provider must also take some responsibility for the client system and should support the security software if installed.

Plug-Ins

Browsers may not contain all of the functions required for strong security; for example, digital signatures might not be supported as a standard feature. In such cases, vendors can design plug-ins to enhance the browser. The plug-in runs using the browser as a platform, making it possible to use PKI features with legacy applications, even though the back-end application server does not explicitly support these features.

However, Netscape's leading form-signing plug-in is typically limited to a specific method of payment and to a particular browser version. The support for smart cards and the practical issues around deploying certificates will also be an unsolved problem if the plug-in is not supported by a good helper application extending the browser's PKI functionality.

Unlike Netscape, the Microsoft browser has no native plug-in, but uses Active X, which does not work well in Navigator. Luckily there are plug-in designs that work in both environments. A "universal plug-in" is an easily deployable tool that provides the most important feature of PKI: the digital signature to a broad Internet community where you do not control the end-user browser environment. The alternative is picking one browser version and design accordingly.

One of the requirements for a plug-in that supports digital signing is that a leading standard, such as S/MIME/PKCS#7, is supported. A separate verification application/toolkit also needs to be present to provide an easy and secure way to evoke the plug-in and verify the signature in the Web or application server.

Digital Signature Plug-In

Today, digital signatures are the only secure and manageable way to provide legally binding proof of an electronic document/transaction. The digital signature works as an electronic equivalent to an ordinary signature, but is much more secure and reliable. By using digital signatures, you achieve verification of a user's identity, legal proof of authorship, and proof that the data has not been changed. These requirements can only be accomplished if the Web browser used for sending transactions is extended with digital-signing capability.

A digital signature plug-in (such as eSigner from CeloCom) is designed to provide extended digital-signature capabilities for any major Web browser. The digital signature plug-in provides non-repudiation capabilities through S/MIME signature operations on a number of document types, including plain text, HTML, and RTF.

While being able to sign text documents is mainly used for online banking and trading transactions, the HTML plug-in allows signing of entire Web pages. Thus, the latter would, for instance, enable you to sign a contract online, where you would be signing the whole document, including images and so forth. What you see is what you sign!

Figure 13.1 illustrates the digital signing of a contract written in HTML using the CeloCom eSigner plug-in demo.

Figure 13.1 Lease agreement in HTML—digital signature HTML plug-in demo.

The HTML plug-in signs the HTML code as well as images, and displays the Web page to be signed in a miniature browser window that is presented inside the regular browser. The user then selects certificate and is prompted to enter a password.

In Figure 13.2, the results from the performed digital signature verified by the server are displayed, confirming that the agreement was successfully signed.

Digital Signatures for Transaction Security

Let's say you were to perform a digitally signed transaction with the application for online banking with your bank. The necessary steps can be described as shown in Figure 13.3.

Secure Bank Transaction Demo

To see how a digital signature plug-in would work for a bank transaction, you can download the CeloCom Web Demo from the Celo Download Site at www.celocom .com. In this illustration, the plug-in is signing text; whereas in the former, it was for signing an HTML document.

When entering the demo, the user selects certificate and is prompted to enter a password, as shown in Figure 13.4, that will unlock and access the private key needed to sign the data.

You can now use your certificate to digitally sign a transaction as shown in Figure 13.5. Select transaction type (Buy or Sell), Number of shares, Price per share, and other options.

Figure 13.2 Results from digitally signed lease agreement verified by the server.

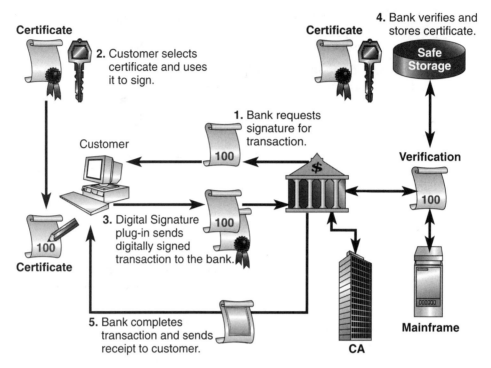

Figure 13.3   Digital signing of a bank transaction.
Source: Celo Communications.

Then the transaction is confirmed with a digital signature as shown in Figure 13.6. Notice the time stamp. For more information, see Chapter 7, "Time Stamps."

The Digital Signature verification server will tell you when the transaction occurred, and how many shares were bought at what price. Figure 13.7 shows the results of the server verification.

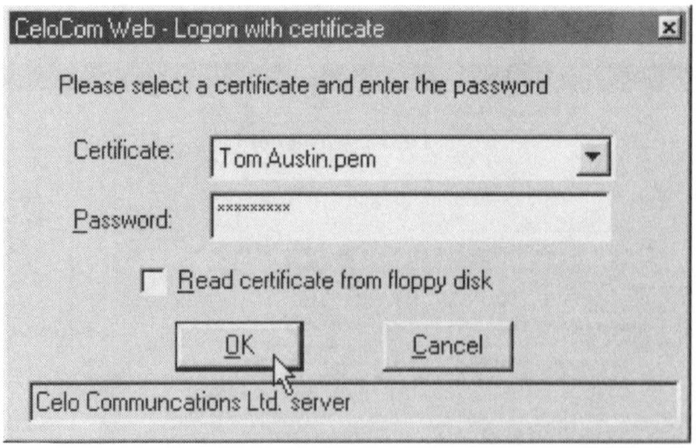

Figure 13.4   Logon with certificate window.

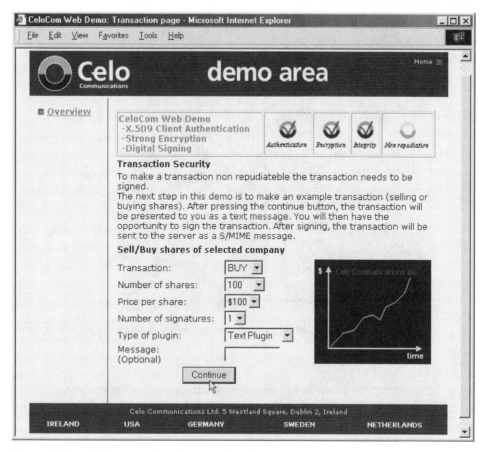

Figure 13.5 Celo's secure bank transaction demo.

With this short demo you've observed the following:

➤ Access of a secure site using strong encryption

➤ User identification to demo bank with client certificate

➤ Performed digitally signed transaction

➤ Received verification from the demo server

Identrus

There is currently an ongoing project promoted by banking and finance organizations worldwide, called *Identrus.* The goal is to enable financial institutions to extend their full range of practices onto the Internet and become trusted third parties for e-commerce transactions. Digital certificates issued by participating institutions will offer customers

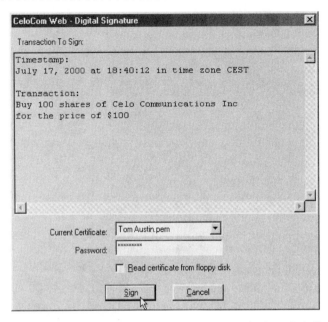

Figure 13.6 Window with final confirmation before digitally signing the transaction.

the certainty they require to conduct negotiations, forge an agreement, and arrange for payment in a trusted and secure manner. For more information about this project and others on PKI, see Chapter 19, "Initiatives, Laws, and Standards."

Web Servers

The Web server is the standard back end for providing services to browsers. As such, it is the nearest thing to a universal, standard server platform available today. By offering Web-based PKI services, organizations make it easier to integrate PKI services with corporate intranets. The checklist for your Web server is:

➤ Can the Web server use client certificate for authentication?

➤ If yes, can we check revocation of the certificates against our CA provider?

➤ How is the certificate mapped against the existing authentication method?

➤ Will the existing CGI program be able to use certificate data, or do you need access to data from the user database, meaning information that is not stored in the certificates?

➤ Are we changing, can we change our Web server environment, or will an upgrade cause other problems, inconsistent features that make the switch of Web servers unlikely in the near future?

➤ Do we need several authentication methods for different user groups at the same time?

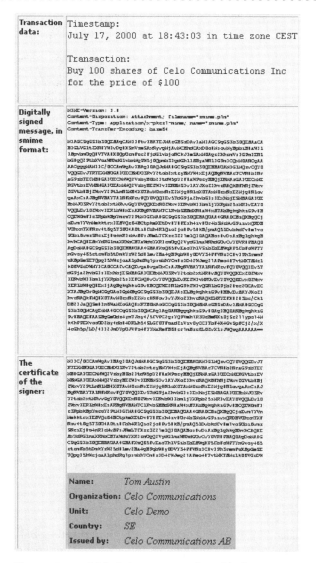

Figure 13.7   Digital signature results with time stamp and transaction details.

➤ Can encryption via SSL and/or verification of signature be handled by existing hardware?

Although many legacy applications have no support or inadequate support for PKI functions, in most cases, support for browsers and integration with Web-based services has become a requirement for continued survival of the application. Thus, in planning a PKI deployment, it is generally reasonable to assume that legacy applications will support browsers and integrate with Web servers via some kind of middleware.

Web servers may also have proxies, typically for three reasons:

➤ To step up the encryption of the server if only 40-bit.

➤ To integrate client verification without changing the existing system.

➤ To integrate a more complex single sign-on (SSO) system. Instead of logging on directly to the application, the user interacts with the proxy. The proxy accepts the logon on behalf of the user to the application server, replacing the universal PKI identity used by the SSO, with an application-specific user credential (user name/password).

Clients and servers may need little or no modification in order to work with a standards-based proxy such as an HTTP/HTTPS (SSL) proxy. Thus, using proxies based on standards can significantly speed up deployment of the PKI.

Access Control

A fully functional access control system is vital in order to successfully PKI enable an existing legacy system. There are some central functionalities and features required in the infrastructure:

➤ X.509 Certificate-based access control

➤ Single sign-on capabilities for login information

➤ Multiprotocol revocation control

➤ LDAP support (Lightweight Directory Access Protocol) for access to data integrity configuration parameters and authentication information in a directory server

➤ Support for hardware cryptographic accelerators and key storage

Figure 13.8 illustrates the access control aspect of a fully PKI-enabled legacy system, with optional means of authentication.

Access Control Server

An access control server, such as CeloCom eAccess, is a high-performing SSL gateway with extended PKI capabilities to be used by any client-server application to achieve strong encryption, revocation control, and PKI-based access control.

Based on an implementation of the TLS/SSL (Transport Layer Security/Secure Socket Layer) protocol that is a global de facto standard for network encryption, it provides a platform for a generic SSL server-side tunnel that can be applied to any static TCP-protocol.

An access control server typically uses a single certificate per user for all applications. The single sign-on feature simplifies and centralizes management of user-level security, improving management scalability: As the number of applications grows, user-level security management does not get more complex, as it does when managing multiple certificates through multiple application-specific interfaces.

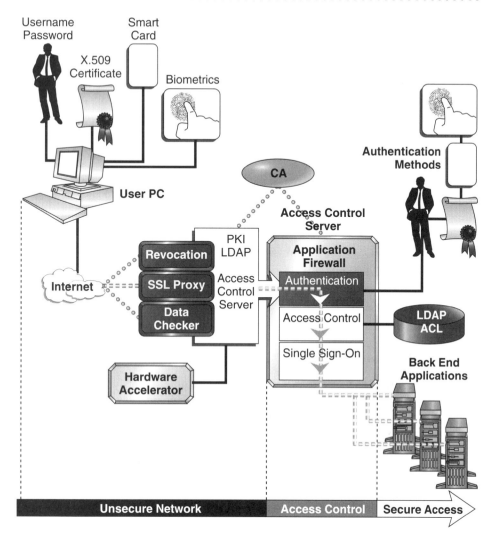

Figure 13.8 Client-server components for a PKI access control system.
Source: Celo Communications.

Both user and application see a simple username/password system, but "under the covers," much stronger PKI-based authentication and authorization are enforced. The fact that clients and applications do not have to change their approaches to security speeds up deployment of PKI functions. In some cases, it may be desirable to change the client, but not the back-end application; for instance, the user may upgrade to smart card authentication. The single sign-on feature accepts the smart card authentication and logs the user on to the application by using username/password security. Again, the fact that the back end doesn't have to change speeds up deployment.

Single Sign-On (SSO)

The single sign-on (SSO) feature allows a user to log on to the entire network once and gain access to all authorized services, such as Web servers, mail systems, and databases. No matter how complex the underlying network, or how the network changes, the user logs on the same way, providing user-friendly logon.

The SSO feature acts as middleware between users and applications; for instance, the SSO performs a PKI-based authentication and authorization for that user, and then via LDAP (Lightweight Directory Access Protocol) provides username/password logon to an application.

SSO also improves reliability and performance, since the SSO system can log on faster and with fewer errors than a user can. Finally, SSO improves productivity, since users don't have to go through logon sequences.

The SSO can also implement various security levels, based on the type of authentication, without having to modify the back end to understand the various types of authentication or the security levels. One example is the SSO might log the user on to the application with a different user ID, depending on which type of authentication is used. The back-end application thinks in terms of different users with different levels of privilege.

Revocation

Authentication is just half of the process; you need to verify that the certificates are still valid. Much as you do for credit cards, if they are lost or tampered with, you revoke them on separate lists, revocation lists. Those could be CRLs (certificate revocation lists), OCSPs (On-Line Certificate Status Protocol), or a proprietary CA solution. Revocation control is needed for every PKI system.

The native PKI revocation features in the standard Web server are normally weak, and need to be complemented with different add-ons. This is a moving target, of course, and better functionality will be built in. The functionally is not only based on the Web server, but also on what service is supported by the CA of choice. If you have a CA that uses OCSP, your Web server will have slim chances of being able to perform the revocation control. The main method for revocation with a CA is OCSP. OCSP can be native in the Web server, or can be a feature of an access control server.

Digital Signature Verification Server

A natural consequence of PKI access control is authentication in combination with transaction security; that is, digital signatures. The possibility to use digital signatures separates PKI-based access control as a superior alternative to just username/password.

A digital signature verification server contains the database that holds the digital signature, the certificate, the revocation control time stamp, the transaction time stamp, and the data both before and after signing. It fulfills digital signing requests, enforcing time limits on the transactions. Implementing digital signing functionality as a separate software module makes it easier to integrate this functionality with legacy systems. The separate module should also reduce access to the database to a minimum, reducing the risk of the database being violated.

Open PKI Standards

Vendor-independent interfaces and protocols are evolving fast. A few target the PKI specifically. A number of others are used in connection with the PKI, although they were not developed for the PKI. Historically, vendor-independent PKI standards have not been complete or robust enough to define a full PKI solution, so software vendors have had to depend on vendor-specific interfaces, at least to some extent. However, vendor-independent interfaces are evolving rapidly, so that organizations can now plan to base solutions primarily on vendor-independent PKI interfaces.

Unfortunately, legacy applications, because they were not designed with a PKI in mind, are generally slow to support PKI-oriented standards. Maximizing openness under these conditions can be difficult.

Another important aspect of openness is looking to the future. Legacy applications are evolving to support more vendor-independent standards. The standards themselves are evolving as well. Organizations need an architecture that will accommodate this evolution efficiently and cost-effectively.

Key Points

A fully functional PKI access control system is vital, as it offers the possibility of PKI-based authentication rather than username/password.

➤ Include digital signatures in your PKI solution. It will give you a stronger position on the market as well as with your customers.

➤ Choose one or preferably two application areas that follow the PKI standard and work with other vendors. Interoperability between PKI vendors and open standards will be vital.

➤ Initially, PKI for business-to-business commerce is a lot easier to deploy than a full-blown business-to-consumer system. The control, as well as the understanding of a PKI system, has more relevance on a B2B level.

➤ Evaluate the possibilities of issuing your own certificates or using a national/international CA as the issuer, depending on your ability to run a CA center.

➤ Create business alliances with other companies that use PKI, in order to offer the user more sites that accept the certificates.

➤ Start by issuing soft certificates (stored on hard disk) for larger volumes, and use smart cards and USB tokens for more carefully selected groups with higher business/transaction values.

Case Studies

These five case studies, which represent both government and private enterprises, should provide you with extraordinary insight into the issues, problems and the complexities that they discovered in implementing their PKI. From their business requirements to how they're measuring the results of their investment, you'll grasp whether they've reached their expectations and what it took for them to achieve them. More importantly, the key points they learned and what they would do differently may help you understand how you could best approach implementing your own PKI.

For the most part, there are little or no references to any one vendor. Of course, you should ask any vendor that you're considering doing business with for solid reference accounts that have implemented their solution. However, you'll probably discover just what I did in writing this book. That is, that some vendors are much better than others in how they market, execute, follow through, and how well they support their clients. If you take away anything from these case studies, vendor support was one of the most critical elements that helped these organizations accomplish what they did.

Unlike cryptographic algorithms that benefit from public scrutiny, when it comes to security, few organizations like to share what they know for fear of creating some vulnerability or losing a competitive edge. This made case studies difficult to obtain and required an effort that spanned well over a year. For each of the case studies, there were many others that fell through citing reasons for security or, in the case of some vendors, being unable to provide any. Therefore, applause goes to the organizations that were not only supportive of this endeavor, but for their willingness to contribute so that others may learn and benefit from their experience.

Bank of Bermuda

● ●

G ive customers what they want, when they want it, and let them get it anywhere in the world. While this may sound difficult, that's exactly the goal of Bank of Bermuda. *Anytime, anyplace, anywhere* customers want access to the bank's staff and services, they can have it. But how can a bank, or any organization for that matter, do this in a cost-effective and secure manner? By taking advantage of the Internet, a public network, and the capabilities of PKI, the bank is enhancing its competitive position and providing new services to its customers (see Figure 14.1).

Background

Founded in 1889 and headquartered in Hamilton, Bank of Bermuda has offices or subsidiaries in 14 countries, including the Cayman Islands, Cook Islands, Dublin, Hong Kong, Luxembourg, New York, New Zealand, and Singapore. It also has representative offices in Bahrain and London.

Bank of Bermuda's four business lines entail global fund services for providing global custody and fund administration services; corporate banking for international corporations with an offshore presence; private client services; and retail banking is offered exclusively in Bermuda. The bank's Treasury and Investment Operations, which were recently consolidated from regional into global operations, provide product support to the divisions.

The success of each division is based on common values of high levels of service, close client relationships, and responsiveness to clients' evolving requirements. Through basing the bank's business on these values, Bank of Bermuda has grown to become one of the world's leading suppliers of trust, administration, and global cus-

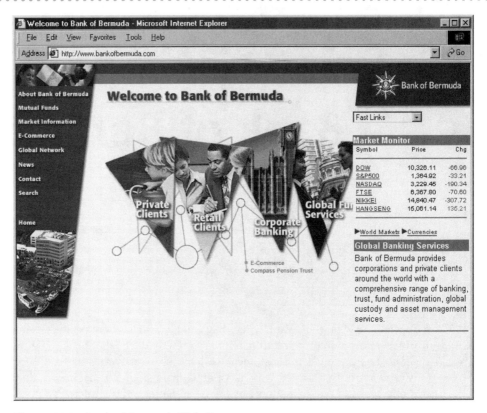

Figure 14.1 Bank of Bermuda Website.

tody services to investment managers and financial institutions. As a global private bank, Bank of Bermuda provides high net-worth individuals and families with trust, private banking, brokerage, advisory, and asset management services. Bank of Bermuda's retail banking operations serve as the largest such institution in Bermuda.

As of March 2000, Bank of Bermuda had net assets of $10.6 billion, and assets under administration in excess of $80 billion.

Business Requirements

From a business perspective, the goal was to provide electronic access to services for customers and staff "anytime, anyplace, anywhere," and in a cost-effective manner.

Being a conservative, risk-averse international financial institution, it is a very necessary part of the bank's business model to allow clients to access their portfolio electronically from anywhere in the world in a secure manner. The bank had already implemented a remote client access infrastructure that allowed clients to access the bank's services via a dial-up or leased-line connection to any of the bank's 14 international points of presence. However, particularly for clients located in jurisdictions where the bank does not have a physical presence, this often proved to be an expensive and unreliable solution. For example, if the bank has a client in South Africa, the client would have to establish a dial-up connection to the London office in order to get online access. For many clients, the cost and reliability implications made this solution prohibitive.

In addition to addressing the immediate connectivity issues, the bank needed to position itself to provide new and expanded services to meet the needs of the changing global economy; for example, global e-commerce transaction processing, secure electronic communications with clients, and accepting electronic instructions that included a strong foundation for non-repudiation.

Business Impact

As a growing international company, the bank has many business processes that are becoming more international in nature, along with business units and divisions that are increasingly dispersed geographically. PKI is laying the foundation for the bank to be able to move swiftly and securely into the future with current and new technology initiatives. Indeed, it is spawning numerous business initiatives and new ways at looking at application development, implementation, and problem solving. From an organizational viewpoint, implementing PKI is resulting in key staff people thinking differently, from both the technology and the business side.

With PKI now in place, these processes can now be automated much more effectively, particularly where authorizations are involved. For example, when a requisition requires approval and review by two levels of management, and one manager is located in a different country or travelling on business, the business processes can be modified to include the fact that authorizations can be given via digital signature. A process that might have otherwise taken days, or that might have relied on a less secure technology (such as transmitting a fax), can now be turned around in hours.

Similarly, business partner relationships are also benefiting. Agreements that could have taken several weeks to process, simply because of administrative delays, are now set to improve in efficiency, security, and reliability. The necessary criteria for partners include a willingness to use the technology, that appropriate contracts be in place, and have the necessary supporting legislation in place in the various international jurisdictions.

Even though customers may not fully appreciate all of the technological and legislative issues involved, they now expect to be able to have the option to conduct any and all business online. They want something that is transparent, easy to use, yet secure and reliable, and viewed the project as a leap forward from the previous electronic offerings. While PKI in itself may not be the "magic pill," when coupled with the appropriate applications and procedures, it does become a very powerful tool for meeting customer expectations.

Some scepticism also did exist over the potential success of the project, but this was allayed by the outstanding results from the internal pilot testing and, for the most part, internal users were excited by the project.

PKI solutions were seen as definitely cross-discipline, and therefore separate from other "pigeon holes in the organizational structure."

The key, says Bank of Bermuda, is to involve the various parties who will be affected or expected to support the architecture early in the process. Although they may not understand all of the concepts, or even see the overall vision, building a team spirit and a sense of involvement is critical to reducing resistance. As a result of moving forward with its PKI, the bank now has a strong authentication and encryption mechanism in place that can be implemented both at the network and application level that is critical to the bank's international success. PKI is providing the standard framework from which new internal and external services can now be developed and deployed.

Moving Forward

Gaining a thorough understanding of business line managers' concerns and frustrations with the current business processes was another important step accomplished, especially by investing time "walking-the-floors" with the operational groups of the business units.

From that point, the bank ensured that the technology being introduced would be consistent with these goals and defined the draft project scope. Potential new business opportunities were also identified that PKI technology would enable.

The approach required working closely with various technology groups in Information Technology (IT) such as Networks, Applications, Help Desk, Operations, as well as EDP Audit, Business Operations Groups, and Legal Counsel.

The direction was to also follow established industry standards where they existed and were consistent with the bank's requirements and goals. For example, the new Electronic Transactions Bill passed in Bermuda recently, and a similar bill passed in Singapore, another key jurisdiction for the bank, helped spark the need for PKI. Working closely with vendors under non-disclosure and ensuring that the bank's strategic partnerships were consistent helped considerably in reconciling any inter-vendor compatibility issues that arose.

Measuring Results

"The bank is already seeing returns in terms of reduced operating and communications costs, new business coming in through the door, and reduced support overheads. While it may be difficult to put a total dollar value on the return on investment, it's expected to be phenomenal."

Bank of Bermuda viewed PKI both as a long-term strategic project as well as one that would also deliver immediate benefits within just six months. Building on an existing global TCP/IP network and state-of-the-art firewall infrastructure, the estimated costs for the PKI element alone is anticipated to be less than $750,000 over a three-year period, with most of the costs being operational. Interestingly enough, the overall support overhead is a fraction of what it was before PKI. The entire project actually reduced operation overhead both in time and man-hours.

The bank's PKI is not an open retail application solution, but is considered a closed community of trust. Even though it's expected to issue some 10,000 certificates through year 2000, the bank didn't consider attaining a certain number to be a success factor. Rather, success is being measured by:

➤ Number of clients that regularly use the infrastructure

➤ Volume of new business that's attained because the PKI is in place

➤ Business and procedural overhead that migrates to a service supported by PKI

➤ Reduced time required for processes that can now be completed as a result of PKI

The immediate benefit PKI achieved was opening up the option to use low-cost international networks for external communication by incorporating encryption technology with client-specific authentication.

For the bank's clients, this meant that they could connect to the bank's extranet services either via the Internet or via a local dial connection to a VPN-dial service provider—whether connecting from a hotel room or from an airport lounge. Clients, using a standard Web browser, now have access to these services via an encrypted connection over the Internet, or via a global VPN-dial service. For the bank's staff, the immediate benefits were much the same. Moreover, deploying the infrastructure allowed the bank to implement legacy host connectivity software.

New applications are already in the process of coming online that have simply sprung out of this infrastructure. In many cases now, the encryption is taking place, with client authentication, without the application even being aware.

Online application access for cash management, share registration, portfolio management, e-mail, messaging, and authenticated network encryption are driving the PKI. The bank now has user-specific keys for authentication and encryption, centralized policy management with distributed administration, and a standard, cross-platform, cross-application authentication architecture.

Implementing the PKI

Implementing a PKI solution enabled the bank to provide client-specific encryption of stored data and data in transit, thus opening up the use of public networks. In addition, by virtue of the digital-signature technology coupled with effective and efficient procedures, the infrastructure would be in place to facilitate the non-repudiation of messages and instructions, and connectivity and communication streams.

Thus, part of the requirement for PKI was to devise an infrastructure that would:

> Allow the secure use of public networks for low-cost access, such as dial networks and the Internet

> Be consistent with new-generation client access applications under development

> Support access to legacy applications

Policies

The bank created a Certificate Practice Statement (CPS) that is readily accessible on its Web site (see "Resources").

People

The project required one project manager who was assigned overall responsibility, with two other technologists involved on a full-time basis. Four added members of the IT staff were involved in the project from various disciplines, investing about 10 to 15 percent of their time. However, for development of the PKI, there was no increase in head count.

For ongoing support, existing administrative staff will be used for managing the PKI. It's also likely that at least one new employee will be taken on to ensure adherence to policy, and to track industry developments and legislative changes as they occur in the various international jurisdictions.

Facility and Equipment

A fully redundant configuration was implemented with fail-over hardware in two separate buildings. The servers themselves are in a secure area of the buildings, which are designed to withstand natural disasters such as hurricanes, and include uninterruptible power supply (UPS) power coverage. The hardware involved in the PKI architecture is hosted in a highly secured location, incorporating physical, procedural, and electronic protective security mechanisms.

Six enterprise-quality servers were deployed: a primary certificate authority (CA), a primary directory, a hot fail-over CA and directory, and a complete development and testing environment. The PKI is basically divided into two parts: the CA itself and the directory, with the former having higher security implications. Both servers are protected and isolated from the production network by a separate firewall. In addition to addressing the security of the PKI infrastructure itself, a complete contingency architecture approach was incorporated along with the usual "high availability" policies that would apply to any mission-critical infrastructure, such as those involved in a trading service, for example.

An argument could be made that the directory in this case could be more critical than the CA. If the CA is down, certificates cannot be issued or revoked, but real-time authentication continues. If the directory is down, real-time authentication stops, so it also has a direct and immediate production impact. Therefore, provisioning the CA with the same high availability would depend on the business model and the criticality of being able to immediately revoke a certificate.

Process

Bank of Bermuda followed a fairly simple and effective 12-step process.

1. Initial proof-of concept

Testing the functionality for:

2. Each piece of the technology
3. Each complete scenario
4. Complete installation, implementation, and upgrade testing
5. Complete test of all procedures
6. Exhaustive Y2K testing
7. UAT for each business unit

Pilot testing:

8. By technical staff (globally)
9. By business staff (globally)
10. By select business partners
11. By select customers
12. Identify clear trouble spots and define a "go-live" plan that would allow certain aspects of the project to go live while others were completing the testing and development phases.

Throughout this process, the critical element was to make full use of the test-lab environment where all possible scenarios for implementation and support could be simulated.

Timeline

From start to finish, it took the bank 25 months to implement the PKI:

Jul 97	Initial consideration
Aug → Jan 98	Criteria development, review
Feb → Apr 98	Vendor selection
May → Jun 98	Pilot implementation started/completed
Aug → Apr 99	Production environment rollout start date/scheduled ramp up
Aug 99	Finish implementation

Issues and Other Specifics

To meet the bank's encryption requirements, there were few alternatives other than PKI. Encryption devices, though providing privacy, were an expensive solution and lack the flexibility in scope and application. Additionally, relying on these for true client authentication was not ideal. Pre-shared keys was also considered, but also rejected due to the higher risk of key compromises and administrative overhead and risk.

Tokens were considered and selected for one-time passwords and the benefits of a physical token requirement for access to be implemented within the PKI architecture to provide strong authentication for certain online services and transaction types.

For existing applications integration, the bank took the approach of providing Web-based access to some legacy systems through an "off-the-shelf" application that was compliant with industry standards for PKI. It then looked to address any remaining legacy requirements on an as-needed basis such as when legacy applications would be due for upgrade or replacement.

The initial implementation is with a single CA with the plan to have a separate CA for staff and external clients once the bank reaches critical mass. Clients and business partners will likely be managed on the same CA, assuming an internal / external model. The bank is initially implementing a Lightweight Directory Access Protocol (LDAP) directory with a migration path to full X.500.

Use of multiple certificates per entity may be used on rare occasions when individuals are members of multiple organizations. Storing of authorization information in any of the extension fields found in the current certificate format is likely to be at least two years away, and would most likely be used for managing authorization levels. Protocols being used to manage the certificates include LDAP, Public Key Cryptography Standards (PKCS), and Cisco's Certificate Enrollment Protocol (CEP).

Initially, one certificate revocation list (CRL) is being used with real-time updates. The CRL includes business partners and other third parties, and resides in the directory with CRL checking occurring automatically. Online Status Checking Protocol (OSCP) may follow later.

Achieving Expectations

The bank did expect that the overall project would be successful and delivered on time. It was also realistic enough to understand that the test phase wouldn't be trouble-free—which it wasn't. The current implementation did, however, match the original plan within about 95 percent of the original design. That 95 percent includes the entire project, and not just the PKI.

Remarkably, the PKI itself fell within 98 percent of the bank's original design. Only a slight change in the original design to facilitate Internet Protocol Security (IPsec) VPN authentication more efficiently needed to be done. Even the CA itself worked fine.

The challenge the bank did face was that some vendors made strategic shifts in direction, dissolved partnerships, and then formed new partnerships. They also hit difficulties when strategic shifts by vendors required slight changes in the implementation at the application level. Software upgrades also had adverse effects on some areas of functionality. Nonetheless, by working closely with quality vendors and by having those vendors work closely with each other, the issues were resolved. Nothing necessitated any fundamental change in the design or strategy of the PKI and CA itself.

There's confidence that the architecture and associated procedures are such that a growing end-user base can be accommodated smoothly. It's now synonymous with the growth of a "telephone on every desk," or "e-mail for everyone." Of course, that's if the technology and procedures are designed from the outset with flexibility and international growth in mind.

Key Points

TOP THREE LESSONS LEARNED

1. Get cross-discipline IT folks involved early enough for them to at least feel like they were involved in the design.

2. Make sure senior managers and executives are willing to make structural changes further down the line if necessary. If the process and structure are wrong, PKI will not be the magic pill to cure all ills.

3. Continuously and repeatedly educate business groups once they are aware of the project.

TOP THREE CRITICAL SUCCESS FACTORS

1. Remember: PKI is not a security solution. It crosses organizational boundaries and is interdicisplinary.

2. Get the buy-in of your key business managers first. Bring all key technology staff, not just managers, into the loop early. Even if they're not going to eat, sleep, and breathe the project, you will need them down the line!

3. Keep a close eye on legislative issues, and make sure your legal audit and legal counsel are apprised. If they don't understand what you're doing, bring someone in to explain it, or find a lawyer who does understand it and that your counsel is comfortable with, and have him or her do some of the legal work.

WOULD DO DIFFERENTLY

➣ Bring other IT groups into the fray earlier, especially those who will be expected to support it.

MOST HELPFUL IN GETTING PKI UP AND RUNNING

1. NDA sessions with technology developers.

2. Strategy discussions with business managers.

3. Hearing sentences that started "Wouldn't it be great if we could…"

4. Having tremendously dedicated and enthusiastic staff. It was just as new to them, but with dedication, conceptual thinking, drive, and a commitment to learn and be successful, they were just brilliant!

5. Excellent vendor support and training, coupled with a motivated and enthusiastic vendor account manager.

Findings

Bank of Bermuda continues to discover the benefits of the "I" in PKI. Customers know that only they have the authorization to access their financial portfolio, and that they can conduct their business in complete privacy. Moreover, they don't even have to learn how to use anything new to do this. They can use a means with which they are already familiar: the browser.

CHAPTER 15

Perot Systems

• •

With an ever-increasing mobile workforce, enabling authorized employees to securely access sensitive company information is a business necessity. Virtual private networks (VPNs), in conjunction with digital certificates, offer a low-cost, strong authentication alternative to high-cost private networks. Indeed, while planning and implementing a solution like PKI presents a degree of complexity, it also fosters opportunity. As such, Perot Systems is finding that PKI is fast becoming a competitive requirement.

Background

Perot Systems is a worldwide provider of information technology services and business solutions to a broad range of clients. Perot Systems serves clients by delivering services and solutions focused on each client's specific needs, with particular emphasis on developing and integrating information systems, operating and improving technology and business processes, and helping clients to transform their business. Perot Systems helps large multinational companies to leverage their traditional strengths and technologies to take full advantage of e-business by capitalizing on the growth and productivity that can be achieved by integrating many companies into common marketplaces. Perot Systems focuses its core business integration, systems integration and application development, and infrastructure services to enable clients to accelerate growth, streamline operations, and create new levels of customer value. With more than 7000 employees and more than 1 billion dollars in revenue, Perot Systems has long-term relationships with clients in the financial services, healthcare, energy, travel and transportation, communications and media, insurance, and manufacturing industries.[1]

[1] Press release, Perot Systems, February 8, 2000: Perot Systems Reports a 36% Increase to Full Year EPS.

Figure 15.1 Perot Systems Web site.

Business Requirements

As part of a fundamental change in Perot's infrastructure, PKI is being implemented as a required tool to enhance authentication to acceptable risk levels associated with remote access over a globally shared media—the Internet.

Perot's original motivation for virtual private networking was to allow confidential and secure access for employees working remotely from customer account sites. In the past, connections were accomplished over private wide area network (WAN) connections using non-standard, tactical VPN solutions. As Internet Protocol Security (IPSec) technology standards became increasingly available in products, Perot wanted to take advantage of the situation and make the move to digital certificates for their second-generation VPN.

Business Impact

Complexity breeds opportunity. PKI is going to allow Perot to do much more than just secure VPN authentication. While it's an enabler today, PKI is becoming a competitive requirement. Plans are to extend authentication to mainstream applications to enable e-mail encryption for confidentiality, digital signatures for non-repudiation, as well as e-forms to eliminate paperwork and expedite transaction processing. Moreover, the same infrastructure will be in place for customers to connect to Perot's network. As its expertise expands, Perot plans to market PKI to its customers, creating even more revenue opportunities.

Moving Forward

Managers at Perot saw PKI as a strategic move, and as a result, took a staged approach to get management support. Where Information Technology (IT) has to first obtain a capital expenditure approval for dollars, the vehicle to move forward was to first develop and present a business plan.

While Perot could have continued with its tactical plans and its associated body of manual administration, VPN brought PKI to the forefront and allowed Perot to bring in the technology in a cost-effective manner. Little doubt now exists that PKI integration will allow for a long-term return on investment (ROI) and provide necessary leverage for other future uses.

Moreover, there was an acknowledgment that without the VPN requirement, it wouldn't have made sense, or a practical business case, to create the PKI (and its associated directory) just for the sake of the technology itself.

Measuring Results

Perot wants to do more with less: more control over their network with fewer people, a lower ratio of system administrators to end users, and larger deployments of sites with less staff. PKI is the tool that Perot believes is the security architecture that's not only scalable, but will also allow them the authentication assurance and the ability to implement secure access throughout its organization.

Furthermore, it's also opening up the potential of having hundreds of thousands of users access Perot's applications. By integrating VPN with directories and taking advantage of tying into emerging standards such as Directory Enabled Networks (DEN) initiative (the schema for representing network elements and services in a directory), Perot is achieving scalability of user authentication. This level of integration is seen as the starting point for leveraging PKI for other uses such as secure e-mail, single sign-on, and smart cards, for using one physical, electronic, picture identification access card.

With over 2000 certificates deployed over a one-year period, measurements are being tied to functionality of the VPN; in effect, whether the users can connect and authenticate. Performance is a close second. Plans are to issue a certificate to each of Perot's 7000 employees as well as selected routers throughout the network.

While cost justification was initially focused on the enhancements of security, Perot quantified better security by demonstrating the lower recurring costs for remote access VPN. Increased performance and productivity were also cited using soft dollar savings. Overarching concerns about competitive advantages also became more evident during the process, as well as eventual business survival by not upgrading existing network operations.

Indeed, Perot had already invested close to six years in VPN design with implementation and support adding another four man-years and growing, a direct infrastructure cost for hardware and software of over $1.2M, and support costs in the range of $2M to $3M over the next three years.

Implementing the PKI

Perot deployed PKI to authenticate users and devices as part of their virtual private network (VPN), such as server-to-server virtual private networking, intranet and extranet, and a client-to-server VPN for remote employees.

In addition to providing a strong authentication mechanism for VPN, Perot's PKI will also be used in conjunction with other tools such as directories, and accessing other network resources to enable a greater level of identification of users and network devices within the Perot organization.

Policies

With the initial use of certificates limited to VPN authentication, no certificate policy or certificate practice statement was created. However, with deployment now underway and expanding, Perot is now putting these policies in place using an internal policy developer with guidance from security and network engineering.

People

Existing resources were used through the design, testing, and rollout of the PKI. With the initial rollout now in the production phase, several teams throughout Perot are working to enable other applications such as e-mail, human resources, and intranet into the PKI.

Facility and Equipment

A 24-hour by 7-day data center was equipped with a fully redundant, no single point of failure VPN server, firewall, certificate authority, and directory.

Process

Perot approached implementing its PKI through a simple, four-step process:
1. Proof of concept
2. Pilot
3. Limited production
4. Production

Timeline

From start to finish, Perot implemented PKI for VPN within 25 months:

Jan 97   Initial consideration
Jan 97   Criteria development, review

Dec 97	Vendor selection
Nov 98	Pilot implementation started/completed
Feb 99	Production environment rollout start date/scheduled ramp up

Issues and Other Specifics

PKI was initially brought in to serve the one specific need of VPN authentication. However, once Perot became comfortable with the technology, it began to look at other functions that PKI offered, such as secure e-mail and secure single sign-on. While applications such as virtual private networking (VPN), secure e-mail, smart cards, single sign-on, and secure desktop were driving the PKI, the major considerations that led to adopting PKI were scalability, security, leveragability, and robustness of the technology. Even though Perot considered alternatives that included username and password, RADIUS/TACACS, and tokens for authentication, certificates were chosen since they represented the future in technology. (Note: RADIUS stands for Remote Authentication Dial In User Service, an authentication application available from various vendors. TACACS, Terminal Access Controller Access Control System, is a protocol providing access control for routers, network access servers, and other networked devices, and is defined in IETF RFC 1492 the Internet Engineering Task Force Request for Comments standard.)

Where Perot had set very restrictive criteria for use, there was some initial pain for users. As the switch occurred to using the Internet for connectivity, end-user resistance to change greatly diminished, since they were now able to leverage higher-speed access of cable, ISDN (Integrated Services Digital Network), wireless, and broadband technologies from home.

Besides a move toward standardization on Windows desktops, Perot's implementation encountered only minor issues for non-IP protocols and other subtle configurations related to melding multiple private networks. Nonetheless, the complexity of integrating all the aspects of the technology was a major unforeseen problem. Often working with beta code, Perot found itself integrating products from as many as 10 to 12 vendors at a time, with many setbacks as code had to be adjusted.

Perot ultimately selected LDAP in conjunction with Novell Directory Services for certificate management, with the directory integrated to work with Perot's current directory direction. Additionally, serial numbers are being stored in the certificate extension fields for Perot's network of Cisco routers. Currently, there is no planned use for multiple certificates per entity or for deploying multiple certificate authorities. Certificate revocation lists (CRLs) are deployed on a distributed basis using CRL Distribution Points technology, all residing in the directory. CRL checking happens automatically within the applications, and CRLs are updated every 24 hours.

Perot intends to further leverage the directory to mix and match authorizations and quality of service once all the devices and users are using certificates. Perot also envisions potential integration with biometrics, roaming certificates (meaning that digital certificates of users are stored on a secure, centralized server, so transient users do not have to carry their identities with them), zero footprint clients (meaning that no files are required on client workstations), and wireless and Personal Digital Assistant (PDA) integration.

Achieving Expectations

Simply, the technology worked as planned. Perot's original criteria included IPsec standards and incorporating directory management for the certificates. However, as Perot progressed to accommodate its enterprise direction, operating system platforms were changed to standardize on Microsoft Windows.

Key Points

TOP THREE LESSONS LEARNED

➢ Select vendors that are well funded, industry leading, and industry recognized.

➢ Set clear expectations for management and end users.

➢ PKI must be operationally maintainable.

TOP THREE CRITICAL SUCCESS FACTORS

➢ Ease of rollout/use

➢ Supportability

➢ Leverageability of resources

WOULD DO DIFFERENTLY

➢ Upfront commitment for large-scale training and deployment to allow for greater positioning.

➢ Consider wireless in the design.

➢ Managing certificates in-house. Perot recommends that others be prepared for a steep learning curve, and consider the value in outsourcing the PKI.

➢ Certificate validation. Perot believes there's an immediate need for verifying the validity of certificates in a simpler fashion, perhaps utilizing Online Certificate Status Protocol (OCSP).

MOST HELPFUL IN GETTING PKI UP AND RUNNING

➢ Vendor and system engineer support

➢ Understanding the possibilities and the theory

Findings

Perot Systems is changing the way employees communicate with their company by making fundamental changes in its infrastructure by incorporating PKI. By taking advantage of the security services PKI technology has to offer, there is now a higher level of assurance of who has access to their network through authentication. Perot now has further protection of confidentiality for that information through encryption, and as a result, is securing its electronic business assets.

CHAPTER 16

Idaho National Engineering and Environmental Laboratory (INEEL)

Every organization wants to eliminate paperwork. With 900,000 signed paper reports each year, the Idaho National Engineering and Environmental Labs (INEEL) is one organization that is going to virtually eliminate it. By replacing the paper-based record system, it's estimated that cost savings of $9M should be achieved through the year 2002 alone. How was this accomplished? By creating a new digital signature technology for databases, in conjunction with PKI, INEEL is now well on its way.

Background

The Idaho National Engineering and Environmental Laboratory, also known as INEEL, is home to the largest concentration of technical professionals in the northern Rocky Mountain region. Operated by Bechtel BXWT Idaho LLC (BBWI) for the U.S. Department of Energy, it is the scene of some of the most advanced research programs in the world. For more than 40 years, the INEEL has made strong technical contributions to regional and national programs in the areas of energy availability, waste management, defense systems, earth sciences, and engineered systems. In recent years, Congress and the Department of Energy (DOE) have recognized that the national laboratories are a valuable resource for industry. Realizing that industrial collaboration will strengthen the nation's economic security, they have expanded their technology transfer role. The present mission of the INEEL is to develop, demonstrate, deploy, and transfer advanced engineering technology and systems to private industry to improve the competitiveness and security of the United States, the efficient production and use of energy, and the quality of life and the environment worldwide (see Figure 16.1).

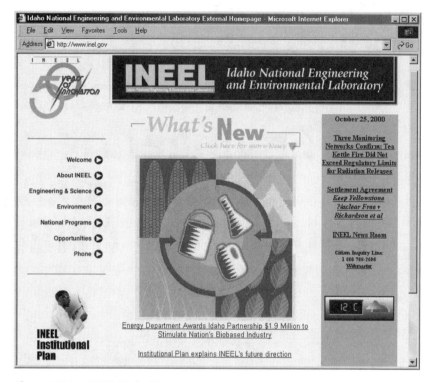

Figure 16.1   INEEL Web site.

Business Requirements

In 1997, DOE's Idaho National Engineering and Environmental Laboratory (INEEL) developed a new digital signature technology for databases as a part of the Transuranic Reporting, Inventory, and Processing System (TRIPS). TRIPS is the primary information system for the Radioactive Waste Management Complex's (RWMC) characterization and waste certification activities at INEEL.

This architecture is currently being enhanced to provide a general case technology that can be applied to other existing databases distributed across an Intranet/Internet. This technology, which is patent pending, removes the need for creating paper historical files and increases the integrity of data at its source, the database. From a user's perspective, the only overhead to "sign" is the authentication of the user. The added benefits are: an automated mechanism to verify the authenticity of both the signed source data, directly on the database, and the data signer; and the numerous storage cost savings and historical search capabilities inherent in electronic systems.

This technology assists in managing a geographically distributed work force that requires signatures from individuals in varied locations. It eliminates the need to create, collect, store, and maintain paper copies of documents generated from databases that require signatures.

This unique technology combines Internet industry standards with a newly developed architecture and protocols to extend these standards to relational databases such as the TRIPS application. Currently, there are limited commercial solutions for providing digital signatures on database elements. Existing products are only for flat documents, which is adequate only for the simplest of electronic approval systems like e-mail or simple signatures on a static data set. The TRIPS implementation permits signing of complex sets of relational data within the context of a complex workflow. It combines different data fields in a different way for each user in the approval process, as defined in the workflow, each of whom is only permitted to sign, change, or reject for rework certain fields presented to them. For example, there is not a single form or document being routed for multiple signatures; each signer's data presentation and control could be unique.

Digitally signing the database data, instead of just external reports, increases data integrity across future reports generated from the database, and permits data validation prior to electronic transfers to other applications requiring TRIPS' waste characterization data.

Business Impact

The Government Paperwork Elimination Act of 1998 requires that all agencies provide the public with the option to submit forms electronically by October 2003. Converting paper forms and electronic data stores to sign-able, routable objects requires many levels of security and integrity checks, only pieces of which exist today and mostly for flat-file paradigms. INEEL is positioning itself as a leader in new applications of public-private key cryptography; that is, the signing of complex entities. Besides databases, the National Security Infrastructure Department at INEEL is developing digital signature systems for digital watermarks on electronic documents, complex multimedia evidence systems, distributed applications, and new forms of secure, dynamic group communications. TRIPS forms are internal only to INEEL currently and are not yet public.

The enormous need at RWMC to control paper processes, data integrity, and INEEL's technological expertise in security systems led to the development of TRIPS and its use of PKI. It will now be a very important part of RWMC facility operations, with more than $100M annual budget out of the INEEL's total budget of about $750M.

The most significant changes to INEEL's internal business processes and customer relations have occurred as a result of going paperless on the processes automated to date. Past database efforts could not address the approval workflow process, because it was so complex and resources were limited. So much of the electronic records work was not utilized to its potential or not kept in sync with the paper.

Indeed, the TRIPS system is highly data intensive with the system storing waste tracking, characterization, certification, and transportation information on up to

140,000 waste containers, which creates about 1000 pages of typed and hand-written documents per waste container. There is also a large amount of output stored from instruments with at least six levels or more of data reviews and approvals that occur, with different personnel involved at each level, and each level combining data in a different way. As many as 40,000 signatures per year can be generated when TRIPS is in full production, and RWMC will be operating 24 hours a day, 7 days a week.

Prior to TRIPS, this data was gathered using paper-based forms, with written comments and signatures on each form. To support report generation at higher levels, some, but not all, of this data was re-entered into legacy database applications. The TRIPS system as a whole will virtually eliminate the need for storing and tracking 900,000 paper copies of signed reports per year. The INEEL Site Program Office (SPO) estimates a paper-based record system will cost $9M through the year 2002, for the paper handling alone.

Although the costs comparing a TRIPS paper-based record system (that is, a new integrated data model for all data collected, but printed and signed reports) to the TRIPS with its digital signature system has not been studied, generic studies have been completed by other government agencies. One such study published by President Clinton's Management Council and its Electronic Processing Initiatives Committee (EPIC) compared a paper-based transaction model with the smart card-based digital signature transaction model. This study, as described in the Federal Smart Card Implementation Plan, noted that the processing costs of the paper-based model were $120 per transaction. The processing costs of the smart card-based digital signature model were $18 per transaction, a savings of 85 percent over the paper-based model.

Many areas of the government had been holding off large implementations pending resolution of Y2K issues, as well as vendor certification for Federal Information Processing Standards (FIPS), and for federal standards, such as Federal PKI, to solidify. As a result, even at this DOE site, PKI has not yet reached its level of importance. This is expected to change significantly over the next one to two years, since all of DOE is tentatively targeted for full PKI implementation by 2002–2003. Moreover, other security-related efforts, like virtual private networks (VPNs) and Internet Protocol Security (IPSec), are only increasing the pressure to establish site and government-wide PKI implementations.

As a consequence, the application of PKI is more important in terms of gaining acceptance to external customers such as the Environmental Protection Agency (EPA), the DOE, and individual states for the concept of electronic approval. The difference between PKI digital signature implementation and a simple approval implementation based on access control measures, such as login to system, has not significantly affected the internal customer or business process. INEEL is also looking to harvest new opportunities from TRIPS' unique PKI efforts on database structures.

Moving Forward

INEEL's overall approach to PKI is based largely on the business need for unique and very complex environmental regulations governing the data in the TRIPS application.

TRIPS and RWMC had significant support by management at INEEL because of public commitments to the State of Idaho by the DOE to process and ship transuranic waste offsite. Meeting those commitments required significant process automation and paperwork elimination. At the same time, regulatory requirements on characterization and approval processes by the EPA and individual states are increasingly becoming more complex. As a result, management was willing to invest significant resources to meet production goals.

In 1997, the DOE complex had not yet established its PKI standards, and INEEL had not implemented a site-wide PKI, so the Research and Development (R&D) staff on TRIPS had some flexibility to use best judgment on balancing anticipated government choices and industry standards.

Engineering and internal IT staffs will now cooperate on deploying PKI at INEEL over the next few years, while R&D will continue to develop other PKI and security-related products for DOE and others. Moreover, PKI now appears to be the favored alternative in many IT areas, both for INEEL and DOE, which are awaiting further guidance through government policies and standards.

Measuring Results

Business results for the PKI side of TRIPS are measured on the cost/efficiency savings achieved from "paperless" signatures. PKI is the primary reason why TRIPS electronic approval was accepted. Similarly, the business results for the entire TRIPS system will be based more on total RWMC process operations, which have a different set of drivers and commitments to DOE and the State of Idaho.

Over a three-year period, about 10 percent of the $15M TRIPS development and maintenance budget was invested in deploying PKI and the TRIPS electronic approval system. The TRIPS system provides significant process efficiency savings needed to meet RWMC production goals, which have not been explicitly quantified yet. Likewise, even though no financial return on investment (ROI) projections have been released, the benefits are such that RWMC operations could not meet production goals without TRIPS—it's simply a matter of survival.

The full-scale TRIPS system as a whole will virtually eliminate the need for storing and tracking 900,000 pages of signed reports every year. The INEEL Site Program Office (SPO) estimates that a paper-based record system, a subset of TRIPS functionality, will cost $9M through the year 2002, just for the paper handling alone. Separate PKI cost/benefit data has not been calculated, and all savings projected for TRIPS are based on the entire TRIPS application, which has re-work and integration savings embedded in the database application itself in addition to new functionality.

Assuredly, the Electronic Processing Initiatives Committee (EPIC) does estimate an 85-percent cost savings when comparing a generic paper-based transaction model with a generic smart card-based digital signature transaction model. It's important to note, however, that these models can be overly simplistic. The environmental programs at RWMC and the TRIPS system do have an extremely complex process to automate, and models cannot present true variations between different levels of application complexity. There is also an unknown portion of TRIPS savings due to the PKI digital signature usage in TRIPS.

Expected return on investment on the electronic approval portion of TRIPS only, plus related PKI research, is about $1.5M to date. Estimated paper savings at full production is $9M over five years. Since PKI for the database structures had to be developed internally at INEEL, most of the cost was in technology development.

Implementing the PKI

PKI is the choice technology because of the need to eliminate paper within the TRIPS system. Moreover, it also provides for authentication of both the signer and the data being signed.

Using the database to generate electronic, or paper reports, and signing these reports creates the potential for discontinuities between the data source, the database, and the signed data report. This weakens the integrity of the source data, which is used by many other levels and many other customers. No one person views the data through the same report, but they all eventually have to sign it.

However, the approval process for waste characterization and certification is extremely detailed and complex. There is not a single "document" that can be routed for the six or more signatures required for each data collection. Each signer combines the data from previous levels in a different way. These data complexities need to be solved using a relational database application with complex queries. INEEL had the expertise and the motivation to develop a new solution that combined PKI with traditional database, client-server applications, as well as sign data with structure. Additionally, non-repudiation of signed data was considered an important benefit. Non-repudiation, along with the use of certificate revocation lists (CRLs), enables signatures to be verified long after a user leaves the company.

The use of smart cards, through Public Key Cryptography Standards (PKCS), also added significant simplification to private key management of internally mobile users. PKCS #11 tokens were chosen for Smart Card interface, Lightweight Directory Access Protocol (LDAP), and International Telecommunication Standard (ITU) X.509 in the certificate authority (CA) and other areas. The RSA (Rivest Shamir Adleman) encryption algorithm was chosen to maximize compliance with the State of New Mexico digital signature statutes and common industry usage.

Compliance with FIPS-140, Security Requirements for Cryptographic Modules, was a concern, but back in 1997, the Smart Card interface was more important. As background, FIPS 140-1 validated cryptographic products' need to meet the provisions of the federal cryptographic security standard. Certification is part of the National Institute of Standards and Technology (NIST) Cryptographic Module Validation (CMV) Program that validates cryptographic modules for conformance with FIPS 140-1, which is the NIST standards document that provides for these requirements. Newer versions of the original vendor's certificate authority now meet various FIPS standards.

Policies

Where INEEL's RWMC Operations do require operating procedures for production systems, a certificate policy for TRIPS was created. The policy was largely based on the Model Certificate Policy, Preliminary Discussion Draft, November '97, available from the Federal PKI Task Force. Other than the certificate policy, no new security policies were added to the standard DOE and INEEL procedures already in place.

As far as a Certificate Practice Statement, while it may become more relevant in future implementations in other areas, it is currently less relevant for a specialized internal application such as TRIPS.

People

INEEL is a large, multiprogram laboratory with about 8000 technically diverse employees. Other than commercial off-the-shelf (COTS) purchases, all internal resources were used for the development work. While the digital signature effort did utilize a few new hires, it was mostly a mixture of the more senior staff at TRIPS.

Facility and Equipment

Two certificate authority servers were deployed, one for development and test, and one for production. Under the development server there are three CA databases: one each for development, test, and training. By TRIPS R5 in 2000, it's anticipated moving to one CA server, with all four certificate databases running on it: development, test, training, and production.

Both servers reside in separate, restricted buildings using standard DOE/INEEL security and access control, and are within computer rooms with additional access control measures. Each server has its own uninterruptible power supply (UPS) with automatic, stable-shutdown software, and diesel generators as part of the production facility. A new certificate authority will use external cryptography tokens to store the root private keys. By storing the private keys on tokens (PCMCIA cards with embedded encryption processors), the root key is never resident in either RAM or a temporary HD file, and all encryptions and signatures by CA are done on external crypto hardware. This prevents a hidden intruder from maliciously capturing a key in the server's temporary memory using search for "randomness" characteristics in keys.

Process

TRIPS release 2.0 was initially fielded in April 1998, with a trial implementation of digital signatures. Release 3.0 followed this in October 1998, which delivered all "Level 1" data collection digital signature roles required by RWMC. This included approximately 40 roles (a user can have multiple "roles") and the first four to five signatures for each data set. TRIPS R4.0 was completed in August and deployed in October 1999, implementing most of the "Level 2" signature process roles, which are the next two to three signatures for each "data set." R5.0 is scheduled for 2000, which will then complete the process roles identified by RWMC to date.

Phased deployment has permitted refinement of the implementation and allowed for important user feedback. However, it has been very complicated to manage on an integrated system like TRIPS, since it serves such a wide variety of personnel all waiting for their portion of the new system. Moreover, parallel management of electronic and paper records, or even parallel management of multiple information systems, all without digital signatures, is extremely complicated, along with designing the migrations of historical data that lack digital signature integrity.

The biggest hurdle to the rollout of digital signatures on this database application has been the management of test data during development. The embedded cross-verification mechanisms that detect unintended or unexpected changes to database values at different stages in the workflow, while an extremely useful feature in production, greatly slows integration testing in development. Developers and testers can't "cheat" the system and set up falsified data for even the most limited test purposes. All data has to be valid from the lowest to the highest signature levels for a given data set to permit further signatures on it. If a piece of data is invalidated due to a design change during development, all previous signatures on the data elements involved have to be re-done before additional work can continue. It shows that the system works as intended, but greatly increased the level of effort to test changes to even the most basic functions.

Timeline

INEEL took just 17 months from conception to its first PKI production rollout:

Nov 96	Digital signature consideration
Jan–Mar 97	Criteria development / TRIPS architectural design
Aug 97	Vender selection
Dec 97	TRIPS development implementation
Apr 98	First release in TRIPS production, TRIPS R2.0
Sep 98	TRIPS R3.0 enhancements
Jul 99	TRIPS R4.0 expansion
Apr 00	TRIPS R5.0 expansion

Issues and Other Specifics

For TRIPS, the only other alternative considered was approvals based solely on database access controls (meaning user login) and approval status flags. This would have greatly simplified the implementation, but would provide no data verification functions in a complex process of approvals and data re-work. It was also not clear whether this simplistic approval model would be accepted to replace the previously signed work package data, since there is a significant political and legal liability associated with the waste characterization data.

Of course, the preliminary acceptance of internal electronic signatures by the DOE sites in Idaho and New Mexico also tilted the scales in favor of full digital signature implementation. More importantly, INEEL wanted to develop a new technology in this area to support other future R&D efforts.

Besides the new functionality delivered with TRIPS, several legacy databases had their data migrated to the new TRIPS data structures. From a database standpoint, the migrations were significant efforts involving data collected on the waste containers for over 30 years. From a PKI signature perspective, the migration date represents a point where dual signed and electronic records ended, and a single set of signed electronic records began. Because of potential integrity problems inherent in dual data copy systems (electronic and paper copies are different), and TRIPS' requirement for all electronic data to be signed, all data migrated into TRIPS was signed by both engineers performing the migration, during the migration, and the "owners" of that data, after opportunity for comparisons with other paper reports, that did not have all the final approvals at the time of migration.

An initial 75 production users were issued certificates, along with 50 for development, testing, and training IDs through TRIPS release 4. An anticipated 75 to 150 new production users are planned over next two years. Administrators also hold two sets of certificates: one normal application certificate stored on TRIPS smart card, and one administrative certificate to communicate with the certificate authority using SSL client certificate authentication to issue new user certificates. Protocols used for certificate management include LDAP 3.0 for storing X.509 certificates, and PKCS#11 for token interface to smart cards. No extension fields are used beyond standard X.509 entries for storing of authorization information.

One large CRL, which resides as part of the CA database, exists for each of the four certificate authorities. Updates are done as certificates are actually revoked, which is infrequent, due to the stable population of users. CRL performance has not been an issue with such a small user certificate set.

CRL checking also happens automatically, as part of TRIPS software "behind the scenes" to the user, except if a verification error is detected. The CRL does not include any other third parties.

Achieving Expectations

While maintaining strong signature cross-verification functions for historical signatures against current data stored in the database has been more work than originally envisioned, the implementation basically matches the original plan. Of course, this may also be attributed to the phased implementation of the TRIPS application where the data model is revised at each major release.

. . . .

Key Points

TOP 3 LESSONS LEARNED

➤ Certificate expiration times and policies for both users and server certificates (SSL, root, CA certificates) need to be well thought out. Expiration of a server root certificate during peak production times is not necessarily a good thing, especially if production administrators don't know about it!

➤ Early versions of Microsoft Internet Explorer and other Microsoft PKI modules did not always work well with the more open standard Internet implementations. Experiment with Microsoft IE too much, and you have to reload your non-Microsoft PKI software.

➤ PKI technologies are just now starting to mature into general-purpose, production-quality systems, and there are lots more opportunities for applications of PKI than just e-mail and flat document signatures.

TOP 3 CRITICAL SUCCESS FACTORS

➤ Customer support of application effort and frequent informal user evaluations in addition to the more formal design reviews.

➤ Many months of thought and architectural and detailed designs combined with rapid prototype experiments to guide details (Gestalt round-trip engineering).

➤ Open standards (LDAP, PKCS, x.509) and availability of free source code.

WOULD DO DIFFERENTLY

More emphasis on user-friendly error messages and other administrative tools to assist the people who have to administer the production system. Although signature/verification/configuration errors do not occur that frequently, the number of production people familiar with PKI and the TRIPS electronic approval structures to do basic diagnosis is limited.

MOST HELPFUL IN GETTING PKI UP AND RUNNING

➤ The use of smart cards has greatly simplified the management of private keys. It is an important technology in applications like TRIPS where users move across multiple secure stations, distributed over multiple computers, buildings, and sites. (There are also security advantages to keeping the private key on an external token, not stored in computer memory.)

➤ "Digital Signature Guidelines: Legal Infrastructure for Certification Authorities and Secure Electronic Commerce," American Bar Association, ISBN 1-57073-250-1.

➤ Model Certificate Policy, Preliminary Discussion Draft, November 1997, Federal PKI Task Force.

➤ PKCS #11 Standard, RSA Laboratories.

Findings

PKI was INEEL's choice not only because of the need to eliminate paper, but to provide the necessary authentication of both the signer and the data being signed. What INEEL is doing presents an excellent example of layering PKI on top of existing business processes. Besides the need for online trust to mimic real-world trust, INEEL's solution is being utilized to implement the business rules as well.

Disclaimer

"References herein to any specific commercial product, process, or service by trade name, trademark, manufacturer, or otherwise, does not necessarily constitute or imply its endorsement, recommendation, or favoring by the U.S. Government or any agency thereof."

CHAPTER 17

U.S. Patent and Trademark Office (USPTO)

B e more responsive, improve service, and provide better access. Meanwhile, start cutting down on that annual $36 million dollar publishing cost. Difficult, yes. Impossible? Not for the USPTO. In fact, it's aiming at capturing honors for "best practice" for assurance in electronic commerce. With 17,000 registered patent practitioners, the USPTO has a unique set of customers to satisfy. When it comes to patents and trademarks, the USPTO has to know who they're dealing with online, be able to do it confidentially, and do it in a trustworthy manner. To meet these business requirements, they chose PKI technology.

Background

The USPTO's mission is to administer laws relating to patents and trademarks, and promote industrial and technical progress in the United States. The USPTO provides inventors and entrepreneurs with the protection and encouragement they need to take their inventive and creative ideas to the marketplace. Primary services provided by USPTO include processing patents and trademarks, and disseminating patent and trademark information.

In recognizing the increasing importance of intellectual property protection in a global and technology-based economy, the USPTO established two strategic goals designed to focus agency priorities to accomplish this vision:

➤ Play a leadership role in intellectual property rights policy, including trade-related intellectual property issues for which we have responsibility.

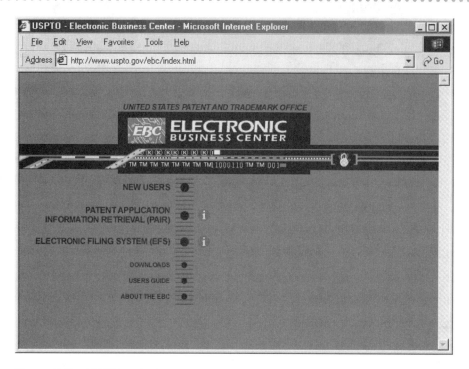

Figure 17.1 USPTO web site.

➤ Provide USPTO customers with the highest level of quality and service in all aspects of the USPTO operations.

To meet the challenges of the future, the USPTO has developed an ambitious strategic agenda to help position the agency to operate more successfully and efficiently in the twenty-first century. An especially important component of USPTO's agenda is to leverage information technology. In particular, this agenda is enabling the USPTO to:

➤ Enhance current business through electronic commerce

➤ Maintain current business production processing

➤ Meet the legal requirements of:

    ➤ American Inventors Protection Act (AIPA)

    ➤ Public Law 106-113

    ➤ Madrid Protocol Implementation Act

Additionally, USPTO's agenda allows for new capability by migrating automated information systems to operate on an open system information technology infrastructure. Ultimately, this will lead to reductions in patent and trademark cycle times, elimination of paper-based processing, and evolution of the businesses to electronic commerce and an electronic workplace.

Under the Omnibus Budget Reconciliation Act (OBRA) of 1990, the USPTO began operating more like a private business in 1991, providing products and services of value to customers in exchange for fees that are used to fully fund operations. Moreover, in March 2000, AIPA made USPTO a performance-based organization. This made the USPTO a results-driven organization for delivering the best possible services to its customers. It also makes USPTO accountable for results by having clear objectives, specific measurable goals, customer service standards, and targets for improved performance. In exchange for this commitment to accountability, the USPTO is granted managerial flexibilities to achieve these goals and operate more like a business with greater autonomy over its budget, hiring, and procurement.

Business Requirements

Confidence in the USPTO's electronic information and supporting information technology infrastructure is essential for creating a trusted environment so that the USPTO can exchange sensitive data electronically with customers and national and international business partners. Implementation of Public Key Infrastructure (PKI) technologies is a prerequisite to build the trusted environment needed to successfully implement electronic commerce.

The PKI provides the security services that are vital for USPTO e-commerce initiatives: confidentiality, authentication, and integrity and non-repudiation. The product of a patent application filing and examination is a legal record that may be introduced into later administrative or judicial proceeding. The integrity of this record is crucial and central to USPTO's business function. PKI implementations will benefit the USPTO by assuring the authenticity and integrity of the patent record, along with other pertinent USPTO created records.

The USPTO must maintain the confidentiality of pending patent applications. The Patent Application Information Retrieval system (PAIR) was deployed to enable confidentiality by establishing an encrypted session from the user's desktop to the USPTO server. PAIR facilitates cost avoidance for both USPTO and its customers by replacing a time-consuming process with secure authenticated electronic access by using digital certificates to authenticate access to patent application information. Now a production system, PAIR is the result of the initial PKI that started as a pilot.

The use of a PKI promises improved service delivery in response to USPTO customer expectations. Since 1994, the USPTO applicant and attorney community has asked for better access to patent application status information. Improving responsiveness for answering status questions is one of USPTO's Customer Service Commitments that are measured annually. The 1999 customer satisfaction rate was only 38 percent for this commitment. PAIR was implemented to address this need through convenient and prompt transactions over the Internet, while meeting the requirements for authenticity and confidentiality. By contrast, non-automated status information requests are by letter or telephone and are time consuming for both the customer and the USPTO, so the implementation of PAIR will save substantial time for both USPTO and its customers.

With full production planned for February 2001, the USPTO will expand the pilot to further include more participants and additional types of transactions.

A second effort, the Electronic Filing System (EFS), holds the greatest potential for significant cost avoidance. EFS supports the authoring and authenticated, secure filing of patent applications. Now in pilot phase, EFS makes use of both encryption and digital signatures to preserve the confidentiality, authenticity, integrity, and non-repudiation of patent application data submissions.

Together, the PAIR and EFS are the driving force for choosing PKI technology. The need for the security services that PKI provides also became more important when the American Inventors Protection Act required the USPTO to publish some patent applications 18 months after filing, but also permitted the reduction of parts of such applications in some instances. With such time-sensitive activity at stake, this process could only be accomplished by relying on electronic transactions supported by a PKI. Starting at the end of November 2000, electronic filing will be required to take advantage of some of the provisions of the AIPA.

Moreover, the product of a patent of trademark application filing and examination is a legal record that may be introduced into administrative or judicial proceeding. The integrity of this record is vital and central to the USPTO's mission. Implementing PKI benefits the USPTO by assuring the authenticity and integrity of the patent record and the other records that the USPTO creates.

As a result, PKI was identified as a security "best practice" for assurance in electronic commerce by both the commercial and Federal sectors. The Patent Law and Patent Cooperation Treaties also require that patent applications be preserved in confidence. Implementing PKI indicates that the USPTO is making a major commitment to preserving the integrity and confidentiality of its transactions, as well as identifying the parties to an electronic transaction. Confidentiality and inventorship, while important to all USPTO patent customers, is of particular sensitivity to the independent inventor community that has great concerns about application confidentiality.

Lastly, an enterprise PKI helps to meet the information assurance requirements established in the May 1998 Presidential Decision Directive 63 "Critical Infrastructure Protection."

Business Impact

The implementation of the PKI is essential to moving the paper-based patent prosecution process to an electronic one. The use of a PKI promises improved service delivery in response to articulated USPTO customer expectations. Based on customer input, the USPTO established a customer service commitment in 1995 to provide applicants with the status of their application within 30 days.

In January 2000, PTO customers submitted nearly 24,000 queries to obtain the status of their patent application—which means that the PTO did not have to prepare 24,000 post cards to send to patent applicants with the current status of their application. This also enables the USPTO to reduce the "30 day" customer service commitment for patent application status to seconds.

The PKI provides the basis for implementing secure e-commerce solutions for both our internal and external processes as we move from a primarily paper-based system to an electronic one. The USPTO PKI will ultimately support secure and authenticated communications and commerce with the USPTO patent applicant community, Registered Patent Attorneys and Patent Agents, international business partners including other Intellectual Property Offices, Patent and Trademark Depository Libraries, USPTO employees and support contractors, and others with whom the USPTO does business that requires guarantees of authenticity and confidentiality.

Currently, it costs $196 to prepare each patent granted for publication. Much of this cost can be avoided by receiving patent applications in electronic form. For example, if USPTO processes as little as 10 percent of the 300,000 patent applications electronically, it can achieve $58.8M in cost savings alone. The projected savings easily offset the $4 million investment for deploying PKI and the electronic mail room.

The USPTO PKI is being implemented as part of an integrated information technology infrastructure to provide for both internal and external uses of public key technology. This enables the USPTO to have a single, highly scaleable security infrastructure to support both internal and external applications regardless of risk level. The implementation of a single PKI will provide security and authentication for a wide range of business applications, rather than providing separate, stove-piped security solutions for individual applications.

The USPTO enterprise PKI will provide a single integrated set of enhanced security services that will be relied upon by current and developing systems. The PKI will serve the needs of developing systems, as well as provide a path for migration of legacy systems.

PKI has been accepted as the security technology of choice by the USPTO's three largest trading partners: the Japanese and European Patent Offices, and the International Bureau of the Patent Cooperation Treaty at the World Intellectual Property Office in Geneva, Switzerland.

This forms the basis for moving the paper-based processes that often involve confidential patent information to secure electronic processes. This also creates a driving force to investigate and resolve the interoperability issues between the differing PKI vendor choices of the Offices.

The PKI builds upon the existing trust that the USPTO customers have in the Office to maintain the confidentiality of their patent applications and related data. It promises to be the basis for meeting customer service commitments, decreasing the time it takes to examine and issue a patent or register a trademark, while assuring the customer that a high-security solution was implemented to protect the customer's intellectual property in transit and while in USPTO custody.

Subject to budget constraints in the next three years, the USPTO anticipates developing PKI-based security services for at least 12 automated information technology infrastructure systems and services:

- Patent Application Capture and Review
- Patent Cooperation Treaty (PCT) Operations Workflow and Electronic Review
- International Priority Document Exchange
- Office Action and Correspondence System
- Tools for Electronic Application Management
- Enterprise-wide Login
- Patent and Trademark Assignment System
- Patent and Trademark Depository Libraries
- Human Resource Information System
- Revenue Accounting Management
- Trademark Work-At-Home
- Patent Work-At-Home

Moving Forward

The 1995 USPTO strategic vision was for business to be carried on via the Internet, in which electronic information would be captured or created once and reused through the business process. PKI provided the necessary authentication, integrity, and confidentiality that was required by law, and thus helped realize the vision.

Business management approached the USPTO Executive Council, which approves USPTO enterprise initiatives. The Chief Information Officer as head of IT management recognized the match of the services provided by an enterprise PKI and the security needs of the USPTO Patent business process.

The Patent Act and the Trademark Act establish the basis for domestic patent and trademark practice, while the Patent Cooperation Treaty and the Madrid Protocol establish the basis for international patent and trademark practice.

The American Inventors Protection Act (AIPA) was signed into law on November 29, 1999. Title IV of the legislation is intended to minimize the delay of disclosure of technology contained in patent applications. This section of the law requires the publishing of patent applications 18 months after the effective filing date for applications filed, or expected to be filed, in a foreign patent office, while permitting the applicant to redact certain information. The legislation applies to utility and plant patent applications.

In addition to the Patent and Trademark Law, other federal regulations and guidance documents influenced the strategic information technology planning and implementation process. These laws, regulations, and policy directives are intended to improve congressional decision-making, and the efficiency, effectiveness, and public accountability of federal agencies.

➤ *Do Business Electronically*

The *Government Paperwork Elimination Act* enacted in 1998 instructs Federal agencies, by October 21, 2003, to allow individuals or entities that deal with the agencies the option to submit information or transact with the agency electronically, and to maintain records electronically, when practicable. The Act specifically states that electronic records and their related electronic signatures are not to be denied legal effect, validity, or enforceability merely because they are in electronic form, and specifically sanctions Federal government use of a range of electronic signature alternatives.

➤ *Improve Service Delivery*

The *Government Performance and Results Act* of 1993 establishes performance reporting as part of an integrated planning, budgeting, management, and performance assessment system. GPRA emphasizes improved service delivery by requiring agencies to focus on results, service quality, and customer satisfaction.

➤ *Integrate Information Technology*

The Information Technology Management Reform Act of 1996, referred to as the Clinger-Cohen Act, provides for the integration of the information technology management process with the processes for making budget, financial, and program management decisions. Annually, an agency prepares a report, to be included in the budget submission to Congress, on the progress in achieving the goals.

➤ *Manage IT Investments*

Referred to as the "Raines Rules," the Office of Management and Budget issued guidance in October 1996 to agencies on how to manage information technology investments in keeping with the provisions of the GPRA and Clinger-Cohen Act.

➤ *Develop an IT Architecture*

The Office of Management and Budget issued guidance in June 1997 (M-97-16) to agencies on the development and implementation of Information Technology Architectures.

➤ *Plan and Manage*

The Office of Management and Budget issued the Capital Programming Guide to provide a process for portfolio analysis, risk management, planning, performance management, budgeting, and other related activities.

Additionally, the USPTO PKI was designed to meet as many applicable technology industry standards as possible, which included:

➤ X.509, version 3 certificates

➤ X.509 version 2 certificate revocation lists

➤ Public Key Infrastructure X.509 Certificate Management Protocol (PKIX-CMP)

➤ Public Key Cryptography Standard (PKCS) #7 and PKCS #10 certificate request/receipt protocol

➤ Fully compliant X.500 directories

➤ Lightweight Directory Access Protocol (LDAP) version 2

➤ Federal Information Processing Standard (FIPS) 140-1

➤ Support for Secure Multipurpose Internet Mail Extensions (S/MIME)

Additionally, the current efforts of the Federal PKI Working Group were considered during the design of the infrastructure.

Measuring Results

It's difficult to calculate a return on investment for building an enterprise security architecture. The USPTO at any one time has a huge quantity of intellectual property in its possession, and the loss of the information could be valued at many millions of dollars. USPTO also believes that PKI is a strategic asset to provide for enterprise security services for internal and external customers, and changes in the patent laws have made e-commerce solutions necessary for the survival of the business process of filing, examining and publishing patent documents.

Currently, the USPTO spends $36 million annually to publish the granted patents, with the principal cost being $196 to put each patent application into publishable form. Receiving the text from the patent applicant in electronic form will substantially save money by reducing the time spent preparing the documents for publication and increasing the quality by reducing the errors introduced in text capture. The USPTO plans to move the publication of its patent documents to a fully electronic one to reduce this cost. Consequently, if as few as 10 percent of the 300,000 patent applications are filed electronically, the cost avoidance will more than equal the USPTO PKI related investment.

The $4 million USPTO has invested in PKI and the electronic mail room for the transmission, receipt, validation, and acknowledgment of correspondence represents an investment of approximately 0.4 percent of the USPTO annual budget, or 0.15 percent per year spread over a three-year period (see Table 17.1).

USPTO believes this investment will yield substantial savings and improved service delivery. For example, when a patent application is filed containing nucleotide or amino acid sequences, it may contain thousands of pages of sequence information. The physical mass of paper is difficult to maintain and use. The implementation of EFS permits the electronic filing of these sequence listings in place of the paper as part of the legal patent application record, and saves the customer and USPTO the time and expense of providing a voluminous paper copy. These PKI services permit the USPTO to hold only the electronic file as the official record. Another area of savings is due in part to the "Intellectual Property and Communications Omnibus Reform Act of

Table 17.1 Overall Budget to Deploy PKI over a Three-Year Period

	FY 1999	FY 2000	FY 2001 (ESTIMATED)
HW and infrastructure	$1,055,630	$0	$0
PKI software licenses and maintenance	$700,000	$1,426,810	~$320,000
Engineering support	$839,060	$60,000	~$150,000
Totals	$2,594,690	$1,486,810	~$470,000

Note: These figures include both the PKI and electronic mail room costs.

1999," which was signed into law in November 1999 and requires publishing of the filed U.S. applications in specified circumstances, but permits redaction of portions of the applications. The submission of applications in electronic form will substantially reduce costs for printing and redaction of these patent applications.

Implementing the PKI

The primary objective in establishing an enterprise PKI is to address all internal and external USPTO enterprise requirements for security, non-repudiation authentication, and integrity in its electronic commerce and electronic workplace initiatives. As such, the enterprise PKI will provide a uniform way for the USPTO to engage in secure communication with applicants, the public, and other Intellectual Property Offices. A second objective is to implement a PKI that will address enterprise-wide (as opposed to single isolated stovepipe applications) needs. Confidence in the USPTO's electronic information and supporting information technology infrastructure is essential for creating a trusted environment whereby the USPTO can exchange sensitive data electronically with customers and business partners. Implementation of Public Key Infrastructure technologies can help build the trusted environment needed to successfully implement electronic commerce.

Since a patent is basically a contract between the USPTO and the patent applicant, the capability to do non-repudiation was an important factor in choosing PKI. This becomes more important when the official record becomes electronic in the next few years.

Moreover, the patent law and patent cooperation treaty also imposes the need for guarantees in electronic communication of patent information, and PKI provides the best technical approach for meeting these needs. In brief, the USPTO needs to be able to:

➢ Preserve the confidentiality of information exchanges

➢ Ensure the integrity of patent application submissions, since the content of a patent application and related communication defines the patent holder's rights

➢ Authenticate who USPTO is dealing with electronically, since the patent law restricts who may access information relating to a pending patent application

Password-based systems and Personal Identification Numbers (PIN) were considered but rejected, due to the known vulnerabilities of these systems. In addition to the need to dedicate resources for ongoing user support to deal with forgotten or mislaid passwords, there were also the potential vulnerabilities of poor authentication guarantees in password-based systems or a PIN.

Fortunately, the USPTO was able to gain experience early on with the completion of two Federal PKI Steering Committee demonstration projects over the past three years. These projects were able to demonstrate the use of PKI to provide security and authentication services in the filing of patent applications and in the international exchange of confidential patent application information.

The USPTO then conducted a market study in February 1999 to evaluate various vendors against the criteria developed from USPTO requirements. The requirements and criteria are detailed in the USPTO document "Preliminary Public Key Infrastructure Market Survey (updated). Keep in mind that since this survey was completed, both strategy and product offerings by many vendors may have changed considerably, to include mergers and acquisitions.

Policies

Implementing PKI led the USPTO to restructure the e-commerce security architecture to center around PKI-based solutions and to easily allow for new e-commerce systems as necessary without requiring major firewall policy redesign. It also required the development and implementation of new procedures. In particular, policy was changed to permit real-time access to internal data in a secure manner.

Where USPTO is the only relying party, and the PKI is a closed system, it did not create a certificate policy. Certificates are granted only to individuals according to USPTO identity proofing procedures. The complex mixture of legal and technical information in a certificate policy would not add value to the existing trust relationship between the USPTO and its external customers. Nor would the policy fit into the official System Development Methodology required for the development and maintenance of its automated information systems.

The essential document in a PKI is the subscriber agreement, which is a signed contract between the subscriber and the certificate authority, including the identity proofing requirements for subscribers and the limits of use of and reliance on the PKI.

USPTO did, however, create a PKI Services Manual that details the operation of the PKI and serves the function of a Certificate Practice Statement. It provides the process and the details of granting and maintaining certificates in support of USPTO business practices, and includes a subscriber agreement.

People

Existing personnel are providing the PKI registration authority and certificate authority services with plans to increase staff as needed. The existing division of responsibilities between the USPTO Network Operations Division and Information Security

Services Division also lends itself well to the separation of functions sought after in a PKI environment.

Facility and Equipment

Staging was done mostly in the USPTO development lab that is separate from the production facility. A total of 16 servers were deployed, with 4 used for development. The remaining 12 operate the PKI, which is located in a secure facility on existing USPTO premises.

Process

USPTO followed its system Life Cycle Management methodology (LCM) to develop and implement its PKI. The LCM establishes management policies, procedures, and practices governing the initiation, definition, design, development, deployment, operation, maintenance, enhancement, and retirement of automated information systems at the USPTO.

Timeline

It took USPTO just three months from the time it finished developing its master plan to deploying its first PKI pilot, and an additional 15 months for its first deployment for internal operations:

Jan 99	Develop PKI master plan
Sep 99	Identify required PKI services for Individual Automated Information Systems (AIS) and infrastructure projects
May 99	Train staff
May 99	Deploy PKI hardware, software
Jun 99	Develop PKI services manual
Jul 99	Pilot Patent Application Information Retrieval (PAIR) system
Sep 99	Pilot Electronic Filing System (EFS)
Mar 00	Develop migration strategy and plans for legacy systems
Aug 00	Deploy PKI for internal operations
Aug 00	Test for interoperability and cross-certification with trilateral offices

Issues and Other Specifics

Over 750 certificates were issued through June 2000 to registered patent attorneys, agents, and independent inventors. With some 17,000 patent practitioners registered with USPTO, the USPTO expects to issue between 6000 and 10,000 certificates by year-end. This is based primarily on the overwhelmingly positive response by users and the express interest of patent practitioners.

Recognizing a business reality in the legal profession, USPTO permits the use of the certificate by an employee of the patent attorney or agent for limited purposes. However, the patent practitioner remains legally responsible for the use. To obtain a digital certificate, identity-proofing requirements vary. For independent inventors, presentation of two forms of identification to the USPTO or to a notary is needed. For patent attorneys and agents, identity records and signature specimens, which the USPTO keeps for each party, are used. For employees of the patent attorney or agent, the attorney or agent verifies identity. The client software on the user's computer protects the private keys and, at the user's option, the private key and certificate may be transferred to a smart card or other token. USPTO also places the encryption key in escrow.

To issue certificates, the USPTO created two certificate authorities (CAs), with one focused on employees, and the other for external customers and business partners. USPTO operates the CA directory and application servers in security zones protected by firewalls and further secured by versions of compartmented mode workstation software. There are both hot and cold backups for the CAs in case of failure. Equally important, the CA's private keys are protected using commercially available technology for physical and network security. The two CAs are cross-certified and also incorporate a system of shadow directories so that they can be easily restored in event of failure or attack. A sophisticated X.500 directory infrastructure supports USPTO's high reliability requirements with additional support for Lightweight Directory Access Protocol (LDAP). Other protocols deployed include PKIX-CMP, PKCS 7, and PKCS 10.

The need to manage authorization separately from authentication was somewhat of a surprise to developers. While PKI can provide for assuring identity, there's also a need to map that identity and access to other permissions and authorization. The major challenge in PAIR was to provide real-time access to internal data, which is stored in a critical internal legacy system. Applications that were modified to utilize PKI services currently manage their own authorization information and maintain their own access control lists. An enterprise-wide login was also implemented to simplify management of multiple authorizations for internal users who will migrate to applications served by PKI. There are no plans to carry authorization information in the certificate extension fields.

As part of the standard software, USPTO is using multiple certificate revocation lists (CRLs), which are accessed via CRL distribution points. CRLs presently reside in the directory, with updates being done on a 24-hour basis. CRL checking is automatically deployed. Only USPTO certificate revocation information in included in the CRL. Lastly, while Online Certificate Status Protocol (OSCP) is also available in the product architecture, it's not being used.

Achieving Expectations

Like most organizations that have deployed complex information technology (IT) projects, USPTO assumed that implementing PKI would have been quicker and cheaper than it actually turned out to be. For one, USPTO initially expected to follow other agencies in implementing PKI secured transactions, but found themselves assuming a leadership position. USPTO soon had to recognize and resolve policy problems and issues such as identity-proofing strategies and requirements, clearances, and privacy and paperwork reduction act notices.

The major change to the proposed implementation schedule was an acceleration of the planned date for full implementation of electronic filing of patent applications to February of 2001, due to the requirement of the American Inventors Protection Act of 1999 for publication of redacted versions of many patent applications 18 months after filing. The need for time-critical authenticated secure transactions between the USPTO and its customers involving the patent application text to be published cannot be implemented without electronic filing.

Moreover, USPTO also had to determine the technical details of implementing an enterprise PKI for both external and internal users as part of an overall security infrastructure. It soon learned the need to market and educate both internal and external customers on basic computer security practices and the value of PKI to support e-commerce. This meant explaining how PKI provides for the necessary security and authentication services such as digital signatures to support the patent business process, as well as future automation of the patent examination and publication process.

For example, the internal user community had difficulty understanding that the digital certificate was intended to be bound to a single external user identity, and that identity proofing was necessary for external users to establish a strong link between the human identity and the digital certificate to support authentication and non-repudiation. There was an initial resistance to change in that too much emphasis was initially placed on the complex nature of how cryptosystems function. Of course, this left many with the impression that PKI was just too difficult to really work. To dispel initial resistance by internal users, it meant demonstrating that the browser plug-in was easy to install for end users, and that PKI is an underlying basis for doing business. Educated on the benefits of the services provided by PKI, these users have become strong advocates.

There was also a tendency to avoid reengineering existing processes and exploring the flexibility in interpreting the patent law and regulations to take better advantage of the PKI services. The business, legal, and IT communities often miscommunicated. They viewed the same processes from very different perspectives, and terminology such as "audit trail" and "digital signature" often carried different meanings for the different communities. Intervention by upper management helped break any logjams that developed.

Conversely, external users appeared to have a greater acceptance based on the existing trust in the USPTO, and the improvement of securing their business process that interactions with PKI would offer. However, where many large law firms and corporations have already implemented their own firewall and security solutions, USPTO discovered that changes in firewall rules were required. USPTO also found that many patent application files exceeded the file size limits of the PKI vendor software that was soon corrected in cooperation with the vendor. Growing USPTO's end-user base also meant rising costs, since licensing agreements required payments for each certificate, along with other transaction elements such as time stamping.

Despite these obstacles, USPTO's PKI is demonstrating success. There is apparent high customer demand for PKI secured access to patent status information, and great interest in electronic filing of patent applications. It's become a leader in the international patent community regarding PKI.

Key Points

TOP 3 LESSONS LEARNED

➤ Need for close cooperation and mutual understanding among the business, legal, and IT functions

➤ Need to fit smoothly into our customers' business processes

➤ Importance of electronic record management issues in the overall system design

TOP 3 CRITICAL SUCCESS FACTORS

➤ Customer acceptance (ease of use)

➤ Satisfy legal requirements for confidentiality, authentication, integrity, and non-repudiation

➤ Provide a cost-effective security infrastructure to conduct business with our external customers and business partners.

WOULD DO DIFFERENTLY

➤ It would have been better if circumstances permitted USPTO to have waited some years before starting the implementation. To meet the USPTO's strategic business goals, it required them to be on the leading edge. While there was sample theory written about how to implement PKI, there was no validated body of experience to draw upon in their effort.

MOST HELPFUL IN GETTING PKI UP AND RUNNING

➤ The policy work of the Government of Canada in their PKI implementation for providing the model that served as the starting point for our Subscriber Agreement; and the separation of functions in running the USPTO PKI.

➤ Identity proofing strategies developed by the Social Security Administration and the Passport Office provided the basis for USPTO requirements for independent inventors. The USPTO System Development Methodology for providing a path for developing the PKI system.

➤ Assistance from the vendor and experienced contractors proved to be invaluable.

➤ Guidance manuals and training provided by the vendor.

LEAST HELPFUL IN GETTING PKI UP AND RUNNING

➤ A PKI secures the business process of an organization, and the implementation of a PKI must recognize the organizational IT system development methodology and the internal business practices of both the organization and the customer.

➤ USPTO found that many of the model documents or strategies were lacking in providing guidance regarding the electronic record-keeping needs for a PKI. The focus of much of the legal writing on the topic of PKI is on the topic of liability in the private sector. The problems posed to the liability models by the legally limited liability of the Federal Government have largely been ignored. The other missing element was any guidance or body of writings regarding the implementation of secure systems of electronic records for the management of the records of the PKI, and the PKI facilitated e-commerce transactions over time.

Findings

The USPTO expects to have almost 60 percent of patent practitioners using digital certificates before 2001. That would be an achievement in itself, but there are more ways to measure success. With 300,000 patents filed every year, if these practitioners file only 10 percent of that number online, the USPTO's financial investment will have paid off. At the same time, the USPTO is reducing costs and improving service. Given the highly positive response to date, the USPTO is also getting closer to meeting its customers' goals of better service and reaching its own goals for "best practice."

CHAPTER 18

Ruesch

With so much at stake in the financial services industry, Ruesch believes that without a PKI, there's little possibility of business-to-business e-commerce. It's also finding that from a security standpoint, doing business online using a PKI-enabled solution is now more preferable than calls coming in over the telephone.

Background

Ruesch International, a financial institution specializing in international payments and related services, manages more than $10 billion in cross-border transactions a year. As a leading provider of foreign exchange risk management strategies, it monitors currency markets for over 30,000 clients worldwide. Ruesch maintains offices in Atlanta, Boston, Chicago, Los Angeles, New York, and Prague, and operates trading departments at its headquarters in Washington as well as London and Zurich.

Business Requirements

Since its start in 1980, Ruesch's mission as a financial institution is to provide business-to-business global payment services and risk management tools to corporations. In 1994, Ruesch began development of its plan to launch its e-business—what it called its "electronic client interaction proposition."

Ruesch was well motivated to develop its e-business, because its competitors, mostly banks, started to offer electronic services that Ruesch itself could not deliver. As business

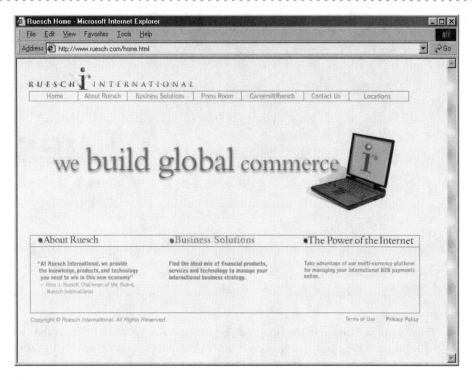

Figure 18.1   Ruesch Web site.

use of the Internet started surging in 1996, Ruesch launched its "proof of concept" project to prove that the Internet, and the World Wide Web, could be used for high-value financial transactions.

With successful results in hand, it began a multiple stage approach to:

➤ Transform Ruesch into an e-business

➤ Offer an e-commerce proposition to its clients

➤ Be at the forefront of Internet-based financial services

Business Impact

According to Ruesch, the importance of PKI can be calculated in an easy manner because of the following equation:

No PKI = No B2B commerce

Simply put, without a PKI, there would be no business-to-business (B2B) commerce. For Ruesch, there's just too much at stake in the financial services industry to ignore it.

To be sure, PKI provides a very strong argument to its client companies that transactions are secure in a manner that no competitor can match. It's a winning advantage.

Indeed, security is critical for financial transactions. A financial institution such as Ruesch cannot exist if it does not have a relationship based on trust with its clients. Conducting business online requires even a higher level of trust. For Ruesch, PKI is the essential component in its online venture that protects that trust.

Ruesch also found itself leading the way in its PKI vision and implementation for its business partners and clients. Since it was at the forefront, Ruesch didn't have to change internal processes to accommodate external requirements of others.

There's also a much greater awareness of security issues within Ruesch. With PKI, Ruesch realized that online transactions are actually more secure than telephone or fax transactions in many aspects. For example, Ruesch now believes that it can authenticate users with more accuracy when they're online with PKI than it can with a voice on the telephone. As a result, Ruesch now concludes that online PKI-enabled solutions are preferable, especially from a security standpoint, to "offline" solutions.

Moving Forward

As a financial institution, all employees, not just executive management, realize the importance of security both online and offline. As such, there was never a question of management support. Early in the planning stage for PKI, a group of executives and managers met to:

➤ Determine the policies that would guide its e-business efforts

➤ Assess current policies, business and security, for potential changes

➤ Focus on the policy issues in how the site would operate

Moreover, it began its discussions with the following proposition:

> "Ruesch will use "state of the art" security technologies in order to secure the resulting transactions and to ensure that the client and the transaction information would not be compromised in any way."

Developments that Ruesch continues to watch are the efforts to make digital signatures legally binding. Such legislation could open up additional opportunities for Ruesch. Its e-commerce site, RueschLINK, would be ready to take advantage of the situation since it is already in compliance with regulations issued by the U.S. Department of Treasury, various state banking commissions, and regulatory agencies of three other countries.

For example, because its digital certificates are S/MIME compatible, Ruesch plans to use signed e-mail to interact electronically with its clients. Deploying this capability would guarantee its clients that the e-mail message was not altered in transit, a key point in any financial communication.

Measuring Results

What's it worth to a financial institution to guarantee its financial transactions? While Ruesch processes more than $10 billion in transactions a year, it invested just $100,000 to implement and deploy PKI as part of its business model.

Ruesch suggests that it may be impossible to make an ROI argument for deployment of PKI in any B2B context. Although RueschLINK accounts for only 15 percent of its activity, the percentage is rapidly increasing each month. Within a year, it's expected that RueschLINK will grow 50 to 75 percent of its total transactional volume, easily justifying the investment. Ruesch further discovered that the majority of its PKI deployment costs are for supporting its internal staff and clients.

Ruesch looks at PKI as a business enabler, with risk avoidance being a consequence of using certificates. To be sure, Ruesch has found that PKI is enabling it to provide potential client companies with the piece of mind and modicum of trust that their transactions will be securely conducted.

Operating since May 1999, RueschLINK has already signed up over 1400 client companies and issued over 2500 digital certificates through June 2000. While these numbers are not large compared to the Business to Consumer (B2C) space, Ruesch is dominant in the B2B space. For certain, with regard to PKI and digital certificates, few companies have yet matched Ruesch's accomplishments. With one of the larger PKI implementations in the business-to-business space right now, no other corporation handles more business-to-business processing than Ruesch does.

Furthermore, Ruesch has a strategic competitive advantage. PKI makes transactions over the Internet for RueschLINK safe for its clients, since certificates offer confidentiality through encryption, non-repudiation through digital signatures, as well as control of the process. In the next three years, Ruesch expects to add secure e-mail (S/MIME), and to extend the PKI framework to all phases of its business, both internal and external.

Implementing the PKI

Conceptually, Ruesch thought through what possibilities could fulfill its mission statement requirement for "state of the art." Ruesch considered biometrics and smart cards, which could also be part of the PKI, as alternatives. With each requiring some type of physical device that its clients would have to track, Ruesch believed that this would be a burden to its clients, and become a roadblock to any implementation. For sure, these components would be considered physical assets that someone would need to purchase and manage. Ruesch viewed digital certificates as the solution that would meet the need to be secure and also provide ease of use.

Ruesch also developed what it called a "shared three-tier" security framework for its Web site, where Ruesch shares security responsibilities with its clients. These three tiers consist of:

➤ Individually issued digital certificates to each user within its client companies

➤ A corporate ID, a user ID, and a user password

➤ Individual user access permissions that include transaction limits per user, and per company, over a 24-hour period

Ruesch further required its security framework to:

➤ Be based on public open standards

➤ Be independent of any one vendor, so that if Ruesch decided to switch vendors in the future, disruption to the operation of the site would be minimal

➤ Be state of the art

➤ Combine relative ease of implementation with strong security

PKI fulfilled the security framework requirements. As part of this approach, Ruesch requested that each client company also appoint an administrator to be responsible for adding and deleting users, as well as granting certain permissions.

Two major applications are driving the PKI effort. First is RueschLINK, which demands a high level of security, and second is secure e-mail for communications with clients. Ruesch is also considering another implementation of PKI to support and enhance authentication for its internal applications along with integrated directory services.

Policies

Ruesch developed security polices and procedures that are incorporated into its client agreement for using RueschLINK.

People

Initially, existing staff was used for all phases of deployment. To address technology issues associated with implementation of the digital certificates, Ruesch then hired additional employees to form what Ruesch calls its "RueschLINK Response Team."

Facility and Equipment

Ruesch outsources both its certificate authority (CA) hosting service and the RueschLINK Web site to two different vendors. A virtual private network (VPN) connects the Web server to production systems at a Ruesch facility. As it broadens its e-business initiatives, Ruesch may consider the use of multiple CAs for various strategic business partners.

Process

Ruesch initially thought that its deployment would be relatively simple and straightforward. As the rollout proceeded, however, the following issues surfaced:

➤ Browser version differences kept coming up. Microsoft Internet Explorer and Netscape Navigator handle digital certificates differently.

➤ The hosted certificate authority (CA) site would not be available occasionally during normal business hours. This presented an extra obstacle for Ruesch's clients to overcome during the sign-up process.

➤ Since the vendor was UNIX-oriented, it lacked knowledge of the Microsoft NT operating system environment.

➤ Client and employee education on the importance of certificates. Many employees felt that the use of digital certificates constituted a barrier, since it was one more thing that a client had to do in order to use RueschLINK.

Indeed, Ruesch was reminded of what it heard a speaker once say, *"The PK part works great... it's the "I" part that is problematic."* To Ruesch, it appears that everyone, vendors as well as businesses, are "learning" as they go.

Timeline

Where Ruesch knew that it would use some form of authentication and encryption, it took the company only six months to implement its PKI from start to finish:

Dec 98   Initial consideration and decision to use certificates

Dec 98   Criteria development, review

Dec 98   Vendor selection

Mar 99   Pilot implementation started/completed

May 99   Production environment rollout start date/scheduled ramp-up

Jun 99   Certificates mandatory for all clients

Ruesch allowed clients 30 days to apply for certificates, starting in May 1999. This allowed sufficient time for Ruesch to approve certificate requests and for clients to download the certificate into their browser to start using it.

Issues and Other Specifics

Through June 2000, Ruesch has issued over 2500 certificates to employees at 1400 client companies. Over the next 18 months, it's anticipated that 10,000 certificates will be in use. With the RueschLINK model, Ruesch issues one certificate per user, per branch, of a client company. For example, a client company with 40 branch offices would have 40 certificates, one for each of the authorized users in each branch that uses RueschLINK. Currently, there is authorization information stored in any of the extension fields found in the certificate format.

As part of the CA hosting service, the certificate revocation list (CRL) resides in a database at the hosting facility. There's currently one CRL that Ruesch maintains with updates being done on a daily basis. Although CRL checking happens automatically, the registration authorities (RAs) at the hosting service can also examine the CRL at any time.

Because the PKI solution is in the Internet space, no real legacy issues surfaced other than browser compliance. Moreover, the architecture of RueschLINK is fully integrated with its back-end systems, where transactions and sessions are at the point that they are already authenticated and encrypted.

Achieving Expectations

No significant changes needed to be made for the PKI side of RueschLINK, and the results mapped right to the plan. Ruesch did, however, have to make major organizational changes to support its employees "selling" RueschLINK, because they tended to see it as a "software sell," and not a "solution sell." To resolve this, it appointed, trained, and certified at least one "RueschLINK Product Specialist" in each of its offices to act as a resource for other office employees. Once this was done, use of certificates grew quickly among its client base.

Key Points

TOP 3 LESSONS LEARNED

➤ Deploying PKI takes careful planning and exquisite execution to do it properly.

➤ Both the vendor and we have to approach the project with humility and a tolerance for learning.

➤ PKI is not only a technological advantage; it is a strategic one as well.

TOP 3 CRITICAL SUCCESS FACTORS

➤ Selecting the right product and the right vendor.

➤ Determination to execute and deploy properly.

➤ Training and having the right staff to address client issues. Moreover, having a process in place so that the client experience is favorable.

WOULD DO DIFFERENTLY

➤ Given that hindsight is 20/20, Ruesch should have spent more time beta-testing the certificate deployment across different environments; for example, different browsers, different browser versions, and different operating systems. This would have allowed Ruesch to better anticipate the type of problems its clients experienced.

➤ Second, Ruesch had to recalibrate its expectations after it had begun the rollout. It had assumed that its clients would be more familiar with commercial Web sites than many actually were.

MOST HELPFUL IN GETTING PKI UP AND RUNNING

➤ Ruesch found the willingness of the vendor to work with them to be the single most helpful element in deploying PKI. Because of the scope of its implementation,

Ruesch came across problems that it didn't expect and that the vendor had not experienced before. The vendor sent staff to train Ruesch staff, and to help troubleshoot and solve difficult problems.

Findings

For Ruesch, PKI was never a question—it was business requirement. Clearly, more functionality and security than what a typical Web site provides is required when a financial institution is processing million-dollar payments.

Ruesch was confident that PKI could provide the solution it needed. PKI met the need for credentials through authentication, confidentiality through encryption, and integrity through digital signatures.

Case Studies Summary

Technology, people, and time.

While this book and these case studies are focused on PKI, what comes across in the case studies is really about much more than just the technology itself. Most likely, technology is the reason why you're reading this book in the first place, but if that is all you're concerned about, you may be missing a great deal.

It's amazing how many of us realize the impact that technology has on people, but not the impact that people have on technology. Regardless of how well designed an architecture may be, it is always dependent on the people who create it, deploy it, and manage it. In case you missed it, leaf back through the case studies, and you'll find some of the more critical components: commitment, cooperation, determination, discipline, and expectations. Without these attributes, you'll have difficulty achieving a secure PKI implementation.

As the saying goes, time waits for no one—and neither does the competition, or that next version of software. The organizations that shared their experiences with you didn't have the benefit of more time, or the experience of others to learn from. It would have been great for them to have more time to plan, test, and wait for more established standards or improved technologies.

No doubt, you've learned that the "I" in PKI represents the most complexity. No one knows it all, and we're dependent on others to make any PKI deployment a success. One thought, offered by Ron Szoc of Ruesch, sums it all up: " . . . *that both the vendor and the organization deploying the project approach it with humility and a tolerance for learning.*"

PART FIVE

PKI Efforts:
Present and Future

CHAPTER 19

Initiatives, Laws, and Standards

Initiatives

"Overwhelming" describes what many PKI initiatives are accomplishing. Canada, long regarded as a pioneer in leading PKI implementation activities, is working diligently to maintain a leadership position. Likewise, United States government agencies are also quickly forging ahead with PKI deployments to increase efficiencies and reduce costs.

Industry, always looking for that competitive edge, is coming on strong, especially in the financial arena. As such, Identrus is leading the way in facilitating global electronic commerce with over 15 multinational banking partners. Moreover, the Internet Council of the National Automated Clearing House Association is developing guidelines to help state governments and other organizations adopt PKI. Technology vendors, understanding the need to grow the adoption and enhance the value of PKI for their customers, have also formed their own alliance, the PKI Forum.

These initiatives are a signal to other governments, industries, and organizations that the need to work together is greater than ever when it comes to deploying PKI technology. The benefits of secure communications between authenticated parties, coupled with the market advantages of increased productivity and lower costs, are clear to these organizations. Companies need to draw on the collective expertise to ensure that their technology strategies and plans map to, and work effectively, with others. No man is an island, and today, no organization can afford to be out of step with a non-interoperable technology. Here are the top organizations that are leading the way to the future.

Government

Canada

A Secretariat was created in April 1998 to support and coordinate implementation activities for the Government of Canada's PKI (GOC PKI). Sponsored by the Chief Information Officer Branch of the Treasury Board of Canada, the GOC PKI became operational in May 1999. Among its many goals, it's chartered to promote understanding and acceptance of PKI between the branches of the federal government. Its mission includes developing a corporate management and policy structure for the GOC PKI, and resolving any legal, technical, and operational issues.

One of Canada's major contributions in advancing PKI is its extensive work in certificate policies. In fact, the GOC PKI has made eight separate certificate policies available since December 1998, with four levels of assurance for both digital signature and confidentiality certificates: Rudimentary, Basic, Medium, and High. This allows for flexibility in differentiating how the certificates are actually being used.

In addition to assisting with the development of technical infrastructure standards and migration strategies, GOC PKI is also working toward cross-certification between GOC branches as well as territorial governments and foreign countries. May 1999 also saw the first cross-certification between the Communications Security Establishment and Health Canada through the Canadian Central Facility, the primary certification authority for GOC PKI. By proceeding with its work in PKI, the Government of Canada is eliminating the drawbacks of high-cost private communications, and moving Canada to the low-cost electronic services delivery and commerce.

United States

Established in 1996 originally under the Government Information Technology Services Board, the Federal PKI (FPKI) Steering Committee now operates under the Enterprise Interoperability and Emerging Information Technology Committee of the Federal Chief Information Officers (CIO) Council.

Much like its Canadian counterpart, the FPKI is focused on promoting interoperable PKI solutions, developing common guidance, and communicating its expertise to others considering or actually deploying PKI. What's interesting is that the FPKI is not an agency in itself, but a voluntary interagency group consisting of over 50 members from over two-dozen agencies. There are three working groups—Business, Technical, and Legal and Policy—and all regularly publish their activities and meeting minutes on the FPKI Web site. The need to achieve long-term cost savings, conform with trading partner practices, meet international competition, and comply with federal regulations are just some of the issues driving the FPKI effort.

The impetus for federal agencies to move toward electronic transactions and delivery of services was strengthened with the Government Paperwork Elimination Act

(GPEA) of 1998, which requires agencies to accept forms electronically with electronic signatures by October 2003, when practicable.

In May 2000, as required by GPEA, the Office of Management and Budget (OMB) issued guidance in the Federal Register regarding electronic signature mechanisms. According to the report, "The Evolving Federal Public Key Infrastructure," OMB's guidance recognizes *that digital signatures provide a particularly robust means for authenticating individuals, and doing so in an interoperable fashion— that is, one electronic credential (a digital certificate) can readily serve multiple applications…"* Now, the OMB is increasing the momentum by soliciting agencies to have plans submitted by October 2000 detailing how they'll comply with GPEA.

Given the efforts of the FPKI Steering Committee, many agencies have already adopted and deployed their own PKIs. These agencies include the Department of Defense (DoD), the Federal Aviation Administration (FAA), the Federal Deposit Insurance Corporation (FDIC), National Aeronautics and Space Administration (NASA), and the U.S. Patent and Trademark Office (USPTO). Together, they've already issued over a quarter-million certificates with plans to exceed four million by 2002. To learn more about efforts within the federal government, see the case studies presented in Chapter 17, "U.S. Patent and Trademark Office (USPTO)," and Chapter 16, "Idaho National Engineering and Environmental Laboratory (INEEL)."

As such, the FPKI Steering Committee is moving forward to meet the needs of the various agencies by establishing a Federal Bridge Certification Authority (FBCA). The FBCA serves as a non-hierarchical, peer-to-peer hub that will support interagency PKI technical interoperability using commercial off-the-shelf software. A Federal PKI Policy Authority (PA) would serve to establish the conditions where a specific federal agency could interoperate with the FBCA and hence, efficiently interoperate with all other parties who are doing likewise. The PA maps certificate policies of each agency to the FBCA certificate policy, allowing agencies to determine which certificates from other agencies have the level of assurance needed for each transaction.

To demonstrate this interoperability, a prototype FBCA successfully supported test S/MIME messaging among five disparate PKI domains that were cross-certified with the FBCA (see Figure 19.1). Moreover, the demonstration included a total of five different CA products and five different X.500 directory products. This demonstration proved that using the FBCA to communicate across multiple federal agencies works, which could prompt a faster adoption of PKI in the federal government and serve as a model for other organizations to follow.

Industry

Identrus

Identrus is enabling business to manage their risks in e-commerce through trusted relationships with their financial institutions, and is providing business recourse

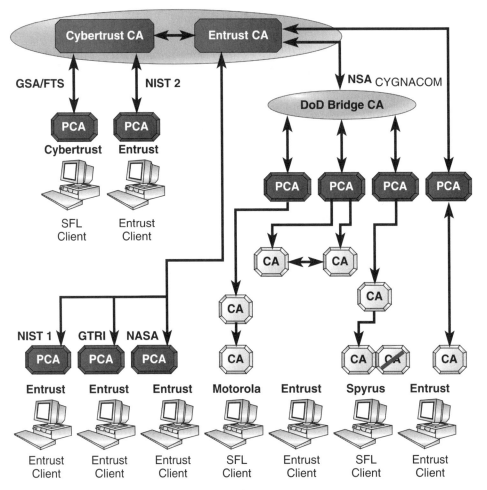

Figure 19.1 Federal Bridge Certification Authority.
Source: Federal CIO Council.

capability when discrepancies occur within its framework. Through Identrus, business can exploit the Internet to conclusively identify trading partners and conduct trusted business to business e-commerce with any participant in the Identrus network. What's more, it's also offloading the complexity of creating the trusted relationships with trading partners and eliminating transaction costs.

Identrus, which originated in 1997, is now a limited liability company (LLC) headquartered in New York. Founding financial institutions include:

➢ ABN AMRO Bank

➢ Bank of America

➢ Barclays PLC

- ➤ Chase Manhattan Bank
- ➤ Citigroup
- ➤ Deutsche Bank
- ➤ Hypo Vereinsbank

Since its inception, these eight other major financial institutions have become members:

- ➤ Canadian Imperial Bank of Commerce
- ➤ Commerzbank
- ➤ HSBC Group
- ➤ Industrial Bank of Japan, Limited
- ➤ NatWest Group
- ➤ Sanwa Bank
- ➤ Scotiabank
- ➤ Wells Fargo Wholesale Internet Services

Historically, financial institutions have acted as trusted intermediaries in traditional commerce for payments and signature guarantors. With their extensive experience in deploying and managing security solutions such as funds transfer and online treasury workstations, they're in a position to provide the element of trust required for e-commerce and reduce risk. Moreover, their broad customer reach, from large corporations to small business, further enables them to provide identity certification that's fundamental to developing trusted relationships and permit critical e-commerce services. Figure 19.2 illustrates at a high level some of the stages of a generic transaction where identity risk exists and where trusted third-party financial institutions can apply their risk management expertise. Furthermore, where Identrus provides a system with rigorous oversight along with policies, practices, and legal framework, any recourse is accomplished internally, thereby eliminating any dependence on legislation for adjudication or very difficult, depending on key controls and trusted cryptographic modules.

Where technology must support the business requirements, Identrus chose PKI because it utilizes two asymmetric related keys that can provide the necessary controls and form the basis for non-repudiation. Prior to PKI, the problem of key distribution and shared secrets made non-repudiation impossible.

As shown in Figure 19.3, Identrus provides the root certificate authority that verifies the identities of the participating member financial institutions. In turn, these member institutions then issue certificates to their customers. Each party in a transaction receives a digitally signed attestation certificate with validation done in real time that also serves as a basis for any potential recourse.

What's different about the Identrus initiative is that it is global in scope, uses open standards and interoperability, and provides a single identity certificate that enables a high level of trust that is supported by major financial institutions.

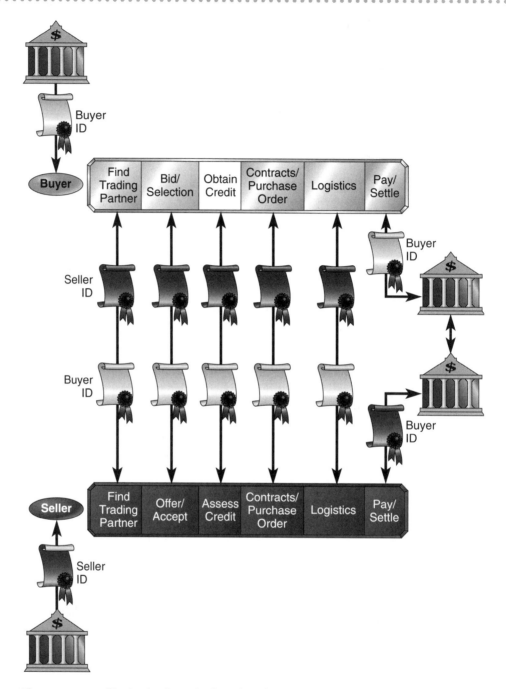

Figure19.2 Facilitating business in the value chain.
Source: Identrus.

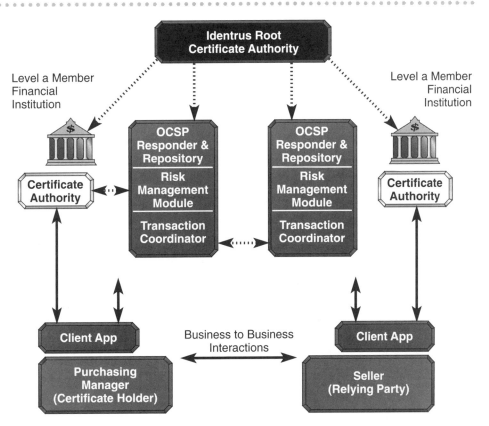

Figure 19.3   Integrated technology architecture.
Source: Identrus.

National Automated Clearing House Association

The Internet Council of the National Automated Clearing House Association (NACHA) has prepared guidelines for review in an effort to help state governments and other organizations adopt PKI. Aptly, the document is referred to by the same name as the task force that created it: the Certification Authority Rating and Trust (CARAT) Task Force.

As the document's subtitle states, the CARAT Guidelines are *Guidelines for Constructing Policies Governing the Use of Identity-Based Public Key Certificates,* and it is publicly available from the NACHA Web site. It includes an introduction to PKI, the role and form of a policy authority, business and legal models, and the role of a certificate policy in context of the business environment. NACHA welcomes interested parties to provide their comments regarding the helpfulness of the guidelines.

PKI Forum

The PKI Forum (PKIF) is an international, vendor-neutral, not-for-profit organization managed by its members with administrative support services provided by The Open Group.

The key objectives of PKIF are to:

➤ Grow the adoption and use of PKI as a critical enabler of e-business

➤ Enhance the value of PKI for customers by enabling them to harness its use in their business applications

➤ Increase revenue opportunities for PKI products and services

To accomplish this, PKIF plans to:

➤ Provide a forum for vendors to demonstrate their support for standards-based PKI that's necessary as a foundation for e-business

➤ Bring customers and vendors together in a neutral setting to increase customer knowledge about PKI, security, and migration issues

➤ Foster interoperability by interacting with appropriate standards bodies, and initiate projects that demonstrate the value of PKI

Membership in the Forum is open to PKI vendors, technology companies building value around PKI, end-user organizations from industry segments such as finance and healthcare, as well as leaders from government and business.

Laws and Regulations

Confidentiality and integrity, two of the essential security services that PKI enables, are attributes that most business people recognize and require. Not only is keeping information private and reliable important for maintaining a corporation's image and reputation, but it's also vital for its ongoing operations. Moreover, the need for both secrecy and reliability has become so important that legislation is being enacted to ensure that it is. While there are numerous laws in effect or pending, what follows are some of the more major legal requirements and issues that have a significant impact on how you protect information and how PKI addresses those requirements.

United States

Economic Espionage Act

The U.S. Economic Espionage Act of 1996 (EEA) is especially noteworthy for its broad definition of a trade secret and what constitutes due diligence for its protection. How to develop a program to comply with the EEA is further provided through the Federal Sentencing Guidelines.

What's important to realize is that the EEA effectively broadens how a trade secret is defined and the protection it receives under federal law. In effect, Title 18, United States Code, Section 1839, states *"the term 'trade secret' means... all forms and types of financial, business, scientific, technical, economic, or engineering information... whether tangible or intangible, and whether or how stored, compiled, or memorialized physically, electronically... if the owner thereof has taken reasonable measures to keep such information secret."*

The EEA further provides for civil and criminal penalties for corporations as well as individuals. Depending on the violation, fines range upward to $10M and 15 years in prison. However, by implementing and enforcing an EEA compliance program, you can minimize your risk and exposure. According to the U.S. Sentencing Commission, there are seven fundamentals required to demonstrate due diligence and are considered to be the minimum standards for an effective compliance program. Briefly, these fundamentals include:

Policy and procedures. Establishing standards and procedures.

Management leadership. Assigning specific, high-level individuals with responsibility.

Limit discretion. Cautioning regarding a propensity to engage in illegal activities.

Communication and training. Effectively communicate standards and procedures.

Auditing and reporting. Reasonable steps to achieve compliance.

Enforcement and discipline. Enforcing appropriate disciplinary mechanisms.

Continuous improvement. Reasonable steps to prevent further occurrences.

In short, the traditional business objective of ensuring confidentiality has now become a matter of legal compliance. Basic security measures must be followed, and organizations need to go a step further by ensuring that procedures are in place to meet recognized standards of practice. The need to maintain confidentiality and integrity of electronic information can be achieved through encryption and digital signatures, both basic functions of a PKI.

Electronic Signatures in Global and National Commerce Act

Effective October 1, 2000, online contracts in the United States will have the same legal force as equivalent paper contracts. This new law states that *"a signature, contract, or other record relating to such transaction may not be denied legal effect, validity, or enforcement solely because it is in electronic form; and... a contract relating to such transaction may not be denied legal effect, validity, or enforceability solely because an electronic signature was used in its formation."*

The law further defines an electronic signature to mean "an electronic sound, symbol, or process, attached to or logically associated with a contract or other record and executed or adopted by a person with the intent to sign the record." There is no provision in the law that specifically calls for any one type of technology. It does, however, say that electronic contracts and records are only legally enforceable if they're "in a form that is capable of being retained and accurately reproduced for later reference by all parties or persons who are entitled to retain the contract or other record."

Although the law doesn't specify what technology may be used, there aren't many options available that can be as ubiquitous and practical as PKI is. PKI not only offers a high level of scalability, but it also incorporates assurance for authentication in establishing the parties involved, as well as the integrity required by law for accurately reproducing documents at a later date.

Health Insurance Portability and Accountability Act of 1996 (HIPAA)

Public Law 104-191 was enacted to ensure the protection for privacy of medical information. The goal of the law is to reduce the cost of administration, encourage the widespread use of electronic transmission, and ensure the security and integrity of healthcare information. In fact, sections 261 through 264 of HIPAA are known as the Administrative Simplification provisions. Since Congress failed to meet its August 1999 deadline to enact legislation governing necessary standards, the law mandated the Department of Health and Human Services to propose regulations. As a result, it published its proposed rule, Standards for Privacy of Individually Identifiable Health Information, in the Federal Register in November 1999. Final rules for security are still pending.

21 Code of Federal Regulations (CFR) Part 11, U.S. Food and Drug Administration (FDA)

Unlike HIPAA, the FDA issued its final rule in March 1997 regarding the criteria that must be met for electronic signatures. Part 11 *"applies to any paper records required by statute or agency regulations and supercedes any existing paper record requirements by providing that electronic records may be used in lieu of paper records."* The FDA issued this regulation as a result of requests by the pharmaceutical industry to accommodate paperless record systems under the current good manufacturing practice (CGMP).

Particularly interesting reading is the Comments on the Proposed Rule, Section III, regarding Personnel Integrity. It's here that the FDA addresses the role of individual honesty and trust in ensuring that electronic records are reliable, trustworthy, and authentic. The FDA states that the *"agency agrees that the integrity of any electronic signature/electronic record system depends heavily upon the honesty of employees and that most persons are not motivated to falsify records. However, the agency's experience… demonstrates that some people do falsify information under certain circumstances."* Part 11 is intended to minimize these opportunities.

Europe

European Union Data Protection Directive

Directive 95/46/EC of the European Parliament and of the Council of 24 October 1995

What's important about the European Directive are the consequences for multinational business organizations in how they currently handle information about individuals. Specifically, the Directive provides that *"transfer to a third country of personal data which are undergoing processing… may take place only if… the third country in question ensures an adequate level of protection."* Unfortunately, for organizations in the United States, the reliance on self-regulation does not meet the Directive's criteria, and there are no government regulations or policies yet in place.

Additionally, Section VIII of the Directive requires confidentiality and security of processing personal data, and calls for *"sufficient guarantees in respect of the technical security measures… governing the processing…"* Moreover, assurances must be made that the responsible individual *"must implement appropriate technical and organizational measures to protect personal data against accidental or unlawful destruction or accidental loss, alteration, unauthorized disclosure or access, in particular where the processing involves the transmission of data over a network…"*

PKI, through the use of digital signatures, can detect any alteration of data. Similarly, issuing certificates can also control authorized access and provide for confidentiality through encryption over a public network such as the Internet.

European Union Electronic Signature Directive

Directive 1999/93/EC of the European Parliament and of the Council of 13 December 1999 on a Community framework for electronic signatures.

According to the scope of this Directive, its purpose is to *"facilitate the use of electronic signatures and to contribute to their legal recognition."* It establishes the basis for electronic signatures, and provides some interesting definitions as to types of electronic signatures. For example,

" 'advanced electronic signature' means an electronic signature which meets the following requirements:

(a) it is uniquely linked to the signatory;

(b) it is capable of identifying the signatory;

(c) it is created using means that the signatory can maintain under his sole control; and

(d) it is linked to the data to which it relates in such a manner that any subsequent change of the data is detectable."

Unlike the Electronic Signatures in Global and National Commerce Act, this Directive goes much further in that it provides critical definitions, covers liability, and, not surprisingly, data protection based upon the European Union Data Protection Directive. In far fewer words than its U.S. counterpart, Article 5 quickly states in two paragraphs what establishes the legal effects of electronic signatures.

Indeed, Article 6 goes far beyond in regard to liability language. It states *"As a minimum, Member States shall ensure that by issuing a certificate as a qualified certificate to the public or by guaranteeing such a certificate to the public a certification-service-provider is liable for damage caused to any entity or legal or natural person who reasonably relies on that certificate…"* There are some caveats, but at least there's some language within the Directive.

Lastly, personal data protection is ensured once more by incorporating compliance with the requirements of the Data Protection Directive. *A "certification-service-provider which issues certificates to the public may collect personal data only directly from the data subject, or after the explicit consent of the data subject, and only insofar as it is necessary for the purposes of issuing and maintaining the certificate."* Once again, this will present yet another issue for multinational organizations that are planning to issue certificates within Europe.

Standards

Benchmarking is nothing new in the business world. Organizations constantly check their performance to see how they measure up against others and what they consider to be "best practice" in the industry. They're always on the lookout for ways to improve and validate operations to increase market share and profitability. No doubt, many of us have seen banners on many buildings touting "ISO 9001 certified" as an example of a company's manufacturing competency. Likewise, the Underwriters Lab (UL) seal of approval is also found on many of the products we use every day. Within the fast-paced computer industry, however, standards are somewhat more elusive, with the market playing a much greater role in determining what becomes a standard more than technical specifications by any one manufacturer or group. Therefore, it's surprising that when it comes to the Internet, standards are common parlance, especially regarding PKI.

For example, the International Telecommunications Union's X.509 is frequently cited as the de facto certificate format, and the Public-Key Cryptography Standards (PKCS) specifications are widely accepted for syntax and various interfaces in deploying certificates. Consequently, it's important to have a basic understanding of what major standards are utilized, and how they meet your requirements when evaluating PKI products and solutions.

Moreover, other organizations such as the National Institute of Standards and Technology perform critical roles in how products are classified and tested for functionality. The Common Criteria, now an International Standard, offers a mechanism to specify and evaluate products. Be sure to also recognize standards specifically adopted for your industry, such as those published by the Accredited Standards Committee.

While the following listing of standards is not all-inclusive, they're significant, since most vendors are developing and marketing their products based on most of them. Even with this existing plethora of standards, more are being discussed and submitted for approval to address newer protocols such as wireless. Unquestionably, this is a reflection of the ever-changing ways we use the Internet for business and communications.

Accredited Standards Committee X9—Financial Services

Accredited in 1984 by the American National Standards Institute, X9 Financial Services is also the U.S. Technical Advisory Group to the International Technical Committee on Banking and Related Services under the International Organization for Standardization (ISO). As the secretariat, the American Bankers Association (ABA) provides administrative support for X9.

American National Standard X9.49: Secure Remote Access to Financial Services for the Financial Industry

Regardless of what industry you're in, this standard presents an excellent framework for assessing threats, vulnerabilities, and risks. It further elaborates on minimum-security requirements for secure communications between a user and a financial service provider.

American National Standard X9.55: Public Key Cryptography: Extensions to Public Key Certificates and Certificate Revocation Lists

Covers the specifications of the extension fields, descriptions of the underlying requirements, and descriptions of their intended use.

American National Standard X9.57: Public Key Cryptography for the Financial Services Industry, Certificate Management

Specifies the contents of certificates and the credentials required to obtain a certificate as well as procedures for certificate generation, validation, and revocation.

American National Standard X9.79: Public Key Infrastructure, Practices, and Policy Framework

This standard defines the components of a PKI and contains a framework of practices and policy requirements. It allows for the implementation of operational, baseline PKI practices that satisfy industry-accepted information systems control objectives.

Common Criteria

This standard provides for a common, technical basis for Information Technology (IT) security. The Common Criteria recently became ISO Standard 15408 with countries such as Canada, France, Germany, the Netherlands, United Kingdom, and the United States as participants. Other countries now implementing the criteria include Australia, Japan, Korea, and New Zealand.

The Criteria permits comparability through a common set of requirements, and comes in three parts:

> Part I is the Introduction and General Model that defines concepts, principles, and constructs for expressing security objectives.

> Part II provides a catalog for a standardized way of expressing requirements.

> Part III contains a catalog that establishes a set of assurance components along with seven evaluation assurance levels (EAL).

What's more, the criterion preserves concepts drawn from the Trusted Computer Systems Evaluation Criteria (TCSEC), the Information Technology Security Evaluation Criteria (ITSEC), and the Canadian Trusted Computer Product Evaluation Guide (CTCPEG).

What's important to recognize is that much like the validations under FIPS 140 (see the following section), this new ISO Standard will soon be the default evaluation criterion to measure the level of security in products from PKI vendors. For more on evaluation criteria, see Chapter 3, "Securing the Environment for PKI."

International Telecommunications Union (ITU-T)

Recommendation X.500: The Directory: Overview of Concepts, Models, and Services

This standard provides directory and directory information base concepts. It contains a services and capabilities overview that describes user-friendly naming, name-to-address mapping, dynamic binding between objects and locations, and self-configuring networks. For more on information, see Chapter 6, "Directories."

Recommendation X.509: The Directory: Authentication Framework

Although known more for specifying the format for certificates, X.509 provides a considerable amount of information regarding strong and weak authentication. It suggests that only strong authentication—that is, credentials using cryptography—should be used as the basis for providing secure services.

In essence, X.509 defines a framework for the provision of authentication services by the directory. It also includes information regarding management of keys and certificates, certificate and certificate revocation list (CRL) extensions, CRL distribution points and delta-CRLs, and attribute certificates.

For additional information, see the section on digital certificates in Chapter 2, and authentication in Chapter 1.

Internet Engineering Task Force, Request for Comments (IETF RFCs)

The following RFC documents either present a framework, describe, profile, or specify the given subject. Note that standardization status varies among these documents.

Directories

The major alternative directory to the ITU X.500 Directory, the Lightweight Directory Access Protocol (LDAP) encompasses several standards as listed next. RFC 1777, introduced in March 1995, refers specifically to the Lightweight Directory Access Protocol with RFC 2251, introducing version 3 in December 1997. For more on information, see Chapter 6.

➤ RFC 1777: Lightweight Directory Access Protocol (Obsoletes 1487)

➤ RFC 1778: The String Representation of Standard Attribute Syntaxes

➤ RFC 2251: Lightweight Directory Access Protocol v3

➤ RFC 2252: Lightweight Directory Access Protocol (v3): Attribute Syntax Definitions

➤ RFC 2253: Lightweight Directory Access Protocol (v3): UTF-8 String Representation of Distinguished Names

➤ RFC 2254: The String Representation of LDAP Search Filters

➤ RFC 2255: The LDAP URL Format

➤ RFC 2256: A Summary of the X.500(96) User Schema for Use with LDAPv3

Domain Name Security

Describes further use for the Domain Name System (DNS).

➤ RFC 2538: Storing Certificates in the Domain Name System

➤ RFC 2539: Storage of Diffie-Hellman Keys in the Domain Name System

Generic Security Service Application Program Interface

Provides security services with a range of underlying mechanisms to allow application portability to different environments.

➤ RFC 1509: Generic Security Service Application Program Interface (GSS-API): C-Bindings

➤ RFC 2025: The Simple Public-Key GSS-API Mechanism (SPKM)

➤ RFC 2078: Generic Service (GSS-API) (obsoletes RFC 1508)

➤ RFC 2479: Independent Data Unit Protection Generic Security Service API (IDUP-GSS-API)

Public Key Infrastructure X.509 (PKIX) Working Group

The stated goal of the PKIX working group is to facilitate the use of X.509 certificates in multiple Internet-related applications, and to promote interoperability among different implementations that make use of X.509 certificates. The intent is to provide a framework that supports a range of trust and usage environments.

➤ RFC 2459: Internet X.509 Public Key Infrastructure, Certificate and CRL Profile

➤ RFC 2510: Internet X.509 Public Key Infrastructure, Certificate Management Protocols

➤ RFC 2511: Internet X.509 Certificate Request Message Format

➤ RFC 2527: Internet X.509 Public Key Infrastructure, Certificate Policy and Certification Practices Framework

❖ RFC 2559: Internet X.509 Public Key Infrastructure, Operational Protocols— LDAPv2 (updates RFC 1778)

➤ RFC 2560: Internet X.509 Public Key Infrastructure, Online Certificate Status Protocol—OCSP

➤ RFC 2585: Internet X.509 Public Key Infrastructure, Operational Protocols: FTP and HTTP

➤ RFC 2587: Internet X.509 Public Key Infrastructure, LDAPv2 Schema

➤ RFC 2797: Certificate Management Messages over CMS (Cryptographic Message Syntax)

Secure Multipurpose Internet Mail Extensions (S/MIME)

Describes the various supporting specifications for creating and using secure MIME messages.

➤ RFC 2311: S/MIME Version 2 Message Specification

➤ RFC 2312: S/MIME Version 2 Certificate Handling

➤ RFC 2630: Cryptographic Message Syntax

➤ RFC 2631: Diffie-Hellman Key Agreement Method

➤ RFC 2632: S/MIME Version 3 Certificate Handling

➤ RFC 2633: S/MIME Version 3 Message Specification

➤ RFC 2634: Enhanced Security Services for S/MIME

Time Stamping

➤ RFC 1305: Network Time Protocol (NTP) Version 3

➤ RFC 2030: Simple Network Time Protocol (SNTP) Version 4, for IPv4, IPv6, and OSI

➤ Time Stamp Protocol (TSP); Internet Draft, June 2000, PKIX Working Group

Other

➤ Key management architecture that specified the basis of an X.509-based PKI

RFC 1422: Privacy Enhancement for Internet Electronic Mail: Part II: Certificate-Based Key Management

➤ For allowing client/server communications privacy

RFC 2246: The Transport Layer Security Protocol (TLS) v1

➤ Working Group tasked with producing a certificate structure for trust management

RFC 2692: Simple PKI Requirements

➤ For using certificates for authorization versus authentication (as opposed to X.509-based PKI)

RFC 2693: Simple PKI Certificate Theory

National Institute of Standards and Technology, Federal Information Processing Standards Publications (FIPS Pub)

FIPS PUB 140-1, Security Requirements for Cryptographic Modules

As it is commonly known, FIPS 140 describes the security requirements that need to be satisfied by vendors of cryptographic modules. It is THE standard that's used by government organizations to specify cryptographic-based security systems for providing protection for sensitive data or valuable data. FIPS 140 provides for four increasing levels of security, ranging from Security Level 1 at the lowest level to Security Level 4 at the highest. The security requirements cover many areas and include items such as basic design and documentation, authorized roles and services, physical security, software security, and key management. For more on FIPS 140-1, see Chapter 2 for the section on cryptography, and Chapter 8, on hardware.

Public-Key Cryptography Standards (PKCS)

Starting in 1991, RSA Laboratories first developed Public-Key Cryptography Standards specifications to accelerate the deployment of public-key cryptography. Widely referenced and implemented, they are generally known simply as PKCS and the particular sequence number. Not only do they form the basis for interoperable security based on public key cryptographic techniques, they are part of many other standards such as the IETF's PKIX and S/MIME. The standards currently include:

➤ PKCS #1: RSA Cryptography Standard
➤ PKCS #2: Incorporated into PKCS #1
➤ PKCS #3: Diffie-Hellman Key Agreement Standard

➤ PKCS #4: Incorporated into PKCS #1

➤ PKCS #5: Password-Based Cryptography Standard

➤ PKCS #6: Extended-Certificate Syntax Standard (to be changed to historical status)

➤ PKCS #7: Cryptographic Message Syntax Standard

➤ PKCS #8: Private-Key Information Syntax Standard

➤ PKCS #9: Selected Attribute Types

➤ PKCS #10: Certification Request Syntax Standard

➤ PKCS #11: Cryptographic Token Interface Standard

➤ PKCS #12: Personal Information Exchange Syntax Standard

➤ PKCS #13: Elliptic Curve Cryptography Standard (in development)

➤ PKCS #15: Cryptographic Token Information Format Standard

CHAPTER 20

Biometrics and PKI

Biometrics is a means of determining or verifying identity based on a physiological or behavioral characteristic. Mainstream biometric disciplines include finger scan, voice verification, facial scan, iris scan, hand geometry, and signature verification. The process flow of biometric authentication begins with enrollment, wherein the distinctive characteristics of a given body part (finger, face, iris, and hand) or feature (voice, signature) are converted into a relatively small template. This enrollment template is stored for use in subsequent authentication. Authentication also requires the conversion of distinctive characteristics into templates, after which the verification and enrollment templates are compared to determine their similarity.

Biometrics cannot be lost, forgotten, or stolen, and they provide verification of identity well beyond that of any other authentication mechanism. The levels of accuracy they provide can approach 100 percent for certain technologies (see *Accuracy of Biometric Technology*). They are almost entirely resistant to spoofing, such that presenting a false sample will not fool the device. Originally used for physical security or time and attendance, biometric technologies have grown smaller, less expensive, more user friendly, and more accurate. Biometrics is now a full-fledged solution for most PC and IT authentication needs, and is well suited for integration with PKI.

Biometric authentication also provides flexibility not possible in any other authentication infrastructure. In biometric verification, a score is returned indicating the degree of similarity between the verification and enrollment templates. *Thresholds* can be set to require higher or lower scores; in other words, levels of accuracy, based on variables such as the value of a given transaction, the time of day, and the identity of the user. In PKI, this flexibility can be a powerful tool.

Accuracy of Biometrics Technology

Though no biometric technology can claim to provide 100-percent authentication, certain technologies can provide extremely high levels of accuracy under good conditions. Accuracy can be defined many ways in the context of biometrics and PKI, and each PK infrastructure may have different accuracy requirements essential to the certificate system's overall performance. The different measures of accuracy include FAR, FRR, and FTE.

False Acceptance Rate (FAR). This is the most commonly understood definition of authentication accuracy: the ability to keep out unauthorized personnel or users. FAR measures the likelihood that a user not enrolled in the system is mistaken for someone who is. For many PK infrastructures, especially those ensuring the integrity, privacy, and authenticity of high-value transactions or sensitive data, this will be the most important measure of the biometric technology's performance. Iris scan, retinal scan, and finger scan technologies are generally most accurate in this respect, providing FARs as small as 0.01 to 0.001 percent.

False Rejection Rate (FRR). The likelihood that an authorized user will be incorrectly rejected by the system is represented by the FRR. FARs and FRRs are inversely related: as FARs decrease, and unauthorized users are being kept out at a high rate, FRRs will increase, and authorized users will be increasingly likely to be rejected. For PK infrastructures whose primary objective is not high security, but are intended as a means to serve customers, a low FRR is essential to user satisfaction, and is the key measure of accuracy. FRRs are always slightly higher than FARs due to misplaced fingers, failure to speak clearly, not looking at the camera, and so on.

Failure to Enroll (FTE) rate. A frequently overlooked component of accuracy is the failure to enroll. Some technologies present difficulties for certain populations, such as elderly users with finger scan devices. FTE rates can be especially problematic for PK infrastructure administrators, as every user unable to enroll must be accommodated by alternative authentication mechanisms such as passwords or PINs. Whether an enrollment is supervised or remote will also bear directly on the FTE rate.

Clearly, when considering the importance of privacy and data integrity, those implementing PKI must also define their requirements for authentication accuracy. Selecting the correct technology, and intelligently integrating it into the PK infrastructure, greatly increases the likelihood that these requirements will be met.

Which Biometrics Technologies Are Best for PKI?

Depending on the need for security versus convenience, PKI can accommodate a variety of biometric technologies. Deciding on the technology doesn't mean that there are no other decisions to make; there are over 70 finger scan companies with competing technologies and strengths. Many factors will come into play when making these decisions:

> ➤ Accuracy requirements

> ➤ Demographic makeup of potential users

> ➤ Environment in which PKI will be used (e-commerce, employee access to intranets and e-mail, mobile devices)

> ➤ Network architecture, including throughput capability

> ➤ Physical site where authentication will take place

> ➤ Cost

Finger scan technology has several qualities that make it appropriate for use in PK infrastructures, such as low FAR, fairly low FRR, low cost, and in most cases, ease of use. Finger scan does pose usage problems for certain demographics, and dirty or cut fingers can hinder performance. Iris scan can provide astronomically small FARs, and is an excellent solution for high-value or high-security PK infrastructures. Unfortunately, it is expensive, and works best in controlled environments. Facial scan provides a lower degree of accuracy, but if ease of use is a primary consideration, it is a very intuitive and easy-to-use technology.

Behavioral technologies such as voice or signature tend to be too prone to false rejections to be trusted with all but the lowest-risk PKI transactions. Similarly, retinal scan is very difficult to use, and would frustrate all but the most determined user.

Many biometric companies have developed an alternative solution, using multiple biometric technologies to authenticate users. Face and finger, or voice and face, are common combinations. This reduces the likelihood of false acceptance, as a user will be exceptionally unlikely to effectively mimic two characteristics simultaneously. With populations for whom a finger scan is problematic, this may be an effective method for PKI authentication.

As the technology continues to become more accurate and less expensive, the decision whether to incorporate biometrics in PKI will be replaced with the decision on which technology to use. This question can only be answered by careful consideration of the entire PK infrastructure.

Risk Factors

Biometrics must be implemented carefully in order to maximize the authentication capabilities of PKI.

Many factors can adversely affect the performance of a biometric system, including the following:

Choosing a biometric technology not compatible with your particular PKI needs.
Certain technologies may provide sufficient levels of accuracy for use in high-security PKI architectures, but have an unacceptably high false rejection rate, costing a company time and money. Of course, the inverse of this is establishing lax requirements and allowing access to unauthorized personnel, thereby defeating the purpose of PKI.

Failure to train personnel correctly. Finding the ideal biometric device, integrating it with your current architecture, and setting the thresholds to the correct levels will all prove fruitless if users are not trained on correct enrollment and verification procedures. No biometric technology will perform well without cooperative users who understand the proper way to verify on the system.

Failure to take into account environmental, ease-of-use, and user perception. Using facial scan in a variably lit room, using finger scan for use with manual laborers, or using voice verification in a noisy environment greatly diminishes the accuracy of the biometric and thus the PKI. Similarly, users may be wary of using finger scan or iris scan devices if they are not given information on how the devices work, that they are safe, and that they are not used to track personal data.

Template management. Administrators and IT professionals will have one more area to manage when they decide to implement biometric authentication. The templates representing each user are not large, only 250–800 bytes under most circumstances, but they must be held secure; as opposed to a private key, which can be revoked if compromised, a finger scan is a permanent record. Although there is little that can be done with a biometric template, it is the perception of risk that must be avoided.

Device obsolescence. Biometric devices and technologies are not interoperable, and no standard has been fully accepted that simplifies application development across devices or platforms. The technology advances so quickly that what currently appears to be a cutting-edge solution will likely be surpassed by newer, better devices in short order, perhaps within a year. Any very large expenditure must be executed with extreme caution to avoid being saddled with old, incompatible technology.

Biometrics are a crucial part of, but not a substitute for, a well-designed IT security infrastructure. They cannot claim to eliminate all security risks, especially in an age when hackers may see the presence of biometric authentication as a challenge to be overcome. They do, however, offer the best chance for secure, reliable authentication.

Biometrics and Privacy

People unfamiliar with biometrics, but comfortable with PKI, often wonder if the use of biometrics could be a threat to their privacy. This is definitely a reasonable question, one which biometric vendors go to great lengths to address. In biometric technologies, the fingerprints, iris patterns, and voice patterns are not stored. Instead, their templates, files from $1/10^{th}$ to $1/1000^{th}$ the size of the raw biometric data, are stored. It is important to note that you cannot reconstruct the image of a person's body part or feature from the template. These templates are normally encrypted and stored in biometric vendors' proprietary databases or file structures. Those familiar with biometrics see it as a means, along with PKI, of ensuring and increasing privacy in an age where privacy concerns are paramount.

PKI: Sample Biometric Approaches

The existing PKI is an excellent mechanism to ensure that data remains (1) confidential, and (2) unchanged during transit over non-secure networks such as the Internet.

PKI's premise is that a user has two mathematically related numerical keys, a private key and a public key, which serve to encrypt and decrypt data. A user can secure a message by encrypting it with his private key and the receiver's public key. The receiver reads the message by decrypting it with his private key and the sender's public key.

Local Biometric Protection of the Private Key

To maximize the security of the private key, it is necessary that it be secured with a biometric instead of a password or pin. By securing private keys with a biometric, the *senders* can assure themselves that messages appearing to be from them will not be fraudulently originated. Likewise, the *receivers* protecting their private keys with a biometric can be assured that no one will be able to read messages that are intended for their eyes only.

This is a critical step in the overall cycle of authentication, privacy, and data integrity that PKI provides. Whereas non-biometric PKI ensures that the correct private key has been used for encryption, biometrics in conjunction with PKI ensures that the *holder* of the private key logged on to the PC, or held the smart card, that initiated the session or transaction. The private key is only relevant, in most cases, in terms of the identity of the holder; that is, if a private key is stolen or compromised, it is immediately of no value. Biometrics can ensure the relevance of the private key within the PK infrastructure.

Who Benefits?

Depending on the architecture of the PKI, the local biometric protection may be more beneficial to one party than the other. For example, a merchant may derive more benefit from verifying the identity of an online purchaser than will the purchaser in verifying that he or she is indeed purchasing from a large retailer. But in many situations, the benefit will be equivalent, such as the transmission of sensitive data between department heads, or student loan information, or stock trades.

It is also possible that merchants will offer special discounts for users of PKI and biometrics, as the likelihood of fraud or repudiation will be greatly reduced. As it stands currently, the fear of fraud on both sides of the e-commerce chain has hindered, to some degree, the growth of this marketplace. Biometrics and PKI are two proven technologies that could combine to overcome this understandable hesitation to transmit one's credit card and personal information, or to send goods on the basis of a credit card number and an address.

One Step Beyond: Concurrent, Centralized Verification of Biometric Templates

There is one last step to be overcome in order to finalize the biometric security of the valuable transactions PKI facilitates. It pertains to the amount of certainty required in private key transmission secured by biometrics. Although this final step has not yet been fully developed, there are some interesting possibilities that may become definitive solutions.

The local verification scenario contains weaknesses that must be addressed for some types of medium-to-high value or importance transactions. If the sender and receiver could know with certainty that the other's private key is being secured with a biometric, and if they could interpret and rely on a real-time biometric verification, then the local verification approach would be ideal. However, local verification doesn't provide such assurance.

First, in the local scenario, it is not possible to know for sure at a given time that someone else's private key is being actively protected by a biometric. A biometric verification could have taken place, and the computer left unattended and additional unauthorized transactions initiated. Or there could be backup copies of private keys lacking biometric protection.

In addition, the data used in different types of biometrics, and by the many vendors within each of these disciplines, is not interchangeable. If a receiver were to learn that the sender verified on a biometric system from vendor X with a score of .01, they would have difficulty in determining if this was a very good or a very poor match.

Centralizing Biometric Enrollment and Verification

The ability to verify that a submission is live, and that the score required is indeed attained regardless of the device or technology, is the final step in developing the most secure PKI authentication component possible. What is needed is a process for a central enrollment and verification source for biometric transactions. One example, International Biometric Group's CBA (patent pending), or Central Biometric Authority, provides an additional layer of security for many applications, especially remote electronic transactions, and is a potential mechanism to close the loophole in the local biometric authentication scenario. It is important to note that any infrastructure like CBA is designed to maximize the capabilities of biometric authentication, and will do so as a complement to, not a replacement for, PKI.

No doubt, using a central biometric authority can be controversial and arguments have been made against it with some designers citing valid reasons for preferring local validation.

Remote Electronic Transactions

By centralizing the verification of the sender's and/or receiver's biometric sample, each party can be assured of the other's identity. Since there would be control over conditions of enrollment and verification at the CBA, a verification can safely be interpreted as an assurance of identity. In addition, since a message-specific key (in addition to the PKI private key) is used, the concerns of non-biometrically protected copies of private keys are mitigated. The message specific key could also be time-stamped as an extra precaution. Finally, by using a conversion table, users of different biometric systems can set minimum verification thresholds for users of systems different from their own.

Interpretation of Biometric Comparison Results

Verification scores are only valuable if the reader of the score knows how to interpret it. Unfortunately, each biometric vendor reports scores in different ways. In some cases, the scale is a logarithmic 0 to 1; in other cases, the scale is a linear 1 to 100. In some cases, high scores are best, and in others, low scores are best. Even when the same relative scales are used, different technologies and different vendors have different accuracy levels. Thus, a score of 75 out of an ideal 100 on a retina scan unit might be carry a very different confidence level than a 75 out of an ideal 100 on a dynamic signature verification system. As such, what is necessary is a process to reduce vendors' output into easily understandable categories such as "high," "medium," "low," and "fail" with regard to the confidence of the match.

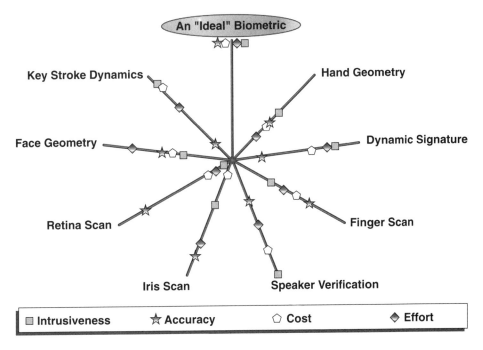

Figure 20.1 Ideal biometrics.

Source: International Biometric Group (www.biometricgroup.com).

Assurance that Biometric Comparison Is Legitimate

Unlike the traditional approach of biometrically securing a private key with a biometric, a centralized infrastructure would assure the legitimacy of the biometric comparison environment. The number of attempts can be documented, since all verifications are taking place at the central authority.

The Zephyr Chart illustrates the comparative strengths and weaknesses of each biometric technology (see Figure 20.1). The eight primary biometric technologies are listed around the outer border, and for each technology the four major evaluation criteria are ranked from outside (better) to inside (worse). Looking at dynamic signature verification (DSV) will illustrate how the Zephyr Chart works. We see that intrusiveness is the farthest out for DSV; as most customers feel very comfortable signing their names to approve transactions, most customers consider DSV non-intrusive. Moving slightly closer to the center of the plot we see effort, still positioned strongly, indicating that the effort to use DSV is not problematic. Cost is further in toward the center; hardware involved with DSV can be as cheap as $80 in the case of an opaque tablet. The accuracy of DSV is the closest to the center of the plot, as it is its greatest disadvantage.

Conclusion

Even without the immediate implementation of this centralized infrastructure, wherein security would be at its highest, it is clear that PKI benefits greatly from integration with biometrics. The decisions regarding how, when, and where to use biometrics will be left up to purchasers, IT directors, and network security professionals. However, it is safe to say that biometrics and PKI will grow increasingly intertwined as the respective industries grow from niche solutions to broad-based enablers of commerce and data flow in the new Internet era.

Request for Proposal for Public Key Infrastructure

Table of Contents

SECTION I

GENERAL INFORMATION

RFP #

1 General Information

1.1 Introduction and Background

This document is a Request for Proposal (hereafter referred to as "RFP") for provision of a Public Key Infrastructure (PKI). This RFP specifies the information which you must provide in your response and sets forth requirements which must be met.

We evaluate suppliers looking for the best match between our requirements and the suppliers' capabilities, pricing, etc. As part of the evaluation process, we may ask you to demonstrate any or all of the capabilities of your products.

The technical requirements of the proposed PKI are described in detail in Section II.

The RFP specifies the information that you must provide in your response and sets forth requirements which any prospective supplier must meet. It includes the following Attachments:

Section I	General Information
Section II	Summary of Requirements
Section III	Specific Questions

Appendix A   Terms and Conditions

As part of the evaluation process, we may ask you to demonstrate any or all of the capabilities of your product and/or the quality of your services.

1.2 General Guidelines

1.2.1 We shall not be responsible or liable in any manner for any risks, costs, or expenses incurred by any prospective supplier, including but not limited to the selected supplier(s).

1.2.2 We may reject any offer which is conditional or incomplete or which contains any irregularities of any kind.

1.2.3 Prior to the due date, we may modify this RFP by one or more addenda issued to all the prospective suppliers to whom we issued this RFP.

1.2.4 We reserve the absolute right to withdraw this RFP by written notice, to reject any oral offers and to reject any and all offers submitted in response to this RFP. We shall incur no liability whatsoever to prospective suppliers by reason of such withdrawal, rejection or acceptance.

1.2.5 A letter of transmittal shall accompany each prospective proposal. Such letter must be signed by a person authorized to obligate the prospective supplier contractually to the scope, terms, specifications and pricing contained in the offer.

1.2.6 All offers and any other materials submitted in response to this RFP will become our property of and may be returned only at our option and at the prospective supplier's expense.

1.2.7 You may modify your offer after you submit it by withdrawing the original and resubmitting a revised offer prior to the due date. We will not consider modifications offered in any other manner, whether written or oral.

1.2.8 We routinely handle all information submitted in response to an RFP with care, use it only for evaluation purposes, and restrict access to the minimum number of persons who have a need to know. However, we assume no obligation and shall incur no liability regarding confidentiality of all or any portion of a quotation or any other material submitted in response to this RFP unless we have expressly agreed in writing to protect specifically identified information.

1.2.9 If you want to delete, add, or change any language in the Terms and Conditions please include in your response the exact contractual language you propose. If you do not spell out these changes, we will expect you to execute the Agreement in the form attached hereto. Setting forth specific proposed contractual language may be grounds for us to reject your offer, and such proposed language may be subject to negotiation prior to the selection of a supplier.

1.2.10 Each prospective supplier shall include a statement in his proposal that the entire proposal (including scope and prices) contained therein are firm for not less than XXX months from the date of the quotation.

1.3 Correspondence

1.3.1 Should a prospective supplier discover materials ambiguity, conflict discrepancy, omission or other error in this RFP, such supplier shall immediately notify us in writing of such discovery with a request for modification or clarification of this RFP. All such requests must cite the area in question. Corrections to any part of this RFP will be provided to all suppliers receiving the RFP.

1.3.2 Any answers provided by us to questions from prospective suppliers will be furnished to each supplier who received the RFP, unless that supplier has indicated that they do not wish to respond.

1.3.3 We reserve the right to refuse to answer any questions.

1.3.4 All correspondence related to this tender should be directed to the contact below:

Name:

Address:

1.4 Proposal Requirements

1.4.1 This RFP outlines our requirements. A prospective supplier should prepare any offer simply and economically, giving a straightforward, concise picture of that supplier's ability to satisfy the requirements of the RFP.

1.4.2 General information about our requirements are provided in Section II.

1.4.3 The first section of a prospective suppliers' response must include a comprehensive description of the proposed solution, and how it meets the general and mandatory requirements in Sections II of this tender. It must be brief, but sufficiently descriptive and supply all of the information directly where required. The second part of your response should answer all of the specific questions as laid out in Section III of this RFP.

1.4.4 Supplemental information about the vendor's products may be included as an addendum to the proposal.

1.4.5 One electronic copy and two hard copies of the response must be submitted.

1.5 Costing Proposal

1.5.1 The vendor must provide a detailed, itemized costing for all proposed goods and services in a separate section of the response.

1.5.2 Costing should be provided for the following number of users…

1.6 Evaluation of Proposals

> 1.6.1 In the initial phase of the evaluation, proposals will be reviewed for completeness and compliance with all other requirements including submittal, instructions, provisions, and terms and conditions of this RFP. Proposals which fail to comply with the essential requirements of the RFP may be rejected as non-responsive and eliminated from further consideration. .

> 1.6.2 Proposals must satisfy each of the mandatory requirements. Proposals that fail to meet any one requirement shall not be considered.

> 1.6.3 List of RFP Evaluation Criteria Accepted proposals will be reviewed by an evaluation committee and scored against the following criteria:

XX%   Ability to meet Mandatory requirements

XX%   Cost

XX%   Company Experience, Financial Stability and References

XX%   Ability to meet general requirements

SECTION II

SUMMARY OF REQUIREMENTS

RFP #

2 General Description of Requirements

The following specifications detail our requirements for a digital Certification Authority and a Public Key Infrastructure (PKI). Please provide a general description of your solution and describe how it meets the general requirements, and each of the mandatory requirements.

2.1 General Requirements

In responding to this section (2.1), please provide a general description of your solution, and a general description of the functionality as it pertains to each of the sub-sections.

This Public Key Infrastructure will be used to provide authentication, confidentiality, non-repudiation and privacy for a variety of applications running on multiple hardware platforms. Encryption and digital signature technology provides many security needs such as data confidentiality, integrity, authentication, and non-repudiation. It is important that the company providing this technology is a strong corporate entity

The Public Key Infrastructure will consist of hardware and software to issue and revoke keys mapped to X.500 objects, and software development tool kits for developing client and server applications.

The PKI will use public key encryption and digital signature technologies to ensure the authenticity and integrity of sensitive information in electronic transactions, to protect the confidentiality of such sensitive information and to support non-repudiation. It will provide a range of services to its users, including digital signature key management services, confidentiality, certificate management services, directory services, end-entity initialization services, support personal tokens if required, and non-repudiation services.

The issuance of digital certificates, does not ensure that a user's access is properly monitored, that privileges associated with access are accurately and currently defined, or that the certificates in question have not been withdrawn or replaced. To address these needs, enterprises require a robust public key infrastructure that supplements the straight certificate issuance functions with full life cycle issuance of public keys. This includes issuance, authentication, storage, retrieval, back-up, recovery, updating and revocation of keys and certificates in an easy-to-use cost-effective manner.

The certificate management capability will maintain and distribute X.509-based public key certificates and certificate revocation lists to ensure secure communications between any pair of entities supported by the PKI. Provision will also be required for inter-operation with end-user systems supported by external PKIs operated by other organizations.

2.1.1 Certification Authority

The *Certification Authority* is a trusted entity whose responsibility is certifying the authenticity of users. In creating certificates, CAs act as agents of trust in a Public Key Infrastructure. CAs create certificates for users by digitally signing set of data, such as the User's Name, a public key of the user, the validity period and the specific operations for which the key is to be used, among other items. The CAs signature on a certificate ensures that any tampering with the contents of the certificate can be easily detected. As long as users trust a CA and its business policies for issuing and managing certificates, they can trust certificates issued by the CA.

2.1.2 Key Generation and User Authorization

Key Generation and User Authorization is the process for setting up new users. Users should have the ability to be enabled easily with minimum effort on their part. Administrators should have the ability to enable users individually or bulk enable. It is important that passwords and keying material are never sent in the clear when setting up new users.

2.1.3 Key Backup/Recovery

Key backup/recovery enables a user to recover their key/certificate material when they forget the password that protects such material in their local environment. It also enables system administrators to gain emergency access to protected data. A comprehensive PKI architecture will typically employ two key pairs per user. In this case, only the encryption key pair should be backed-up. The signing key pair should never be backed-up in order to support non-repudiation of their digital signature.

2.1.4 Certificate Expiration/Renewal

Certificate expiration/renewal enables periodic refreshing of keying material, whereby new key pairs are generated to replace existing (expired) keys. This reduces the risk of various attacks on a user's keys. Certificate expiration also enables certificate issuers to control how long a given user's certificate will be valid. For example, employee certificates might be issued with a longer lifetime than agent certificates. It is very important to ensure that keys are actually updated prior to their expiration.

2.1.5 Certificate Revocation

Certificate revocation is an extremely important capability, as this is the primary means by which user certificates are removed from the PKI. Revoked certificates should be placed on a certificate revocation list (CRL), which is then distributed through a public directory (typically the same directory as the valid public key certificates). It is important to note that merely publishing a CRL is not sufficient; the appropriate application security software must verify whether a certificate is still valid by checking the CRL. Certificate revocation is necessary when a user loses their private key material, or such material is otherwise compromised, stolen, etc.

2.1.6 Cross-Certification

Cross-Certification is a means of establishing third party trust among separate CA domains so that users in one domain can exchange protected files with users in other domains. Technically, it involves the creation of cross-certificates between two CAs.

2.1.7 Client Software

The value of a PKI is tied to the ability to use *intelligent application software* that operates consistently and transparently across the all the applications on the desktop. This client-side software *must* be able to:

➢ Validate the CAs signature on certificates and ensure signature validity by checking a CRL *every time* a certificate is used by a user *(Note: Also consider that other checking may be utilized such as short-lived certificates or OSCP).*

➢ Support non-repudiation by generating the key pairs used for digital signature on the user's computer *(or optionally in hardware)*

➢ Support non-repudiation by also ensuring that the signing keys are never backed-up and remain only under the user's control at all times

➢ Monitor the user's key pairs to ensure that they are updated before expiry

➢ Automatically and transparently handle the updating of the user's key pairs

➤ Keep track of a history (on the user's desktop) of all the private decryption keys ever used by that user to ensure that the user can decrypt data encrypted with previous key pairs. *History could also be offloaded to a directory, protected by users current key and downloaded when needed.*

➤ Automatically and transparently navigate the key history at the desktop to select the proper key needed to decrypt the file to be accessed

➤ Cache all necessary information (certificates & CRLs) to perform all of the functions above without needing to be connected to the network (off-line). *Alternatively, higher security may also be attained if on-line and a server can authenticate user first before granting access and resources.*

2.2 Mandatory Requirements

The following are mandatory requirements for the product. In responding to this section of the RFI, please provide a response to each item, confirming compliance and where appropriate describing how it is provided.

2.2.1 Key and Certificate Management

1. The PKI must be able to be cost effectively deployed and operated.

2. Solutions must provide a minimum of two key pairs: one for signing and one for encrypting. A back-up of the encryption private key(s) will be securely stored so encrypted documents may be historically retrieved. The signing private key will exist only on the key token or profile issued to the individual. This provides support for both non-repudiation for digital signatures and the key recovery requirements for encrypted documents. The solution must provide a means for archival of private decryption keys, and support for the recovery of a private decryption key on request.

3. A key back-up and recovery capability must be provided so that users can quickly be re-instated with their keying material in the event that they lose access to it (i.e., hard drive crash, forgotten password, et cetera)

4. Recognizing complexities of cryptography and key management, the solution must provide these services transparently to the user. It must also provide automatic key rollover to reduce administrative overhead associated with manually managing this process.

5. The solution must provide a means for the revocation of previously distributed public keys, in the event of compromises, such as a change in authorization or suspected key compromise.

6. The solution must support the generation of Certificate Revocation Lists (CRLs), and must ensure that users cannot inadvertently send encrypted information to users whose certificates have been revoked.

7. The solution must support the ability to extend its domain of trust through cross-certification; cross certification with other vendor CAs should also be possible.

8. It must be possible to revoke cross certificates, and have these Authority Revocation Lists (ARLs) checked automatically.

9. The solution must provide a secure means of protecting the private key on the client workstation; it should also support personal token cards, security smart cards, and/or other enhanced authentication devices.

10. Support for Multiple certificate types must be provided in the same infrastructure product; the product must be able to issue certificates to different users, including Web users, VPN users and users of Secure Electronic Transactions.

11. Application Support

12. Toolkits must be provided so that third-party products can be integrated into the PKI to take advantage of its certificate management services; Toolkits must support C, C++ and Java developers. These should be provided on various technology platforms.

13. The PKI must provide support for S/MIME and third party e-mail applications; these applications should be supported on multiple platforms. Additional support should be provided for SAP and PeopleSoft.

14. Certificate Management Services should be seamlessly integrated with the applications supported, such that they are provided consistently across the applications and are transparent to users.

15. Timestamping services should be available for use with the infrastructure to securely associate a trustworthy statement of time with each transaction.

16. Single Logon to multiple PKI applications must be provided.

17. Application support must be provided for Virtual Private Network (VPN) devices.

2.2.2 Deployment

1. Introduction of certificates to the users must be a "user friendly" process.

2. The solution must be scaleable, and have the capability to issue certificates internally, and to external partners and customers.

3. The certificates and security platform must secure internal and external Web applications.

4. The certification authority must be deployable in a 24×7 environment, whereby CA services are available at all times.

5. The solution must be Year 2000 compliant.

2.2.3 Standards Support

1. The PKI should support multiple algorithms for digital signature, including the Digital Signature Standard (DSS, FIPS 186) and the RSA algorithms.

2. The PKI must be independently *validated* to FIPS-140-1 standard by a third party.

3. The architecture must be standards-based, supporting the following, X.509 v3, GSS-API, LDAP, PKCS #11, S/MIME.

4. The solution must support the following platforms and applications:

SECTION III

SPECIFIC QUESTIONS

RFP #

3 Specific Questions

In responding to this section of the RFI, please discuss your products capabilities in the context of each of the requirements. Please restate the question and provide your response in each case.

3.1 Company Description

1. Very briefly, describe your company's areas of expertise, size, number of employees, and most recent revenue figures (financial backing, R&D capability, R&D location(s)).

2. What are the primary areas of development work undertaken by your company?

3. List any product awards won in the last 5 years.

4. Does the company do actual product development in both North America and Europe? Does the vendor have R&D engineers in Europe to ensure 100% European crypto content?

5. Please provide a list of the cryptographic experts on your staff and list the most notable achievement for each.

3.2 Certification Authority

1. Does the vendor support a hardware solution for storage and use of the CA signing private key. If yes, what level of FIPS 140-1 validation does the hardware device support?

2. Do you prevent the distribution of your root key through copyright restrictions?

3. Do you support multiple character sets?

4. What platforms are supported by the CA product?

3.3 Key and Certificate Management

1. Describe the process for setting up new registration clients, including registration client key generation, and the customization of user registration data and certificate profile; include a description of how user anonymity is maintained, in particular in cases of registration occurring with external entities - such as over the Internet.

2. Define the processes used to authenticate administration/security officers when logging on to the system. The product/service must, at a minimum, support physical dual control over significant system events.

3. Describe protection measures for Private Key Security. Describe the architecture, and specify which physical and logical mechanisms are supported (e.g., hardware devices, key splitting and distribution, re-distribution of the representation of the key) and conformance to US FIPS 140-1.

3.4 Key Pairs

1. Does the solution securely manage the generation and usage of key pairs to support key backup and non-repudiation without involving the end user beyond entering a shared secret?

2. Does the solution support both dual key pair and single key pair systems?

3. If the solution supports dual key pairs, can the key pairs for signing and encryption have independent expiry dates?

3.5 User Initialization

1. Does the system provide a safe distribution method of the CA public key? If yes, please explain. If no, how does the vendor assure that end-users can trust the CA key, and how does the vendor control what other CA keys can be introduced, and prevent those that would potentially weaken the trust and the security of the organization.

2. Can the user initialization process be made to support automated registration and initialization? What tools are available to allow this?

3.6 Certificates

1. Does the solution support X.509v3 certificates?

2. Does the vendor allow flexibility in certificates, so that you can enter your own certificate extensions? Does the vendor allow any number of custom extensions to be included in the certificates issued by the CA? If yes, can these extensions be set on a per user basis?

3. Does the solution support a single set of Public-Key credentials for each user that can be used across all applications in the organization that require security (i.e., file/folder encryption, desktop authentication, secure email, remote access, web browsing, e-forms et cetera)? If yes, explain further. If no, please describe how the solution will enforce consistent security policies across the applications, and minimize the management effort required for users of different applications across multiple security products.

3.7 Password Management

1. Does the solution ensure users' private keys are protected by (at least) passwords? If yes, please provide further applicable information.

2. Does the solution provide password rules (for example, length, number of upper/lowercase characters, ...) that are configurable by a central administrator and can be applied consistently across applications? If yes, what password rules are configurable?

3. Does the solution ensure that passwords are not transmitted 'in the clear' over a network (open or otherwise), or stored in the clear at any time? If yes, please indicate the general methodology for avoiding transmission of passwords and residual passwords in memory.

4. Does the product provide the user visual feedback that their password matches all the password rules?

3.8 Certificate Revocation

1. Does the solution have the ability to automatically issue a certificate revocation list after a certificate is revoked?

2. Does the solution provide a revocation solution that is scaleable to millions of users (i.e. CRL distribution points)?

3. Does your product allow users to perform revocation checking of certificates while off-line (not connected to a network)?

4. Does your solution ensure that a user cannot make use of a revoked certificate? If so, is the user required to perform any steps? Please explain how this mechanism works.

5. Does the solution allow revoked and expired certificates optionally be left on the CRL to allow verification of historical signatures.

3.9 Key Update and Certificate Update

1. Does the solution provide automatic and transparent update of both keys and certificates for users? If not, please describe the process, including how the updating of the key pair is achieved.

2. Is the lifetime of a certificate configurable to meet an organization's security policy? If so, is there an extra cost associated with this?

3.10 Key Backup/Recovery

1. Does the solution allow for backup of encryption keys? If so, is there an extra cost to provide this functionality? Are there additional third party costs associated with the key backup and recovery process?

2. Describe the process for key recovery.

3. Does the vendor provide a scaleable solution for key backup which allows the recovery of decryption keys for all of a user's historical encrypted data in one operation. If a user's keys and certificates have been renewed is previously encrypted data (under an expired keys and certificates) still available.

4. How does the user recover keys if their keys have become lost or corrupted? What process do they have to go through and how long would it take to get the individual back up and running again?

3.11 Cross-Certification

1. Does the product provide support for cross-certification?

2. Does the solution support the ability to perform off-line cross-certification? If yes, please explain the means and standards used. If no, please describe how the vendor will provide the flexibility to interoperate with other CA products.

3. Can unilateral, as well as, bilateral off-line cross-certification be performed? If so, please explain how this is done.

4. Are you able to revoke a cross-certified CA? If so, can the revocation information be passed immediately on to users?

5. Is your support for cross certification such that you can be the superior CA? Do you support being the subordinate CA?

6. If your root, or top level, CA is compromised, what would need to take place for the subordinate CAs to re-establish trust with other peer CAs?

3.12 Trust Model Support

1. Can the product explicitly dictate end-user trust decisions as per corporate policies? If so, explain how this works.

3.13 Administration

1. Is the vendor in complete control of the security software applied in administration of the system? If yes, explain further. If no, please describe precisely what

security is used in administration of the system and what vendors provide that security.

2. Are key management and administration services still available during CA backups?

3. Can a user change their name (DN), but still retain their key history, allowing them to decrypt all previously encrypted files? Is user intervention required?

4. Does the solution support the capability for multiple remote registration authorities to securely execute administrative functions on the PKI system simultaneously? If yes, please describe the features of the security administration application with the security functions and controls that it provides.

5. Can multiple authorizations be required to perform sensitive administrative functions?

3.14 Reporting

1. Describe any audit trail capabilities and reporting capabilities provided by your solution; include a discussion of security protection for these audit logs.

2. Can a report be generated that describes all administrative operations performed?

3. Can a report be generated that describes all certificates that are within a specified period from expiry?

4. Does the solution allow reporting information be imported into a customer-defined application via ODBC for additional querying?

3.15 Standards

1. Does your company use and promote the use of open standards, work with standards boards to come up with new industry solutions, and commit to provide their patented technology for free to support and benefit open standards?

2. Does the solution support the following common standards: X.509 v3, GSS-API, LDAP, PKCS #11, and S/MIME?

3. List all standards bodies you are represented on (are involved with?)

3.16 Interoperability

1. Describe your support for Interoperability

2. Can the product issue certificates to any X.509-enabled application including web-based, VPN-based, SET-based and dual-key-based?

3. Describe your support for the SET protocol.

4. Describe your ability to issue certificates to VPN devices.

5. Can the product work with certificates from another vendor's Certification Authority

3.17 Cryptographic Algorithms

1. List all cryptographic algorithms *(encryption, hashing, digital signature)* supported by your product.

2. Is the vendor in complete control of the software used to implement the cryptographic algorithms, or are parts of it licensed in object code form from other parties?

3. Does the vendor provide a choice of algorithms or are you locked in to one or two?

4. Does the solution allow interoperability between domestic and exportable key management certificates, where both are 1024-bit (RSA) encryption keys?

5. Do you support signing using DSA and encryption using RSA ?

6. What evidence does the vendor have that the implementation of the random number generator and cryptographic algorithms within the solution are implemented securely? Has any third party verified these implementations?

7. Is all the client-side cryptographic software used in your solution FIPS 140 validated?

8. Is your CA capable of supporting FIPS 140 tokens using FIPS 140 algorithms?

3.18 Protocols

1. Does the product have an SNC library that supports single login to SAP client applications as well as other applications (or to SAP applications only) ?

2. Does the product have an SNC library which completely integrates with a managed PKI infrastructure which provides automated and transparent key management and certificate management including automatic CRL issuing and checking, support for non-repudiation, transparent key backup and recovery, and automatic and transparent key and certificate update prior to expiry?

3.19 Smart Card, PC Card, and Biometric Support

1. Does the product allow for multiple authentication techniques for a single individual (i.e., SmartCard, Biometric, Password only)?

2. Does the vendor have a hardware qualification program in place to ensure security and quality or do they accept devices from any vendor without question?

3. Does the solution's client software support the use of smartcards for authentication? If so, which ones?

4. Do the smart cards supported include cards that perform cryptographic operations? Which ones?

5. Does the solution's client software support the use of biometric devices for authentication? If so, which ones?

3.20 Directory Support

1. Describe the Directory support provided. Please list the X.500 or LDAP directories that you have successfully implemented with your product ? Include a list of leading commercial directories that are supported by the product.
2. Can the vendor offer a packaged directory with the PKI.
3. Does the solution use standards-based directory access?
4. Can the vendor support integration with an existing directory, that is already populated with names and attributes?
5. Does the vendor support communication with multiple LDAP servers (for load balancing, redundancy and scalability)?

3.21 Timestamping

1. Does the solution combine a Timestamping service with the authentication and revocation mechanisms in the PKI?
2. Do you support timestamping of DSA signatures?
3. Do you support timestamping of RSA signatures?

3.22 Client Software

1. Does the solution system include client-side application software to ensure consistent security policies and one common security mechanism across multiple applications and multiple platforms?
2. Does the solution support single login across the applications for which it provides security? If so, please explain how this works.
3. Does the solution provide a secure means of protecting the private keys on the client workstation? If yes, please explain what methods are used to protect the private keys.
4. Does the solution provide the necessary mechanisms to ensure that an end user running a client application, based on your solution for security, will never have to know about public and private keys and certificates? In other words, does the solution hide from the end user, the need to know about how to get a certificate, how to use a certificate, what private key they need to decrypt data, when to renew a certificate, and how to renew a certificate?

5. Does your product allow users to perform encryption and revocation checking of certificates while off-line (not connected to a network)?

6. Is client software installation required in all cases? Is there an option for a browser-based alternative with plug-ins rather than installed software to simplify configuration control?

3.23 Application Solutions

1. Does the vendor have relationships with leading application vendors who have endorsed the solution by incorporating support for it into their applications? What other applications are available for the product; ie: e-mail, e-forms…

2. Do you provide encryption services at the client side?

3. Does the vendor have a secure email solution available now? Is it available on multiple email clients? Does the product have a secure email application that transparently and seamlessly retrieves other users' public key certificates from a central directory when required?

4. Does the vendor have a Virtual Private Network solution available now? Is it available on multiple remote access clients? If so, list the clients supported.

5. Does the vendor have a desktop security solution available now? Is it available on multiple operating systems?

6. Does the product allow multiple client-applications to make use of the same set of public-key credentials in a consistent manner?

3.24 Development Tools for PKI

1. Can access to the Certification Authority administrative functions be customized using an API? If so, describe the API.

2. Describe the toolkits that are available, and the languages supported. Does the product and toolkits provide royalty free use of cryptographic algorithms? If not, how much extra cost is involved?

3. Do organizations pay a royalty for applications developed with these toolkits?

3.25 Customer References

1. Describe the availability of User Groups, and support for them by the company

2. Do you have any customers with PKIs installed longer than 4 years?

3. Do you have any customers with more than 50,000 active users?

4. Does the vendor have any single customer with a commercial deployment beyond 100,000 certificates?

3.26 General Support

1. Please describe the training provided with your product

2. Describe the documentation that is provided with the product

3. What is the warranty provided (please enclose a copy of your support agreement); also describe your customer support arrangements; discuss problem escalation and response times; also discuss your measures for upgrades and new releases of your product.

4. Does the vendor provide Support in more than one language?

5. Does the vendor provide 24×7 Support services?

6. Does the vendor provide an Internet-based knowledge base that can be securely accessed by customers, without having to send their password over the Internet?

3.27 Implementation

1. Describe the type of support provided to implement your solution as well as the estimated time to accomplish this.

2. What are the major steps in implementation of a solution?

3.28 Product Verification

1. Is the solution Year 2000 compliant?

2. Does the vendor have a partner-product certification program where products are vigorously tested to ensure interoperability?

3. Please list the dates when you shipped products with the following major versions (1.0? 2.0? 3.0? 4.0? 5.0?)

3.29 Pricing

1. Does the vendor offer both per-seat and per-certificate licensing?

2. Is there an incremental cost for each new certificate?

Selected Definitions

activation data   Data values, other than keys, that are required to operate cryptographic modules and that need to be protected (e.g., a PIN, a passphrase, or a manually held key share).

CA-certificate   A certificate for one CA's public key issued by another CA.

certificate policy (CP)   A named set of rules that indicates the applicability of a certificate to a particular community and/or class of application with common security requirements. For example, a particular certificate policy might indicate applicability of a type of certificate to the authentication of electronic data interchange transactions for the trading of goods within a given price range.

certification path   An ordered sequence of certificates which, together with the public key of the initial object in the path, can be processed to validate the certificate of the final object in the path.

certification practice statement (CPS)   A statement of the practices that a certification authority employs in issuing certificates.

date/time stamp   The date and time a transaction or document is initiated or submitted to a computer system, or the time at which a transaction is logged or archived. Often it is important that the stamp be certified by some authority to establish legal or other special status. Such a service can be provided by a cryptographic procedure. Source: *Cryptography's Role in Securing the Information Society.*

hexadecimal   Hexadecimal means using a number scheme base 16. We use base 10 in our everyday lives. Computers use base 2. For computers, there are only two characters we call bits, 0 and 1, upon which all numbers are expressed. For humans, there are 10 characters, 0 through 9, upon which all numbers are expressed. Hexadecimal is actually a shorthand notation for binary (base 2), where there are 16 characters: 0 through 9, and the letters A through F. Each hexadecimal character represents four bits; for example, 0 = 0000, 1 = 0001, 2 = 0010, through F = 1111.

issuing certification authority (issuing CA) In the context of a particular certificate, the issuing CA is the CA that issued the certificate (*see also* subject certification authority).

policy mapping Recognizing that, when a CA in one domain certifies a CA in another domain, a particular certificate policy in the second domain may be considered by the authority of the first domain to be equivalent (but not necessarily identical in all respects) to a particular certificate policy in the first domain.

policy qualifier Policy-dependent information that accompanies a certificate policy identifier in an X.509 certificate.

practices and policy specification A list of practice and/or policy statements, spanning a range of standard topics, for use in expressing a certificate policy definition or CPS employing the approach described in this framework.

registration authority (RA) An entity that is responsible for identification and authentication of certificate subscribers, but that does not sign or issue certificates (i.e., an RA is delegated certain tasks on behalf of a CA).

relying party A recipient of a certificate who relies on certificates and/or digital signatures verified using that certificate. In this document, the terms "certificate user" and "relying party" are used interchangeably.

subject certification authority (subject CA) In the context of a particular CA-certificate, the subject CA is the CA whose public key is certified in the certificate (*also see* issuing certification authority).

subscriber An entity who is the subject of a certificate and is not a CA or RA. The terms "subject" and "subscriber" are used interchangeably.

References and Further Reading

Business Issues

Information Technology Security: A Challenge for Directors, Director's Monthly, June2000, National Association of Corporate Directors, Washington D.C. www.nacdonline.org

Top Security Threats And Management Issues Facing Corporate America, Year 2000 Survey of Fortune 1000 Companies, Pinkerton Service Corporation, 2000. www.pinkertons.com

Certificate Policy

American Bar Association, Digital Signature Guidelines: Legal Infrastructure for Certification Authorities and Electronic Commerce, Draft 1995

Bank of Bermuda Certificate Practice Statement
http://clientaccess.bankofbermuda.com/

Certificate Policy and Certification Practices Framework, S. Chokhani and W. Ford, IETF RFC 2527

Digital Signature and Confidentiality Policy for the Government of Canada PKI
www.cio-dpi.gc.ca/pki-icp/documents/Certificate_Policy/introduction_e.asp

FPKI Model Certificate Policy
http://gits-sec.treas.gov/model_cert_policy_intro.htm

Internet Public Key Infrastructure, X.509 Certificate and CRL Profile, R. Housley, W. Ford, W. Polk, D. Solo, RFC 2459, January 1999.

Privacy Enhancement for Internet Electronic Mail, S. Kent, Part II: Certificate-Based Key Management," Internet RFC 1422, 1993.

Security Baseline Recommendations For The Specification And Operation Of Public Key Infrastructure (PKI) Components, National Institute of Standards and Technology, May 1998.

Cost of Ownership

A Total Economic Impact Analysis of Two PKI Vendors: Entrust and VeriSign, Giga Information Group, September 1998.

Cryptography

D.G. Abraham, G.M. Dolan, G.P. Double, and J.V. Stevens, *Transaction Security System*, IBM Systems Journal, volume 30 number 2, 1991.

Menezes, Alfred J., et al. *Handbook of Applied Cryptography* (CRC Press; ISBN 0849385237).

Schneier, Bruce, *Applied Cryptography: Protocols, Algorithms and Source Code in C* (John Wiley & Sons; ISBN: 0471117099).

Smith, Richard E., *Internet Cryptography* (Addison-Wesley; ISBN 0201924803).

Stinson, Douglas R., *Cryptography Theory and Practice* (CRC Press; ISBN 0849385210).

Directories

"A System Administator's View of LDAP" by Bruce Markey, http://people.netscape.com/bjm/whyLDAP.html

Howes, Tim, et al. *Understanding and Deploying Ldap Directory Services*, MacMillan Network Architecture and Development Series (Macmillan Technical Publishing; ISBN: 1578700701).

ISO/IEC 9594-8/ITU-T Recommendation X.509, "Information Technology – Open Systems Interconnection: The Directory: Authentication Framework," June 1997.

Kampman, Kevin, *All About Network Directories: Understanding Directory Services and Business Applications* (John Wiley & Sons, ISBN: 0471333638).

LDAP Duplication/Replication/Update Protocols (ldup) Working Group www.ietf.org/html.charters/ldup-charter.html

LDAP: Fulfilling the Promise for Directory-Enabled Networks, Creative Networks, Inc., www.cnilive.com/impact/specials/ldap/index.htm

Microsoft Active Directory www.microsoft.com/windows2000/guide/server/features/dirlist.asp

Netscape Directory Server http://home.netscape.com/directory/v4.0/index.html

NDS eDirectory www.novell.com/products/nds/

Reed, Archie, *Implementing Directory Services* (McGraw-Hill, ISBN: 007134408X).

Schema Standardization Efforts, 3COM, Inc.
   www.3com.com/technology/tech_net/white_papers/500665a.html

University of Michigan LDAP mailing list:
   http://listserver.itd.umich.edu/cgi-bin/lyris.pl?visit=ldap.
   To subscribe to the mailing list:
   http://listserver.itd.umich.edu/cgi-bin/lyris.pl?enter=ldap&text_mode=0

Wilcox, Mark, *Implementing LDAP* (Wrox Press Inc, ISBN: 1861002211).

Getting Certificates

Help Desk for Digital IDs, VeriSign
   www.verisign.com/client/help/index.html

Secure E-Mail Reference Guide, VeriSign
   www.verisign.com/securemail/guide

Hardware Mechanisms

Bracco, Tere'."Tales from the crypto", Network World, 22 May 2000.
   www.nwfusion.com/reviews/2000/0522rev1.html

Brown, Doug. "Encryption Keys Vulnerable, Researchers Warn." ZDNet Inter@ctive
   Week Online, Talkback, 5 January 2000.
   www.zdnet.com/intweek/stories/news/0,4164,2417628,00.html

Intel Corporation. "Advantages of IA-64 for Security Applications", October 1999.
   http://developer.intel.com/software/idap/media/pdf/Security91599.pdf

Intel Corporation. "Itanium™ Processor Overview and IA-64 Roadmap", March 2000.
   http://developer.intel.com/design/IA-64/Downloads/itaniumAndIA64Roadmap.pdf

MacVittie, Lori. "Cryptographic Accelerators Provide Quick Encryption", Network
   Computing, 19 April 1999.
   www.networkcomputing.com/1008/1008r1.html

National Institute of Standards and Technology. *Federal Information Processing Standards Publication 140-1: SECURITY REQUIREMENTS FOR CRYPTOGRAPHIC
   MODULES*, 1994. www.itl.nist.gov/fipspubs/fip140-1.htm

National Institute of Standards and Technology. *FIPS 140-1 Cryptographic Modules Validation List*, June 13, 2000. http://csrc.ncsl.nist.gov/cryptval/140-1/1401val.htm

van Someren, Nicko. "The need for cryptographic accelerators in electronic commerce."
   White paper, 1997. www.ncipher.com/products/resources.html

van Someren, Nicko, and Shamir, Adi. "Playing hide and seek with stored keys."
   White paper, 1998. www.ncipher.com/products/resources.html

Initiatives

Identrus
   www.identrus.com/

Government of Canada PKI
www.cio-dpi.gc.ca/

Government of Canada PKI Certificate Policies
www.cio-dpi.gc.ca/pki/Documents/Certificate%20Policy/aboutCP_e.html

Internet Council of the National Automated Clearing House Association (NACHA)
http://internetcouncil.nacha.org/Projects/CARAT/carat.htm

PKI Forum
www.pkiforum.org/

The Evolving Federal Public Key Infrastructure, June 2000, U.S. FPKI Steering Committee, http://gits-sec.treas.gov/

United States Federal PKI Government Information Technology Services
http://gits-sec.treas.gov/

Laws and Regulations

Directive 1999/93/EC of the European Parliament and of the Council of 13 December 1999, www.ict.etsi.org/eessi/e-sign-directive.pdf

Directive 95/46/EC of the European Parliament and of the Council of 24 October 1995, http://europa.eu.int/eur-lex/en/lif/dat/1995/en_395L0046.html

Electronic Records; Electronic Signatures; Final Rule. Electronic Submissions; Establishment of Public Docket; Notice. Department of Health and Human Services, Food and Drug Administration, 21 CFR Part 11, March 20, 1997.

Medical Records Privacy, Uses and Oversight of Patient Information in Research, U.S. General Accounting Office, Testimony Before the Committee on Health, Education, Labor and Pensions, U.S Senate, February 24, 1999, GAO/T-HEHS-99-70.

Standards for Privacy of Individually Identifiable Health Information; Proposed Rule, 45 CFR Parts 160 through 164, Department of Health and Human Service, Office of the Secretary, November 3, 1999.

Summary of Electronic Commerce and Digital Signature Legislation, McBride, Baker & Coles
www.mbc.com/ecommerce.htm

Qualifying Vendors

Sample Request for Proposal (RFP) electronic text version
www.ibg.com/pki

USPTO Systems Engineering and Technical Assistance, Preliminary PKI Market Survey (updated) for U.S. Department of Commerce, U.S. Patent and Trademark Office, 50-PBPT-8-00005, February 17, 1999 (8 pages).

Security and PKI

Adams, Carlisle and Lloyd, Steve, *Understanding Public-Key Infrastructure* (Macmillan Technical Publishing; ISBN 157870166X).

Feghhi, Jalal, et al. *Digital Certificates Applied Internet Security* (Addison-Wesley; ISBN 0201309807).

Ford, Warwick and Baum, Michael S., *Secure Electronic Commerce* (Prentice Hall; ISBN 0134763424).

Standards

American Bankers Association
Attn: X9 secretariat
1120 Connecticut Ave NW
Washington, D.C. 20036
Phone: (202) 663-5284
www.x9.org

International Telecommunications Union (ITU)
www.itu.int/publications/index.html

Internet Engineering Task Force (IETF)
www.ietf.org/rfc.html

Internet Mail Consortium
www.imc.org/rfcs.html

National Institute of Standards and Technology, Federal Information Processing Standards Publications
www.itl.nist.gov/fipspubs/

RSA Public-Key Cryptography Standards (PKCS)
www.rsasecurity.com/rsalabs/pkcs/

Time Stamping

Cryptography's Role in Securing the Information Society, National Research Council (National Academy Press, 1996).

Validation

Introduction to Windows 2000 security (which mentions Certificate Authorities)
www.microsoft.com/WINDOWS2000/guide/server/features/secintro.asp

Valicert
www.valicert.com

VPNs and Windows 2000, including information about the CA
www.microsoft.com/WINDOWS2000/guide/server/solutions/vpn.asp

Windows 2000 CA installation instructions
http://support.microsoft.com/support/kb/articles/Q231/8/81.ASP

Index